The magnificent north face of Jannu (Kumbhakarna), Nepal Himalaya, taken at the beginning of the monsoon, the day we left base camp for home after our ascent, May 2000. The summit, at 7710 metres, is approximately 3700 vertical metres above where this shot was taken. *Author.*

Athol high on the Balfour Face of Mt Tasman,
New Zealand, during a winter ascent in 1993.
Author.

EXPEDITIONS

ANDREW LINDBLADE

Hardie Grant Books

First published in 2001
by Hardie Grant Books
12 Claremont Street
South Yarra VIC 3141

National Library of Australia Cataloguing-in-Publication Data:
Andrew Lindblade, 1971–
Expeditions

ISBN 1 876719 31 1

Lindblade, Andrew, 1971-. 2. Mountaineers – Australia – Biography. I. Title

796.522092

Cover and text design by Phil Campbell
Typeset by Phil Campbell
Edited by Clare Coney
Printed and bound by South China Printing (1988) Co. Ltd

Cover Photographs: Front: Andrew Lindblade descending Thalay Sagar, Indian Himalaya, after he and Athol Whimp made the first ascent of its north face, September 1997. *Athol Whimp.* Back: Athol Whimp high up on a freezing day in his beloved New Zealand Alps. Central buttress, Sheila Face, Mt Cook, January 1996. *Author.*

Author's Note: Mountains are inherently dangerous and frightening places. Do not attempt mountaineering or rock climbing without proper instruction, as mistakes can prove fatal. Even seemingly harmless mistakes made through ignorance can contribute to a potentially catastrophic chain of events. Also, while the glossary defines some items of equipment and a few climbing processes, the reality can often be very different: things go wrong, climbers have to improvise. This is especially so in the mountains where conditions are often a long way from good, let alone perfect.

CONTENTS

Reinforcements   1

1 Three Nights Out: Fitz Roy, north pillar – Patagonia   21

2 Into the Wind: Cerro Torre, the Maestri Route,
    south-east pillar – Patagonia   53

3 Greetings and Retreat: attempting Thalay Sagar,
    north face – Indian Himalaya   77

4 Hidden by Storms: the first ascent of Thalay Sagar,
    north face – Indian Himalaya   109

5 Shadows and Light: Jannu, north face – Nepal Himalaya   149

Going and Returning: Aoraki Mt Cook, New Zealand   205

Glossary   234

'To live dangerously ... is to live naked and unashamed. It means putting one's trust in the life force and ceasing to battle with a phantom called death.'
Henry Miller

'We have accepted the rules of the game, and the game now forms us in its own image. It is within us that the Sahara reveals itself. To approach it is not to visit an oasis, it is to make our religion of a spring.'
Antoine de Saint-Exupéry

Acknowledgements

Athol Whimp gave me the unlimited use of his photographs for this book. For this, all the years of climbing, the crucial moments up high, and all the miserable bivouacs, I offer my heartfelt gratitude.

Special thanks are also due to my parents Sue and Rod, Sangeetha (Gigi) Chandra-Shekeran, Michael Webster, Charles Creese and Gregory Crouch.

REINFORCEMENTS

BETWEEN TRIPS to the mountains there is much time to think, much time to try and work it all out. Dissatisfaction with normal life can creep in. Climbers spend most of their time living in a city, pondering what could be, and expend so much energy in organising ways to get back to the mountains.

So why do people choose the stress, the insecurity and the uncertainty of working toward a mountaineering objective? For me, at least, in a strange, indefinable way, the mountains, despite their own stresses, give solace from restlessness. As soon as the decision is made to begin another expedition, the days preceding departure are transformed. Gradually, domestic details wither away to reveal my primary focus – the tantalising upper reaches of the mountains. Photos of the soon-to-be-arrived-at mountain are stuck to my walls, and my mind constantly endeavours to fill the gap between the photos, imagination, and the hard reality.

My times in the mountains so far have been very intense and at times violent, yet it is in these moments – despite being unaware of it at the time – that I have felt most contented. After returning home I leave the 'presence' of a completed ascent and attach myself to the potential of another. Then there comes an unmistakable time: I feel something in the wind. The peace of home soon subsides, and I champ at the bit to get back into the mountains, back into the thick of things, back where peace and total chaos live side by side. But then, the predatory, paradoxical question surfaces: surely I could find peace and contentment without having to reach out and up into the dangerous mountain world?

Something happens during these expeditions, at moments of crisis, that allows me a powerful insight into not only what I'm doing there, but why I bothered going in the first place. It suddenly all makes alarming sense. Somehow, after months of uncertainty, it has all added up to a few precious moments, a sense of colossal freedom.

On one trip early in my alpine career, my climbing partner Athol and I were descending unroped from the summit of a mountain in the dark. It was winter and bitterly cold. We had no moonlight to guide us, just the glow emanating from the stars and the dim ambient light reflecting off the mountain. We were facing into the steep ice, our boots gripping its surface with their crampons' front points, being careful and methodical with our placements. We had been going a long time, and I was tired and wanted to stop. But there was nowhere to stop; nowhere to sit, no ledges to stand on, just a huge expanse of hard blue ice. The mind unconsciously accepts this: it is one's fate to keep going until there is somewhere to stop. If you fight it you break down.

My head torch battery had given out from the cold. Tiny crystals of snow and ice played about over the blue ice at my face as I breathed in and out. My fingers constantly veered between warm and cold. Usually, one or two fingers on each hand – the ones closest to the ice – would stay numb as I whacked my ice tools in and out time and again. After every ten placements or so I would rest my head against my ice axe, which I had firmly placed into the ice. My eyes were only centimetres from the microcosmic world of the seemingly infinite ice face, the heat from my breath pushing back onto my face. Lifting my head again I would feel a little dizzy, talk reassuringly to myself, and begin moving down again. The sounds of Athol below me rhythmically placing his ice tools and crampons as he descended were absorbed into my mind like music. Our voices went back and forth, slightly breathless. Sometimes I would see Athol's figure as a dark blur in my tiredness, but always what his presence meant to me felt clear. Climbing together like that feels very powerful, instinctive. The memory of this night continually replays in mind, even now. The moments are extremely vivid, the sounds and the sensations of exhaustion paradoxically making me impatient to return to the mountains again.

Only last winter, after months of frustrating work and injury, watching the endless traffic pass by in Melbourne, a sporadically drizzling day climbing on the cliffs of Mt Rosea in Victoria's Grampians provided the perfect acceleration into the future. Constant upward movement on the vertical cliff through the drizzle, dodging the wet patches of rock and waiting out the occasional cloudburst of rain, brought the reward of reaching our packs and food after each climb before launching up the 100-metre wall yet again. Happiness crept in, a warm therapeutic glow after too much time spent waiting for injuries to repair. The warmth spread through my body as we walked down to the car in the gloomy evening laced with pale orange sunset light. Heavy drops of water landed on my shoulders from the towering gum trees, and it felt like a little version of the serene return to a high alpine hut after a long and uncertain day on the mountain.

When life at home is filled with structures that can push me, more and more, toward a certain future, the mountains fill me with uncertainty – and within this lies the paradox, and the real adventure. Ironically, I have been filled with dread walking in to the mountains on early trips, wondering why I couldn't be content to end my foray where the walking track ended and the glacier began. This feeling was always amplified by the presence of walking folk, standing at the lip of the moraine wall where the glacier had deposited its rubble, poking at the crumbling edge with walking sticks and staring afar with binoculars. I remember wanting to be like them, happy to stand and take in the scenery, yet how different I felt when walking out after having been up in the mountains, having made a commitment to a route I was unsure about before I climbed it. Sometimes, in the middle of a bad day in the mountains, I'd promised never to return – 'This is it, I'm retiring', I'd say to Athol. He knew I was kidding myself. But the impact of near-death has hit home at times, real and terrifying. It is during such moments, especially, that I have looked into myself for a way out, an excuse to leave it all.

Towards colder places

I am always amazed how difficult it is to force myself to get up in the numbing cold of a mountain morning, yet when I am at home in the city it is what I often long for. To feel that sting in the fingers, and to take a minute to re-warm them under my arms! How luxurious that seems in retrospect yet in reality it is so painful. I remember feeling the same sense as a boy when I returned from riding my bike around the Melbourne streets on a silent, misty Sunday morning during winter. My hands were numb, and as I rode I had to pull them into the sleeves of my jacket, steering with the heels of my palms. Back in the house, I thrust them in front of the heater. Nausea overtook me as the blood rushed back into my fingers, I whacked them together to try and hurry the process. Later in the day, as the warmer afternoon sun lit the front of the house, I looked at my bike again and remembered how bitterly cold the metal handlebars had been that morning. It seemed so long ago, but was so fresh in my mind, so powerful. It was as though the bike had transported me to another world.

After doing a lot of bushwalking as a young teenager at school, I began to notice photographs of people on mountains and rocks, wondering in an over-enthused, naïve, schoolboy-type way, what it was like. Then, in the forest full of granite boulders alongside my parents' property, I tried (with a few mates) to climb the boulders by imitating the *real* climbers in the books and magazines. We always argued over the right way to do the ropes, the safe way, the *cool* way. Of course, we thought we were far better than we really were. But we *were* really keen.

Leaving the school-gates for the last time in 1988 I had needed a 'valid' excuse to keep away from university and the career that theoretically lay beyond. With school-friend James I spent time climbing at Mt Arapiles in Victoria's Wimmera off and on through the year. My family talked of 'Andrew taking a year off' as they discussed my diversions to rock faces and mountaineering books.

Knowing what I could get away with at university, besides the occasional, even inspired essay in my literature major during 1991–92, I arranged my timetable so as to get maximum time away rock climbing, renewing the friendships I had made with a few New Zealanders I had met in 1989, in particular the alpinist Jeremy Strang. One fine September afternoon in 1991 he wandered about the boulder field at Mt Arapiles, a cold wind pushing over short lengths of wet, green grass. A letter a month previously had only hinted at this trip to Australia from New Zealand, and now he had made a typically understated arrival. I saw him from the cliff above but instead of calling out wandered and scrambled down the back of the cliff for our greeting. He went back home in November and the next time I saw him was at White Horse Hill campground at Mt Cook, in New Zealand's South Island, the first time I went mountaineering (and told myself I never wanted to go back after getting frightened); January 1992.

I had heard about Athol Whimp, a New Zealand alpinist and rock climber, before I actually met him. I can't remember exactly how we met, only the first climbs together at Mt Arapiles in 1991. The campsite was used by a contingent of Kiwi climbers. Athol struck me as quietly spoken and someone who got serious with climbing, yet laced this seriousness with a constant piss-take of himself and others around him. Someone who believed that everything was possible. He was ex-military, specifically the New Zealand SAS, then he had served in the Sultan of Oman's Land

Forces in the Middle East for some years. He was the complete antithesis of the movie-cliché military man, being a reserved individual who only, it seemed to me, reluctantly spoke of his achievements.

As a child he was always hunting and scrambling around the hills and mountains of New Zealand. When he was 14 he had shot a deer way up in the hills around Arthur's Pass, a snow-capped, mountainous area in the South Island. After gutting it, he carried the deer for seven hours over his shoulders, along with his rifle, to the road. Hastily wrapping the deer in some hessian, he flagged down the next bus and rode into town, the deer safely stowed underneath, and a proud smile on his face. His stories from the long-range patrols across the Oman deserts fascinated me, the images of the sand-coloured 4WDs belting out across the flat, rocky terrain in formation sitting vivid and clear in my mind. We seemed to share similar ideas about climbing – simply a feeling about reaching somewhere or something personally unseen and unfelt before. We never talked about this *per se*, but I came to realise it through the long night drives into the Grampians and home again, stopping for coffee before continuing the drive, talking non-stop into the night.

It became easier to justify sacrificing time and money for climbing as the climbing challenges always grew. I was spending more and more time in Victoria's Grampians National Park, home to the amazing Taipan Wall. My fingertips would nervously sweat as I rehearsed the movements on this beautiful ochre-orange wall, a climb called *Serpentine,* while dimly remembering the commitment I had made to university. Athol had gone back to New Zealand to visit his family and make a solo ascent of Mt Cook from the Hooker glacier, and so my non-climbing brother Rob made the Boxing Day drive to Taipan Wall with me so I could attempt a successful ascent of *Serpentine* following eight days of work on the climb. After falling off and having to rest on the rope right near the top of this long, sustained route, I told Rob that I would have to return the next day to have another go, to climb it without falling off. As we walked from the campsite to Taipan Wall early next morning, Rob, in classic brotherly fashion, warned me, 'You'd better not stuff this up because we're not coming back tomorrow.' Suffice to say I climbed it successfully, and we didn't have to go back for another attempt. A few days later I returned with *Serpentine*'s first ascensionist, Malcolm Matheson, and climbed it again while he took some photos for me. A few weeks later, in early 1993, I travelled to Mt Cook for the second time.

It wasn't until the winter of 1993 that Athol and I ventured into the mountains together, making an ascent of Mt Tasman's Balfour Face, in New Zealand's Southern Alps. Our climbing together, particularly in the mountains, as I discovered on this trip, allowed us to communicate without saying much. We implicitly trusted one another in stressful situations, without becoming frustrated or angry. I was surprised, because the difference in our experience was great, yet we worked together without a hitch. It amplified the peace. Even though my inexperience in the mountains would come to the fore at times, primarily when trying to execute alpine technique smoothly and uninterrupted, Athol would calmly wait, as though he were happily affected by a greater mountain experience. I noticed how streamlined and simple his gear was, while I had a cluttered mess around my harness. I learnt quickly, and I relished our climbing together, even on that first difficult trip, when it would have been so easy to feel inadequate as Athol moved on difficult alpine terrain instinctively while I negotiated the same with slow caution.

Our Patagonian expedition at the end of 1993 tipped the scales to some extent, slowly moving me towards a decision about some sort of commitment to my climbing, an advance toward something other than the completion of a degree or subsequent career. The impending reality of stepping onto the plane to go to the distant southern end of South America seemed to shrink the power of the English department at university in my mind, deadlines merely becoming points of negotiation between me and tutors. Withdrawing from my thesis for the year deemed me a failure on paper, but filled me with relief and, paradoxically, a sense of progress. The money for the trip came together in an *ad hoc* fashion, borrowed and earned without rationality or common sense. Details of my future life were quickly relegated to the back of the mind, wrapped in thoughts like 'I'll deal with it when I get back'. Of course, I never considered that we actually might not come back.

On returning, the attachments to home that had become detached while away immediately made themselves felt again. Suddenly it seemed as though it would be an age until the next trip. In the international terminal at midnight, the smell of dry wind-storm eucalyptus mixed with aviation fuel drifted in and out of the automatic doors. My family's questions revolved around where I had flown from, and what we had actually climbed. 'You climbed mountains with all that's in those three bags?!' my younger sister asked innocently. 'Yeah, but Athol is still back there, so he's got a bit of the gear. He's soloing Cerro Torre, the second peak we climbed,' I said, consciously trying to sound matter-of-fact, aware that I couldn't ever communicate what I felt about my time in Patagonia, or about what Athol was doing there on his own. But soon being with my family closed the enormous communication gap between us, because there was no need for me to explain all about the mountains; instead it was important to be in the 'present', at home. It no longer mattered what I did, or where I had been, and my mother was very excited to have the family together for a few days.

Scratching a vertical surface

I delayed my English Honours at university again, and went to Yosemite Valley in California for a four-week visit with Athol.

Yosemite is famous for the barely perceptible scale of its granite walls, a hallowed ground for climbers. The heart-stopper grand feature is El Capitan, a 900 metre-high cliff, much of it overhanging, smooth, and gets a metallic-like sheen in the sun.

The first climbing book I ever owned, *Basic Rockcraft,* (a present from my father) featured photographs from the early, exploratory ascents on El Capitan. I used to wonder how it was possible to climb such a high wall. The photographs indicated that the climbers made upward movements of only, say, a foot at a time – and the entire wall was 3000 feet! Camping at Yosemite in the famous Camp IV, historically a climbers' camp, we ran into Greg Crouch, an American alpinist we'd met in Patagonia. Greg, ex-American Rangers (an outfit of the U.S. Army), was camped in Yosemite for several months, at the beginning of a long commitment to climbing. Greg shared a sense of the appreciation of the mountains and climbing with Athol and me. We talked at night around the fireless camp table and bear-proof food lockers, unprompted laughter always emerging after remembering things from Patagonia. The years have since passed and Greg has returned many times to Patagonia. Meeting again recently in Los Angeles, Greg, Athol and I talked about the mountains, the memories – and the interpretations of the memories, an almost unspoken understanding of their significance as reference points for the future – coming simultaneously from all of us. Then the words about what we'd all been doing since mixed to form a powerful sensation; a sense that there was no real need to explain anything. Walking along the concrete-edged Venice Beach, stepping over battery-powered, crawling-on-their-stomach GI Joe toys, Greg told us of his most recent Patagonian expedition, and what was in the pipeline: a winter attempt on the West Face of Cerro Torre. Some months later the email telling of his success came in – the first American winter ascent of Cerro Torre.

Athol and I spent nearly every day in Yosemite climbing the features and cliffs made famous by Ansel Adams' black and white photographs, moving quicker the more we climbed. It was a pleasure to eventually climb without shredding my hands too much as I jammed them in the sharp, crystallised cracks. The *West Face* of El Capitan sits in my mind as the most beautiful time, moving rope length after rope length up a gently overhanging, shadowed granite wall. As we climbed higher I watched my pack at the base grow smaller and eventually lost sight of it. After eight hours we broke through to the sunlight on the windswept, moon-like summit plateau of El Capitan. Stunted Jeffrey pine trees, their foliage sculpted by the predominant wind, grew where they could find a birthplace in the loose, granular soil. With the rope coiled around my shoulder, and the rack of climbing gear on Athol, we walked over toward the hiking track and rested in the burning sunlight. The view opened out to Half Dome, whose *North West Face* route we had climbed a few days before. Suddenly it hit me: we were so much higher now than at 6 a.m. that day, and all the different climbing movements faded into one. Then, walking down to the valley floor, particular sections of the climb came to mind in precise detail, where perhaps some movement had been uncertain and had been resolved with conviction.

A few days before leaving we walked to the base of the main prow of El Capitan – a subtle protrusion from the main cliff line – where a route called *The Nose* rises to the top via a well-climbed series of cracks and corners, to finish right up the middle of the prow at its very highest point. It is Yosemite's, and one of the world's, most famous climbing routes. It was 6 a.m. when we left the ground wearing shorts and t-shirts, with three litres of water, some energy bars and a fleece jacket each. We had a small photocopied route map with us and charted our progress on it. I remember looking up a wide crack, too wide to jam my hands in easily, and then being amazed that I was soon at the end of the pitch. The day became warmer but, as if on cue, we were shielded from the sun by a layer of slow-moving cloud. We led alternately, in blocks of five pitches, the second person using jumars (the generic name for lightweight clamps that slide up a rope but grip tight when weight is put on them, thus allowing the climber, by weighting two jumars alternately, to move up the rope) to follow. At one point, at the end of the Great Roof, about halfway up, I watched the loops of rope beneath my feet blow out sideways then drop again in the flukey wind. Fifteen and a half hours after leaving the ground we were on top, walking back to the forest to find somewhere to sleep until dawn, joking about where the bears would be sleeping, being woken by the chill and dozing off again.

A few days later nine climbers were caught out two-thirds of the way up *The Nose,* and struggled against rain, sleet and then snowfall. Despite having planned for multi-day ascents, most of them ended up cramped on a tiny ledge, or hanging off the side of it. The rangers and search and rescue crews wheeled a spotlight-on-wheels into the meadow below and pin-pointed the unfolding drama while cables were simultaneously lowered from above. It looked crazy, but it worked, and the climbers were all plucked off, apparently one with minor frostbite.

Greg wasn't around Camp IV when we left, so Athol and I stuffed our foam mattresses into his tent, along with half-empty packets of chocolate biscuits, and anything else we weren't taking home. I phoned home, to be told a letter or two from 'someone, hang on, let me have a look, um, yes, Gigi, in India' was waiting on my desk. In India with family, Gigi was meant to return to Australia some time in the coming summer. When I did get home her letter, from the Himalaya alluding to a journey up the glacier below a mountain called Thalay Sagar, in retrospect seems somewhat prophetic, while her cryptic words poetically symbolised all that was unsaid between us.

Walking to the Yosemite bus stop Athol and I felt that we hadn't even scratched the surface of 'the Valley', and this heightened my awe of it. Our vertical travels felt all the more personally significant

Climbing the outrageous *Serpentine* (grade 29), Taipan Wall, Grampians National Park, Australia, 1992. *Malcolm 'HB' Matheson.*

Right: Climbing the architectural *Cookie Monster* (grade 25), Yosemite Valley, USA, during a brief visit in 1994. *Athol Whimp*.

Below: Athol and I a few minutes after climbing the north-west face of Half Dome, Yosemite Valley, USA, 1994. *Athol Whimp*.

because I knew we were just little dots playing out our own designs in a place of such massive scale. We waited at the dull aluminium-sided bus in the Yosemite Village centre while the driver finished the last three smokes from his packet of Salems, and golf-club-style buggies hitched into trains whizzed past crammed with google-eyed sightseers, their arms overflowing with sun cream, cameras and litre-sized 'cups' of Coke. We pulled away and the bus droned toward San Francisco.

Lessons from higher grounds

Questions about my future by others at home on the career track merely caused my silent withdrawal. Most of the time I couldn't be bothered talking about climbing – it felt too difficult to communicate my experiences, too contrived. As a teenager, my adventures had been dismissed as expected behaviour, but as I delayed university study and work it became difficult to subdue subconscious pangs of guilt about not getting to grips with a career. And would I ever have any money to get to the bigger mountains if I was just getting by on temporary jobs between trips? I rationalised my acceptance of a full-time 'career' by assuming I could climb effectively as well. The advertising agency Saatchi & Saatchi took me on in a graduate position in account management (managing the advertising between agency and client), and after nine months (I'm sure this wasn't meant to be a joke) offered me a job.

A few days either side of Easter in 1995 was just time enough for a perfect rapid trip to Mt Cook with Athol, making the most of a fast-moving high pressure system spied on the weather maps five days in advance. After this trip I was itching, within days, to go back, but tried to divert my attention to the commitment I had made to work. The intensity of the office was only relieved by weekends away climbing in the Grampians, waking to the cold snap of autumn mornings and the almost eerie pre-winter light – all so different to the office of twelve hours before. Back in the city, running through the smog-ridden traffic for training and thinking about future mountaineering plans only made me more frustrated, yet I was caught to some extent in my rationalised situation, not fully aware of the 'greater picture', or that as time passed I was climbing less and less.

In December 1995 I went back to Mt Cook with Athol and we spent Christmas Day slogging it out through a storm up the Hooker glacier. We had waited for five days for the rain to cease, looking up and down the valley every few hours to see what was going on. Then we got sick of waiting and judged the storm would be spent within another day, so we packed up and headed in. Within ten days I had to be back at my desk. Yet I just wanted to sit for a while and work it all out. Quite separate from the desire to relax and do nothing, sleep on the beach, I wanted to understand what was going on inside my head, what was the double-edged sword I kept plunging into myself, trying to make the career I was brought up to do balance with what I thought I really wanted.

The months prior to departing for the Himalaya in 1996 were frantic and uncertain. Did we have the right gear? Where was the money coming from? The managing director of the advertising agency, English Phil, seemed to have some understated philosophical enthusiasm for the idea. He pulled his spectacles from his face, wearily rubbed his eyes and pragmatically asked me, '... so if you left then, you'd be back, when?' Within minutes what I thought might have been impossible became a reality – I was given six weeks off, which wasn't really long enough, but I knew I could stretch it a bit if I had to, make up an excuse about being storm-bound, or something.

Parcels of gear arrived at the agency's reception, at home, and at Athol's house. Wearily trudging home at night, walking down the depressingly familiar streetscape, feeling very restless, I could barely imagine being in base camp in a few weeks' time. Waking up in the night was occasionally accompanied by a nightmare about nothing specific, but fed by the chaotic flow of information and energy whirling about between work and home. I realised that what I was looking forward to was getting on the plane, and forgetting about the mess on my desk. I also had a strong feeling of empowerment, that finally the 'energy' of our expedition was gathering its own momentum, preparing for departure.

A two-day reprieve from the endless phone calls and organisation came when Gigi and I went away to the beach. It was there, as the cold wind raced over the sand wet from the ocean spray, that I began to feel the potential impact of our chosen objective, the north face of Thalay Sagar. In some ways, I felt as though I didn't quite understand what Athol and I were actually going to attempt. It wasn't like we could just walk in and climb the mountain – there were many uncertainties. Therein lay a lot of the attraction, but I probably missed the irony. We were leaving for the Himalaya, somewhere I had dreamed of going for a long time.

The return trip from Thalay Sagar was fraught with pain from my nerve-damaged toes, the result of the onset of frostbite. The concrete kerb at Melbourne Airport provided a place to sit down after arriving. My friend James and sister Jane picked me up, and I hobbled on my heels toward the car, trying to avoid their obvious, nervous glances at my swollen feet. I told them that on the plane I had counted up the painkillers and anti-inflammatory tablets the doctor in Malaysia had given me, and took one every 20 minutes, yet it still only just kept the horrific pain away. Always it threatened, akin to suddenly realising your feet are burning, too close to the fire. The flight from Delhi to Kuala Lumpur had been stupidly done without any painkillers, and I fought back tears the whole way, trying to sustain a resistance to the shooting, electric-shock-type nerve pain, all the while fending off embarrassed glances from the stewards.

After a few days at home I went into the agency and spoke to Phil about leaving, the words flowing without hesitation or nervousness. It was an extension of the calm I had felt at Thalay Sagar base camp in the days before leaving. I now knew that to keep climbing like I wanted to meant that I couldn't keep working the way I had been. All the space and silence of those days waiting out the storms in base camp formed a bedrock of comfort in my mind, and offered me the chance to sit waiting for Phil's response without any concern. I hobbled out feeling grateful, as he'd 'left the door open' in case I wanted to return in the future. I pressed the clutch gently on the car with the heel of my foot, returned home and sheltered in the back of the house from the noise of the street while I began work on a magazine article about the expedition.

Without any immediate plans for climbing I started to feel restless and annoyed, emotionally displaced, searching for something that would offer a release. Athol had already re-booked Thalay Sagar for the next year, but I remained unsure, despite giving him some enthusiasm for the idea. However, deep down I really wanted to be back on Thalay Sagar, bracing against the huge onslaught of suffering. Soon the journeys up to the Grampians took on a familiar feel, the 5 a.m. departures from Melbourne wrapping the car in gentle mist. And then, as the faded dust-green ranges got closer and the air warmed a little, things felt they were falling into place without giving the issues the slightest thought. The touch of the rock was therapeutic, and the warmth of the early summer days incredibly luxurious.

I started training a lot for rock climbing, and returned to a favourite place in the Grampians, Sandinista Wall, where I finally managed to climb *Daniel-Or-Tiger,* a play on the name of the Sandinista rebels' leader, Daniel Ortega. I had initially seen this dramatic route back in 1989 when it was first climbed, and it marked a sense of personal progression for me when I made the final moves to the top anchor and glanced down at the trailing rope behind me. This very steep wall, the days spent climbing there, became the medium to think about the future.

As the autumn of 1997 approached Athol and I decided on the date of departure for our return to Thalay Sagar. Another point of commitment, another deadline to get ready for and structure life around. Time spent up in the Grampians yet again provided a chance to look into the future a little, to feel the past filtering through my mind and result in some sort of direction. Days and days spent working on *Demon Flower,* a difficult climb, came to nought as my final opportunity before going away to Mt Cook ended in failure and immense, depressing frustration. I had managed to climb the route in two sections, but could not climb it without falling off once halfway, resting on the rope for a minute, and then keeping on climbing to the top. The rock wall always rose darkly and steeply above me as I tried to link all the moves together before failing.

Then, surprisingly, the frustration began to dissipate as the excitement of the winter-time adventure at Mt Cook approached. Driving around town was the usual panic, getting together the last-minute pieces of mountain kit – chemical warmers for hands and feet, spare gloves, spare globes for the head torch – the little things that are so easy to forget but become so important on the mountain. The computer display on the plane stood at minus 19°C as we passed through 3500 metres, a little lower than the height of Mt Cook, on our descent into Christchurch. Suddenly my mind projected into the future, of what might or might not happen in the coming weeks at Mt Cook. The piercing cold and the onslaught of the savage winter were affecting me, doubts were creeping in about Thalay Sagar and reaching a crisis point, as all the nagging elements of my memories of Thalay came to the fore. Warnings surfaced again and again, as I tried to sleep through the dark, windy nights up on Mt Cook. It was as if I was in a silent hyper-reality, unaware of what was really happening inside my mind and, more importantly, what I really wanted. What is real? What's merely imagined? What do I *really* want? I carried the

horrendously heavy burden of doubt home on the plane, causing
an uncomfortable silence between Athol and myself.

The next morning I picked up the phone and called Athol:
'Let's go, I'm in,' I said. The conviction between us was understated, as it so often is. I ripped out my kit bags and lined up all my
gear, fresh from the hard two weeks on Mt Cook. I sharpened my
ice tools and crampons, and stared at the remaining bits scattered
over the floor; how incongruous they seemed inside the heated
house. Soon it all took on a semblance of order. A few frantic
weeks through July in Melbourne was all we then had before leaving for India. Every day was consumed with organisational jobs,
ensuring we had everything we'd need for our climb of Thalay
Sagar's north face.

Three months later, it wasn't until I had ten hours to kill on my
own in Singapore's Changi Airport that I felt the presence of
home softly stepping in. My final ten dollars of an already over-
cooked line of credit bought a phone call home to Gigi, a note-
book, a pen and some sweets. Slumped over a small table, next to
my unfinished coffee, I wrote but couldn't concentrate, my hands
still sun burnt and cut from the mountains. The words petered
out with weakness and a deeper feeling that there was nothing to
say. Streams of people merged into more streams of people as
flights left and arrived. It was distinctly and eerily like an inter-
planetary docking station might be, a grey view of fog and mist
outside the tinted windows adding to the cyber-feel. Cable television played round the clock at many and various places. I remembered the phone call to Gigi as I sat there, and thought how the air
of Melbourne would be cooler. I wanted to call again, but I didn't
have a cent.

My clothes smelt of the crisp hot Delhi laundry, clothes I had
received from the laundry man half an hour before riding to the
airport in the darkness. Athol had helped me squash the kit bags
and a barrel of equipment into the boot of the taxi and onto the

roof. I started laughing when he kicked the end of the barrel with his outstretched leg, and the taxi driver gave me a strange look. We bade farewell. Suddenly it was over.

Driving out to the airport, the pollution mist brushed over the windscreen as I talked with the driver. My mind drifted away and I found myself recalling the bus journey from the mountains down to Delhi a few days before, a 23-hour sardine-tin terror-ride. I thought of the conversation I had had with a *saddhu* about the mountains and clouds, or as he said, 'watersmoke'. When he asked I told him we had been climbing a mountain, and he reacted no differently than if I'd said 'just looking around'.

Athol, Patricia, the expedition's doctor and Tristram, Athol's brother, were staying on for a week or so, and even though I had only left my friends in Delhi 12 hours before, I missed them. How strong my memories already were! As I stared at the frantic, rushing scene of Singapore airport, at the business book stands and pocket organiser racks, I began to say something and realised Athol wasn't there. Our life together in the mountains felt detached and temporarily on hold – we both had to attune to our separate lives again.

My shared experiences with Athol in the mountains have been very powerful. We are deeply in tune with one another, so much that happens goes unspoken. We don't have to think about it. And there is also a stronger, simultaneous awareness between us that comes in the moments after a crisis, when we have been near death and too far from help – but have also felt supremely calm and at peace with one another. These times, for me, in the midst of the journey, have always remained far more vivid and intrinsically valuable than any summit I have stood on. But it is the route and the summit we aim for because they give us the means for the journey, an avenue to direct our energy. The mountain, after all, is the source of inspiration.

Time passed since our adventure on Thalay Sagar and we looked for another mountain. Organisation and money will always remain the hindering issues, especially for the Himalaya. The imagination of each new trip dispels my insecurity about the future, of what may or may not be. The purity of those special times when, after much uncertainty and risk, *something* is realised – yet something that remains strangely and beautifully intangible – keeps feeding my belief that there will always be places inside I haven't been.

Athol stands against the Patagonian giant Fitz Roy after our ascent of its north pillar (in profile on the right). Aguja Poincenot is the peak on the left. *Author.*

Beginning another pitch up the initial couloir leading to the north pillar of Fitz Roy, which rises far above. *Author.*

THREE NIGHTS OUT:

Fitz Roy, north pillar

3441 metres
Patagonia, 1994

DOWN THE southern end of the South American continent is
Patagonia. A day and a half by bus out of Rio Gallegos, a wind-ravaged provincial town, was El Chalten, a last outpost. Its sole communication with the outside world was via an out-of-service 747
aircraft radio, patched through to the phone system in El Calafate,
the town that feeds tourists to the famous Moreno Glacier. As we
made the journey to El Chalten the ex-school bus passed through
disused, barely identifiable, sand-washed concrete military instal-
lations from the Falklands War; it was from here many of the
Argentine sorties were launched. Halfway, the bus stopped
to change wheels after a puncture. Athol and I stepped out to
observe the scene: the desert, the *pampa,* panned out to the east,
while ahead of us to the north-west, scarred by grey, low-slung
clouds, were Cerro Torre and Fitz Roy, the two mountains we
were to climb.

Spaghetti-western balls of tumbleweed tumbled past, as if
unaffected by gravity. The bus driver, uniformed from head to
waist, including tie, below in dusty denim, leant into the wind
when he walked – an instinctive reaction. I noticed wind-blown
sand sticking to the grease on his hands when we got back into the
bus after the wheel change. People adjusted their cameras with
backs to the wind and then turned, trying to keep still, and
snapped away toward the skyline of the abrupt mountain range
kept hazy by the ominous, curling cloud.

Tired-eyed trekkers stared out at the desolate but fascinating
scene through the bus's murky windows, relieved to have re-
boarded after the wind-ravaged tyre-changing episode. We passed

over a bridge, the wooden beams slapping the iron supports underneath as the bus lurched across in first gear. Peering out of the sliding window by my shoulder, I was sprayed in river mist, merely a hint of the violent flow below.

Unloading our gear in El Chalten involved no more than getting off the near-empty bus and rescuing our splitting food cartons from the driver's helping hands. The ensuing argument about excess baggage was a painful end to our dusty trip, the driver eventually distracted by the calls of some young trekkers whose packs were wedged against leaking jerry cans of fuel next to the spare tyres. Soon the welcoming flurry (for the locals on board) dissipated and we stood by ourselves, adding up the packs, kit bags and splitting cartons.

Young boys stared from behind trees and American-built 4WD pick-ups sauntered past, dust and dirt stuck to fuel spillages along the vehicles' sides. One youth offered us some sort of help in Spanish; what he was suggesting we could never work out. His t-shirt was only just hanging to his body, on it a graphic one-finger salute directed toward a retreating comic-strip British flag, the only words I understood being 'fuck off' and 'Falklands'.

Once sorted, the kit stashed under some riverside trees, we walked across to Miguel's bar: *cafe con leche,* chocolate, the thick smell of cigars, and the aristocracy's helicopter waiting outside, looking distinctly on loan from the government, its rotors bouncing around in the wind. The pilot was standing in ex-Army fatigues beside his machine, the wind burning his Marlboro faster than he could. It was a laugh a minute at the bar for the Argentine elite. They were a set-piece from a previous generation, with houndstooth jackets, efficient English/Spanish tongues, and red, watering eyes. The women, dripping in gold and diamonds, touched their husbands' hands lightly and leant back giggling. 'Touristo, touristo,' they softly mentioned to one another as they gazed across at us, downing double shots of whisky.

We were ready to hit Fitz Roy with a good deal of energy. The morning after arriving in El Chalten we brewed up early then packed loads for our first carry into base camp. A big jar of honey had of course smashed inside one of the kit bags during the previous day's journey, so we sauntered out across a myriad pebbled streams to a stronger flow of water and washed it all out. The wind sprayed water up on us as we walked back, always keeping the water surface in a rippled frenzy. Back under the trees, sheltered by the riverbank, all we could hear was the dull whistle of the wind overhead.

We carried 30-kilogram loads into base camp, one a day over three days, the three-hour walk giving us time to get in touch with the scene. Winding sandy paths led us into forests, all the time with crisp alpine air washing over us. The dense, soft-floored beech forests were like something out of a botanic garden. Dead wood covered the ground, highlighted by small pools of sunlight breaking through the canopy. Occasionally a local would pass by, or an Argentine trekker from somewhere north, *hola.* The wind stretched and warped clouds into shapes I'd never seen, which scuttled in from the west and hugged the ranges. Walking along, even under a hot sun, it was if we were always on the edge of a storm, as the circling clouds spat off cold drops of rain like a dog shaking itself dry.

The indigenous locals called this mountain *chalten,* or 'volcano'. It was easy to see why. Freezing, fast-moving cloud often pours thickly from the summit, a very ominous impression, and certainly a reason not to approach any closer than the plains below. Looking at Fitz Roy from near its southern side later in our trip, while near the base of Cerro Torre, we witnessed extraordinary plumes of cloud forming on Fitz Roy's summit as massive westerly winds hit the mountain, riding its flanks higher and higher until eventually condensing into cloud as they departed.

It was after a supposed sighting from a ship, the aptly named *Beagle*, that the mountain was named Fitz Roy. In 1834 the *Beagle* sailed up the Santa Cruz River, on the eastern side of the range, and a view must have opened up for all on board, not dissimilar to what Athol and I saw as our diesel-smoke-pluming bus grunted over the dunes toward El Chalten. Vice-Admiral Robert Fitz Roy was the captain of the *Beagle* and had the peak named after him by an Argentine geographer in 1877.

We crossed the roaring Rio Blanco, White River, on a twisted grey log, strands of wire wrapped around the partially rotting wood offering at least some cosmetic security from the freezing, glacier-fresh rapids below, and staggered up a short hill to arrive in the climbers' base camp for Fitz Roy. Long mountain shadows cast an even light everywhere. As we padded across the soft forest floor, a muted roar of wind outside the forest only a few metres away, my ears caught the fragments of sentences from inside a couple of lean-to log huts, words rushing out alongside plumes of grey fireplace smoke.

Base camp was quaint and compact, and we pitched our tents at the end of the area among beech trees, on the soft, dark earth. A cold stream ran past only metres away, but it was outside the barrier of trees, and so trips to get water were often characterised by steps misplaced due to gusts of wind. The rocks we used to build a fireplace had obviously seen many fires before, and I briefly wondered who had been before us and trodden here, who might have gone onto the mountains, leaving small things behind, perhaps a photo from home or a mark in a book where the climber had stopped reading, waiting for his or her return.

On the way into base camp, Athol sat down on some large stones and we talked about our first close-up sighting of Fitz Roy from a clearing back along the track. The north pillar, our destination, appeared dark and huge, even remote. It only seemed a week ago that we had made the decision to go, when Patagonia was a totally remote and ferocious place to me. The night Athol and I talked in the car about going to Fitz Roy rain was falling heavily in Melbourne, and as we drove along in the dark, we shook hands on going to Patagonia. The stereo was playing and we turned it right down so we could hear what we were saying under the noise of the rain hitting the roof. Somewhere in the future lay arduous alpine days, not knowing where we'd be come darkness, being unsure of what lay ahead or what the weather was going to do. All the accumulated myths about Patagonia made it hard to separate fact from fiction.

Some climbers had procured the few 'huts' in base camp and relegated all others to sit out the rain in tents. This bizarre hut 'ownership' concept left us bewildered, Athol and I coming from a culture where huts in the mountains are for all people – 'come inside, weary traveller', and a hot mug of tea being thrust into one's hands.

Our plan to climb Fitz Roy's north pillar took shape as we gained a deeper faith in our reading of the weather. We were gradually coming to understand the patterns of cloud and wind, which gave us some hope for picking the best time to launch up the mountain. There was a lot of talk in base camp, rhetoric of 'This is Patagonia, man, you'll always be waiting for better weather ...' However, we'd only been 'in port' for a few days, had just completed carrying our gear into base camp, when the normally fantastic, rapidly changing, cloudscape came to a halt and vaporised. Suddenly, the recent memories of sipping *maté* beach-side at Mar del Plata in the shadows of partially finished skyscrapers were cast aside. All our energy became focused on making the most of this opportunity in what might be limited time.

We had carried the gear we would need for the climb up to the base of the couloir (a steep, clearly defined gully) leading to the north pillar of Fitz Roy within a few days of setting up in base camp. Even though at the time it was meteorological chaos up high on the *pillar nord,* Athol had had the foresight to climb up the initial granite wall of the couloir; it had been left wet and sad-looking by a schrund, where the snow had dropped away leaving the face exposed. It took him a couple of hours, but leaving a rope at this point meant we'd merely have to use jumars to get quickly up the rope and over the schrund when we were ready to start the climb.

We wanted to complete the route pioneered by two Swiss alpinists, Marco Pedrini and Kurt Locher, in 1985, *Chimmichurri y Tortas Fritas,* a splendid, visionary line up the right side of the pillar. When Pedrini and Locher reached the top col (saddle) 300 metres below the summit, Pedrini slipped on some ice, fell some 20 metres and badly injured himself. They were forced to bivouac that night. Abandoning the attempt, they abseiled down another way, the Casarotto route, where the likelihood of finding anchors to abseil from, mainly pitons, was high, and so made a long and arduous descent to the glacier, 1000 metres below. While Pedrini and Locher were attempting a new route on the north pillar, two other routes up the north pillar already existed – the Casarotto and the Kearney/Knight routes. Both of these routes took the left side of the north pillar, while the Pedrini/Locher route went up the right side of the pillar, all of these routes meeting on the top col below the summit headwall.

There is a huge expanse of granite on the north pillar. We carried with us a much reduced photocopy of a topographical map we had found in *Mountain* magazine, following the Pedrini/Locher route up to the top col. Although we could barely read it by the time we neared the summit, the black lines breaking up as the paper gradually wore away, to our surprise we found the 'topo' vaguely matched some of the main features of the pillar.

Unfortunately, our first foray to the pillar had to be aborted. One of our cookers kept belching and clogging. We turned back to base camp to replace it, having endured a frustrating day of lukewarm brews and cold porridge. On the mountain food consisted of energy bars, chocolate, drink powder, oats and some rice. The cooker is essential equipment – with it we melted ice for hot drinks and food. Some cookers have a gentle flame for campfire cooking and others are like jet engines for melting ice. Ours was, of course, the latter.

That morning, as we had sat on a rocky step heating some oats over the smoking cooker, two Americans, Kennan Harvey and Topher Donahue, were descending to base camp. They seemed too tired to say much, and kept moving down the slope after a few words. They later asked if they could jumar our initial fixed rope, as they were heading back up that evening for a serious attempt on the mountain. No drama. Kennan and Topher climbed the Kearney/Knight route on the north pillar, their figures black specks high on the route as we saw them from the initial couloir two days later.

We'd planned to leave base at 5 a.m. the next day, but Ath gave me a call when the alarms went off not to bother moving as he was busy throwing his guts up. Shortly after dawn he even threw up a weak cup of tea, and I was left with the guilt of eating breakfast on my own. It wasn't what we needed in the perfect climbing conditions of clear sky and no wind, Ath fighting hard to get the poison out of his system. I think he had been taken sick from a pizza we'd made, probably from some suspect salami. Following a close inspection of the label and consultation with the Spanish dictionary, it seemed as though our salami might well have been horse-meat, ex the glue factory.

We had a visit during the afternoon from a local *gaucho*. Neither of us knew what the other wanted, but a coffee and match for his tobacco smoothed things out before he gave up on us. I motioned him to sit down on the ground beside the fire. After he had drained the coffee from the mug, his thick fingers, like a black-smith's, turned the mug end over end under his toothless smile. The spurs on his Cuban-heeled boots dug into the earth, and a roughly sewn leather jacket hung from his shoulders, with a red and white check shirt protruding at the collar. He was bemused that we preferred to carry our gear in from El Chalten rather than have him load it in on horses.

I think he wanted to know how many of us there were and I signalled 'one other', motioned a good vomiting action and pointed to Athol's tent. The *gaucho* then imitated me vomiting and pointed to the tent as well. I thought we understood one another, but I wasn't sure. There was vomiting action all round, Athol's the only ones that were genuine. After a few hesitant smiles the *gaucho* sauntered off, somewhat annoyed he couldn't deliver a proper sales pitch to us, his horses lying in wait.

Around 5 p.m., followed by aggressive March flies in the strangely humid and still air, we started trudging up the hill toward Fitz Roy again. Athol's stomach was still very tender, but he weakly made step after step toward the higher lake and boulder field, Lago de los Tres, about an hour away.

The lake lay before us, motionless, like the glaze on a liqueur-iced cake. At its higher end snow neatly hugged the shore. The air was cooler than at base camp. It wasn't as cold as we had expected – being further south than Mt. Cook in New Zealand, we thought it would be colder; there it can still get to well below zero on a summer night high up. Base camp was mainly shorts and t-shirts temperature, up to 20°C in the sun, while it often went to zero on the mountain, and well below zero, say to minus 5°C, at night.

On most days the lake had some good furrows whipped up on it, and it reminded me of school-day sailing, frantically attempting to steer the 125 out of trouble, tacking before I really knew what would happen once committed. One shore is bounded by a steep moraine wall – the result of rocks deposited by a glacier, fed by the slow collapse of the mountains – the other a tumbling, scattered scree and boulder field. If the lake were in country Australia it would have its picture painted a dozen times a day. Here, beside some boulders, we spent the night. The end of daylight had brought some harmless cloud to the west, and I remember Athol standing on the moraine ridge, his head capped by these luminescent clouds.

We were out before dawn with just a brew, usually tea or coffee, to go on. It was routine terrain, easier than the standard yet arduous New Zealand glacier travel. Going up the first hill above the lake Athol had a good sweat up, although his body was protesting against the poisonous onslaught. We traversed around the ridge line, and paused for a few minutes where we had vainly tried to increase the pathetic efforts of our cooker two days previously.

Pressing on through the col, Paso Superior, we passed some sleeping Spaniards in their tents, and emerged onto the snap-frozen glacier Piedras Blancas. The glacier was almost a mirror to the pale blue sky, the crust frozen over, small drifts of wind picking the rope up between us. Above was Fitz Roy, the magazine photos we remembered being accurately realised in front of us. The colours of the immense walls were almost blurred, but were pulled into focus by my mind. The scale was like a runway – it was hard to tell the distance between features when we were merely 50 feet out. At least it was comforting to find ourselves directly under the mountain with barely a sweat having been raised in the mid-morning cool.

Fitz Roy has a rich climbing history. Back in 1952 the celebrated first ascent was made by the French via the south-east pillar. Even this ascent followed in the pioneering steps of an Italian Count and two other mountaineers, who in 1937 climbed the col leading to the south-east pillar. To this day, the col is known as Brecha de los Italianos, the Italian Col. From where we stood this col was clearly visible, and I found myself imagining those men looking high up at Fitz Roy and trying to work a way up, hearing the Italian voices, feeling the cold wind through their jackets and the spindrift stinging their faces.

The snow rose to meet the base of the pillar as though it were a tsunami frozen at the height of its ascent. We jumared our 50 metres of fixed rope. We hoped not to see this rope again until our descent – that this would be our one and only time up the couloir. The couloir was scary enough – it was about 400 metres long, rocks protruding from the ice. The couloir started out with an 80° step, then fell back to 40°, steepening again to 60–70° at its top. Rockfall was frequent and the ice was riddled with the evidence of it, from pockmarks to deep black scars. We were glad to be wearing our helmets. We held our breaths a good deal longer than we should have as we moved up the couloir, the walls rising up on each side. We were roped together, wearing our waist harnesses, pitching our way up, trying to stay on the ice (it was quicker to climb than the bare rock) in our plastic boots and crampons, using our tools. Football-sized rocks tore down at random, on one occasion a burning impact of stone-on-stone wafting up my nostrils from a rock landing only several metres away.

Of course, the quickest way out was to keep going up, and as soon as we could we hugged the right side of the couloir, protected by its massive, overhanging rock wall. I remember thinking it would be somewhat stupid to move through this gully in the afternoon, when the snow and ice would have softened up a fair bit. We were both carrying packs that were too heavy. We planned to leave our sleeping bags, mats, a decent amount of food and spare clothing on the col at the top of this couloir, the idea being that it would be retrievable if we had to get off in a hurry, while not so far down that it was pointless to take anyway.

A lot of the good ice had drained away during the afternoon heat in the upper reaches of the couloir, preventing easy climbing transfers from rock to ice, and vice versa. The rock was speckled yellow granite, the cracks rounded, inward-looking, providing straightforward hand-jamming for climbing. The pillar overhead stretched so far it could have been written into *2001: A Space Odyssey*. We plugged away, metre by metre, up the steepening 70° ice and rock near the col, swapping delicately between the ice and the rock, facing in all the time. Often we would end up climbing short sections of rock in crampons, dangling the ice tools from our wrists by their leashes and using our bare hands on the cold rock. Shortly before the col, Athol had to climb through a brief section of rock a few metres long as the ice had melted away. He tenuously made progress on the front points of his crampons. I could hear a faint trickle of water above me as he breathed onto his fingers to warm them up. We were deep in the shadow of the massive wall on the right, and everything was damp and cold. I shivered in the late afternoon air, my upper body instinctively scrunching inward for warmth.

Up above the pillar stretched far away, awash with low-angled sunlight. A small rock broke under Athol's crampons and fell past me, making a sound like a small motor. His technique remained solid, and he moved swiftly up to the col after analysing the rest of the pitch. On the col a fresh wind came through from the west, cold and alpine. I was disappointed when I joined Athol not to have arrived on a good flat area; instead we immediately and awk-wardly had to get our gear organised – what we were taking and leaving – while precariously perched under a huge boulder wedged on the col.

We had unknowingly stopped short of Casarotto's stone wall ledge, complete with the remains of his tent, a few parts of the poles and some barely discernible material. In 1979 Renato Casarotto had pioneered a route up the left side of the north pillar – on his own – spending a total of 43 days on the mountain, no doubt for long periods being trapped on this col in bad weather. From our stance it appeared as though the pillar just kept going up – his ledge was carefully concealed only a few metres higher. After sorting the ropes, rack of climbing equipment, and downing a brew, we started up the pillar. The rest of the other gear we were taking was stashed and tied down in one pack.

On our ascent of Fitz Roy, because the second was carrying a heavy pack, he jumared the rope instead of climbing to join the leader at the belay. In the pack we took above the col, we had one pair of plastic boots and crampons, one pair of ice tools, a light-weight down jacket each, plus a cooker with minimal fuel, some oats, rice, Argentine nougat, a little sugar, orange drink powder and some chocolate. We rationed the food, so much so that we often limited ourselves to one square of chocolate at a time. We wore lightweight 'rock shoes' with friction rubber soles for nearly the entire route, excepting the initial couloir.

As the light faded we found a sloping, jagged mess of a ledge – really just a stance, not good enough to be called a ledge – to spend the night on, but before cranking the cooker I climbed up a crack to just below another ledge, fixed a rope there and in the gloom abseiled back down to Athol, who was busy collecting ice for the cooker, chipping it from inside some cracks. Initially we had hoped we might find a better ledge, but as it became obvious this wasn't to be, we thought it was a good idea to get the rope fixed higher anyway, as it would save time in the morning. When I reached our precarious stance I found that Athol, always brilliantly efficient, had prepared a rope for me to tie into (we tied into the rope so we wouldn't fall off, down the mountain, while asleep) and had the cooker roaring.

Wearing our lightweight down jackets, we watched a sunset some film directors would've killed for, the sun's warmth reced-ing faster than the light. We were already beginning to shiver as we had no more clothing, and the temperature was dropping to below zero Celsius. We ate rice sweetened with sugar, milk powder and a little jam. 'I had this as a child,' Athol said to me quietly as we relished the heat of the food. And it struck me that we could have been kids in a tree as we crouched on the stance. It was New Year's Eve, and Athol asked me if I had a party to go to. We both knew how privileged we were to be 'on the way' on a mountain like Fitz Roy with the weather as stable as it was. We repeatedly remarked how incredible the weather was, always with lashings of swear words; somehow this reinforced our reality, reminded us it wasn't just a game.

Around midnight I remember trying to level out the spot I was sitting on with some rope, and attempting to scrape away the ice to stop my backside from staying numb. No matter what I did, caught in the haze of lack of sleep, I couldn't seem to get a 'seat' that worked; I repeatedly slipped forward and the rope ended up pulling on my harness. Eventually sleep overtook me in 20-minute time frames, and through this I accidentally leant my head – with helmet on – against the rope that tied me in, and it stopped me from slipping forward too far.

Before dawn it grew colder, my feet numb, and we both sat on the tiny ledge trying to hurry in our minds the slowly changing colours of the dawn sky. Far below, the distant hum of the glaciers on the north-west side – as heard on mountains everywhere – reached up to us, and my mind's eye imagined Athol and me sitting down on the glacier next to one of the icy ponds I had seen the previous evening, filling our water bottles. The thought reminded me so much of the gruelling days walking the glaciers at Mt Cook and it almost made me feel thankful for having a place to rest, being able to at least try and sleep.

An hour before light the alarm sounded, but we were already wide awake, keen to get a brew down our throats, sick of the shivering from a night spent out with no sleeping bags and little food. As the minutes wore on and more light was thrown onto the scene, moving about on our tiny stance became easier, the blood began circulating again, like a warm, low-voltage charge to the brain. At 6.30 a.m. Ath began jumaring the rope up to the point I'd reached the previous evening. As soon as he was off the rope, I went up as well.

Our plan for the day was that after an initial section of climbing straight up, we would tend right toward a large corner system – a place where two rock faces meet like the seam of an open book – that hit a two-tiered ledge system, which in turn led into another, larger corner system, the crux of the climb and the last pitches to the top col. We would in fact have to descend from the top of the pillar to the col. Once at the top col there was a further 300 metres to the summit, measured vertically, but we would have to cover more ground than that.

It was surprising how much we could see in the brightness of the morning. Even small granite crystals glittered in the light, at one point hundreds of crystals caught the direct sunlight and refracted it into my eyes. As we swapped leads toward the first corner system it felt like we were on the edge of some sort of discovery. Jumaring with the pack was a tiring job, its weight always pulling on our shoulders. By midday my right ankle was aching badly – it was in an elastic brace – so I swallowed a couple of painkillers and pressed on, trying to be careful when jamming it in the continuous cracks but inevitably forgetting this caution when the going got dire.

I'd injured the ankle six weeks before we left Melbourne. Athol and I had got into a chase with some locals while out running, which resulted in us legging it very quickly for some distance, down alleys and across major roads, all the time with a screaming go-fast Honda after us. Our pursuers apparently thought we were trying to damage their car, when in fact we had merely slapped the boot in frustration as the car was blocking the footpath. That had set the car's alarm off, causing them to bolt out of the front door toward us, one with an iron bar in hand. We thought it better not to stop and reason with them over a 'non-issue', so we took off, adrenalin powering our already tired legs. They soon realised they wouldn't catch us on foot, so turned back to the car and renewed their chase. All we heard as we sprinted down a dead-end cobbled alley was the screech of tyres and horns out on the main road as our pursuers ran red lights. We were nearing the end of the alley when it was suddenly filled with the thundering approach of an engine working overtime and fat tyres slapping over the cobblestones. We just cleared the ivy-covered, head-height fence as the men leapt at us from their car. We ripped down the side of a house. We jumped fence after fence, past swimming pools in back yards and families watching television, suspecting the men would be too fat to get us once the chase was on foot. As we crouched in the recesses of someone's back yard, I noticed my ankle swelling out of control. 'Oh fuck,' I said. We giggled and waited until it got darker, and I limped home while Athol surveyed the streets. After several x-rays and scans the doctor pronounced no structural damage done, so there were sighs of relief and laughter all round.

As we climbed we drifted off to sleep for periods while belaying, sitting or hanging while the other climbed onward, paying out the rope while under the influence of a mixture of sleep deprivation, physical tiredness and warm sunlight. Several times I was jolted awake by the pull of the rope from above. The warmth from the sun without any cold mountain wind was incredibly luxurious, and it was all too easy to drift in and out of sleep. I remember a sloping ledge we rested on briefly, sharing a portion of the expensive local chocolate. There wasn't a cloud in the sky, and not even a breath of wind. There was no choice but to keep going up.

The pillar was well visualised in our minds, and as every pitch was completed we filed it away. The only piece of gear we found left by Pedrini and Locher on the route was some webbing tied off around a tapered rock flake about halfway up – it was like seeing something brought out from a time capsule. We were probably the first humans to see this sling since it had been placed by Pedrini and Locher back in 1985. Finally we decided to sit for a short time and eat some chocolate. I still vividly remember the square sitting in the palm of my hand; a perfect sweet square against a scarred, cut and grazed human form. How long could I hold it against my tongue? The perfect culinary catch-22, voraciously needing to eat, yet wanting to keep the thick sucrose-taste impact forever. Not far

The amazing north pillar and summit headwall of Fitz Roy. Our route took the prominently lit 'corners' on the central pillar's right side. We endured three open bivouacs on this route. *David Neilson.*

Above: Jumaring on day two on the north pillar of Fitz Roy. The bottom col is visible in the middle of the photograph. *Athol Whimp.*

Below: With Athol on the summit of Fitz Roy, relieved and obviously happy to have arrived. We soon turned our attention to the interminable abseil descent. *Athol Whimp.*

from where we dined on our chocolate, we needed to move across to the left to gain the final corner system.

While some of these pitches form a speedy blur in my head, others stand proud and separate and are impossible to dislodge from my memory. I glanced down to the belay and then back up to the corner I figured we needed to get to. Sudden, chaotic and almost unconscious calculations about distance and height sparked through my mind: how far had I climbed on the pitch, how much rope was left before it ran out? We were about two-thirds of the way up this 700-metre section of the pillar, and were consumed by a constant flow of climbing and looking for anchors to belay from.

At this stage I was in a shallow corner and faced with moving out and left onto a prow, then across a steep slab for quite some distance before I'd be able to fix an anchor in a horizontal crack. As I looked down to Athol, I could see the glaciers a thousand metres below, looking like old scars. I jammed a couple of wires in a crack at the back of the corner, clipped the rope on to them and hoped they wouldn't lift out as I moved up. However, I could see the rope was threateningly lifting them as I inched higher. It is necessary to try to get the rope flowing smoothly from the belayer to the leader above, not straining at the protection you've put in the rock, but it's not always easy, especially halfway up a big mountain with limited equipment.

As if working in braille, I felt blindly for a good hold around the prow and eventually felt a few crystals that had risen from the slabby plane. I committed myself and put my weight on these fingers. Already they were sweating, getting slippery. As I did so I felt the rack of equipment catching between my chest and the rock. My feet struggled to take any weight, and as my eyes passed the corner I noticed one of the wires holding my rope had lifted out and dropped away. But thanks to that old predicament of being past the point of no return, I *had* to go ahead. Panting rather wretchedly, I began stepping higher before my toes, currently smearing –

flattening as much as possible over the rock, allowing the rubber soles of my shoes to get maximum purchase – on glittering crystals, slipped off the wall. Soon I was in the convex of the slab, my feet well centred under me, once again stable enough to consider the situation – the most hideous of luxuries. I rapidly talked myself into moving, flat out like a jockey on the straight, toward the break.

I had probably only spent one minute at the stance in the convex, but it felt like hours. Then the ache in my straining calf muscles arrested my wandering mind – it was telling me just how horrible my position was, imagining myself running out of time as I stood on the little, glinting crystals. I stood up on my toes and reached up for two gritty, sloping edges, the rope falling out of sight below and around the prow. As I did so flashes went off in my brain, mere fractions of a second long. Images strong and candid of my family, of food on the table, steam rising from the plates as my father loosened his tie. I hauled my weight up on my fingers, and gazed into the now-in-view foot-wide ledge, my feet pawing rather helplessly on the slabby granite, just like a cat trying to turn a door handle. With my face pressed against the wall, I nervously brought a foot up onto the ledge while simultaneously raising a hand higher, scraping it over the speckled yellow surface. My throat rasped dry. I then stood up, and to my astonishment found a crack to place a good anchor, right by my side.

The wall had steepened more by this stage, but because we knew we would end in a race against daylight as we were focused on getting to the top col that night, we didn't even pause on belays. When Athol arrived after jumaring the pitch, he clipped the jumars to my harness while I clipped all the gear onto his, and then he led away. He climbed a few metres to the left until he was into the corner, put some protection in, and began moving more quickly. He stemmed his feet onto opposite sides of the open-book corner, moving swiftly despite the difficulties. The day was drawing on somewhat, but two more pitches and we were motor-ing up easier ground to the top of the pillar.

No doubt we were slowed considerably by dehydration: not far below the top of the pillar I was hanging on the belay and I could hear the trickling of water in the back of a crack in the rock, out of sight, out of reach, and all too close. I forced my mind away from the sound of the water and thought ahead to the coming night on the top col, our second one with no bivouac gear. We quickly climbed some easier terrain until Fitz Roy's upper headwall came into view through the very dim light, a dark wall with frozen sheets of ice smeared over vertical sections.

It suddenly reminded me of some of the dark, wet granite walls of my first climbs as a teenager, when the excitement and fear would wash through my stomach, unaware of how to even try and control it, as if I was getting blown through some bellows, and helplessly into a fire. I felt the intensity of those beginning moments of my climbing, of looking back down the climb *Grimulace,* which was glistening with a skin of thin, damp algae over its white granite, then glancing higher and not knowing how to climb up there, caught in the middle, only just hanging on, hoping I wasn't going to rip out the protection I'd placed in the crack if I fell, panting and saying to myself, 'This hold, then find the next hold, then the next hold, don't forget your feet, try and get the weight onto your feet or you'll fall off.'

My flashback occupied only a few seconds before I noticed we were climbing and scrambling around some tottering blocks together, wedging our hands and fingers into short cracks, then lowering our bodies down further, glancing down and across, searching for the right place to approach the col, not wanting to get caught by the darkness. My memories rapidly retreated, back into a part of my brain that I could never consciously access.

Athol and I were roped together as we moved, always with a few pieces of protection between us should something happen. Fresh air

rushed up from the freezing, monstrously deep voids on either side
of us, and as we stared around, working out how to descend to the
col, we were caught in a dramatic, luminescent twilight. It seemed
as though we could keep seeing right through the ensuing darkness,
so accustomed had we become to the gradually dimming light.

We traversed a bit more in search of the anchor Pedrini and
Locher must have used to abseil down to the col, about 50 metres
below. We spied a single piton about 20 metres down, and figured
we could reach the col from there; if we couldn't, we'd just continue to climb down from it. Both wearing friction boots, we
edged our way to the piton, making use of small ledges. Little
pieces of rock fell away as we moved carefully, whizzing down into
a seeming infinity like ball bearings tumbling down a stairway, and
amplifying our now near-dark predicament. Soon we had to belay,
as it was getting too steep. Once at the piton, we backed it up with
extra protection, a couple of good wires. We hung there, tied the
two ropes together, threaded them through the sling we had
attached to the piton, and threw the ends off. (By abseiling on the
two ropes, we could then pull one rope, and because the ropes
were tied together at the top, both ropes would fall down to us.)
We could just make out the ends swinging in the breeze, as the col
wasn't directly below the piton, but off to one side.

The whole scene was rather derelict, the rope ends looking so
insignificant hanging thousands of feet above the ground. Athol
abseiled first, launching into the abyss. While I waited for Athol a
deep sense of loneliness invaded me. Hunched over in the gloom,
I tried to keep myself awake as though in a long, foolish sleep-
deprived car drive. I kept moving about as I sat there, trying to
relieve the aches in my back, and knocking loose, dried scabs from
the back of my hands. Cold hands. As Athol neared the ends of the
ropes, he worked a solid pendulum swing up, and soon had
enough sideways movement to land on the col. The piton had held
his abseil all right, so I removed the back-up wires before abseiling

as there was a good chance we'd need them higher up. With gloves on, I followed Athol down, abseiling express down the lines to the ends, which Athol had tied into the col – the red carpet treatment.

The top col of the north pillar was a dismal scene. It was only a few metres wide, the drops on either side stomach-churning, thousands of feet deep. In the last light of the day the rock appeared as though it never saw the sun, and was a little frightening. I dreaded the thought of the onset of the colder night temperatures. We quickly prepared a place to sit for the dark hours. It was impossible to move any rocks – they were frozen in place – but we managed to nestle in under the side of a leaning block. Smears of ice hung from the rock like wind chimes from a porch that hadn't been moved in years.

The distance along the col from the pillar to the headwall was no more than ten or so metres. All was cold and dark. The sound of the cooker enveloped us like a blanket, its heat seeming to soften the night air. Above loomed the headwall, and the summit. Still the fine weather held out. That evening only a thin stretch of very high cloud passed over, and there was not a breath of wind. The cyclical pattern of shivering and re-warmth became a familiar rhythm. I would sleep until the convulsions set in and, once warmed slightly by the shivering, drift toward sleep again, the whole cycle taking around half an hour. It was more a question of how best we could pass the time – at least sitting in one spot for a while was rest, and it might as well be done through the dark hours.

At 6.30 a.m. we began the first pitch above the col and up the headwall. Once again, leaving our little temporary home was like abandoning the wreck of a spaceship – we secured the cooker and some gear here, where we had sat, waiting for collection on the way down. The chaotic arrangement of rock, ice and grey granite colours around us took on much more detail as it grew lighter. The neon hue on the eastern Patagonian horizon drifted away. As the light changed so did my perception of distance: the ground was further below, and the glaciers curved with imperceptible detail.

I climbed for approximately five metres before being stopped by heavily verglassed rock (a surface covering of ice over the rocks formed from the melt-water of the previous day). We were still wearing our rock shoes, carefully stepping to avoid the verglas. Quick movements got me to another stance where I could survey what lay ahead. Then by stemming my legs out on opposing walls, and my arms overhead, jamming my fingers and hands into a crack, smears of ice on the wall underneath, I climbed very delicately over more verglas. The crack continued for at least ten metres. I hoped the wires I was using didn't slip or shatter the veneer of verglas coating the coarse granite wall. That would have meant my protection would have torn out, causing me to fall.

It was a good thing I was so tired – it enabled me to step up as high as I could in my aiders (slings that can be clipped to a piece of protection and enable you to step up high by putting weight on the protection) on these horrible placements without too much conscious fear, methodically moving to climb above the verglas barrier. Meanwhile, the night effectively went on for Ath, as he was still on the col, patiently belaying as I found a passage through the verglas and up into some better ground. We were constantly talking to each other, the words softly breaking through the frigid air, 'What's it like up there?', 'How's it going?', 'How's it look around that bulge – hopefully it leads onto that ledge and beyond ...'

Whoever was leading would sometimes only half-hear these words, replying in monosyllables, at least until the situation allowed us to articulate something greater, words fed from a sense of being in control, of belonging: 'You should see it up here! This is fucking outrageous!' At which point whoever was belaying would just about be jumping out of their skin, wanting to get higher and into the thick of it, as if he had just been given the most valuable reinforcement for committing to the mountain and the route.

After the previous day of painful and awkward hanging belays, where it was hard to get our weight off our harnesses as we hung off the rock, it was with audible relief that I slumped onto a small ledge to belay from and get the weight off my harness. I secured a good anchor and gave the call. Athol was soon on the way, jumaring as I panted in the first morning warmth from the sun. He didn't pause long at the belay ledge. We were on the move, well aware we needed to top out before the weather got away from us.

Athol climbed up a vertical crack, the same width for quite a distance, placing protection very sparingly – he sensed he was going to run out of the right-sized protection. Despite his frugality, he still reached a point where he had to commit to climbing a long way above his final piece of protection to reach a safe belay. I felt at that moment that Athol would have kept climbing above his protection for as long as it took to find one. From Athol's belay we climbed two slightly easier pitches, interspersed with short technical sections of steep slab climbing.

Then came the icefields to the summit. I tried to climb only on the rock, the unlikely granite protrusions that stuck out from the ice. It wasn't easy, and I soon became impatient. Still in rock shoes designed for rock climbing and not the plastic boots and crampons we carried for snow and ice, I had to kick steps up the sun-softened ice between the granite tips. At times I clung desperately to the featureless base of a rock tip as my feet stood tenuously below, quite unaware how long they might – or might not – stay there, the intuitive feeling I usually had about the stability of my position being undermined by the unfamiliarity of using rock shoes on the icy crust. I anchored. I was left feeling ragged; my throat cracked and I could barely get enough moisture into my mouth to call out 'OK' and 'Jumar' to Athol. The sun was shining, but I was still wearing the down jacket I'd had on overnight and felt claustrophobically hot. However, with the slings and gear rack over my jacket, I could do nothing but keep moving.

To arrive on top was the only way to end the intense tiredness and discomfort, and to give some peace to my battered hands. I watched Ath as he led on the final pitch toward the summit, his head turning and looking as if some unexpected danger lay nearby, not knowing exactly what was on the other side of the mountain. It was so quiet and peaceful up there, and I soon heard Ath say rather uneventfully, 'This is it,' as he briefly looked about before rigging an anchor. I jumared up to join him on the summit.

The smile on Athol's face betrayed tiredness. 'Well, Andy, here we are,' he quietly said, and a nervous thud went through my heart; a piercing amount of pain, relief and happiness all at once. I vividly recall the final few metres on the jumars, only several metres of rope between me and the anchor, my eyes running through the system – the pieces making the anchor, an end of the rope going to Athol and the rope running down to me. 'You've got to work the hardest for the best ones,' he said. Sitting on the summit there wasn't even a breath of wind, and it wasn't cold. It wasn't *mountain* cold, instead there was the coolness that belongs so much to the air of a lower height. At home we would complain, but here we relished in it. Somehow the entire scene felt very fragile.

The presence of ice and icicles clinging to the undersides of the rocks was ominous. I wondered what little it would take for nature to wreak havoc on this mountain top. We both knew bad weather – extremely high winds and fast-moving, southerly cold fronts – wasn't far away. In Patagonia, there are barely a few fine days every summer. The climbing stories I'd read of Patagonia even before I'd been mountaineering filled me with terror. We could see Cerro Torre and, next to it, Torre Egger and Cerro Standhart. Cerro Torre, for the sake of brevity and affection often referred to as the 'Torre', had taken on a darker colour, and I wondered why. Often from below it looks on the fainter side of yellow, but from the top of Fitz Roy it was rather dark, despite being covered in sunlight. I was overwhelmed with a strange sensation, somewhere between a resigned peacefulness and an anxious anticipation, a feeling of insecurity about the weather that was exacerbated by our remote, vulnerable position.

We rigged the first abseil down only a few metres from the summit. It was around 1.30 p.m. – we had been on the summit for an hour and a half. Abseiling down the icefield was quick and the rope was pulling free after each abseil easily, without catches or tangles. When we reached the steep sections of rock on the headwall, with the cracks bending and dropping away beneath us, the morning verglas had melted and water was spraying down the face, arcing away eastward, resembling slow-motion tracer bullets. Athol abseiled through a section of the freezing waterfall to a tiny stance and got an anchor in as he hung there, with the rope wound around his leg to free his hands. He was the victim of a good dousing on the way through the waterfall as he placed some protection to act as a diversion for the rope. Rather typically, he didn't complain. On my way down I copped the water spray as well when I took his protection out.

From the anchor we couldn't see anywhere to go. The col, plain as day, lay right under our noses, but it was further than 50 metres away – our ropes were only 50 metres – and there wasn't anywhere on the way down we might be able to get another anchor. The only vague hope was a flake – a fin of rock that had partially broken away from the rock buttress – off to the right. After pulling the ropes down from the previous abseil point, which left both of us hanging from the anchor, I set off. By the time I got to where the flake was, I didn't have to swing much from the anchor – a relief as each swing sent me into the waterfall. When I swung onto the flake I immediately yelled back 'No' with resounding disappointment. My heart sunk. The flake was too tight to take any of the gear we had, and its edges too shattered. Slightly lower I noticed a yellow sling around a smaller flake, and my heart beat with a sweet relief. When I reached it I saw the sling had obviously been used as an abseil point before, perhaps years ago. It was a pretty pathetic anchor, now that I think about it. Athol abseiled to join me, and we nervously took turns abseiling to the col.

At the col we sat in the sun, trying to dry our down jackets out, and snacked on Argentine nougat. We both shivered a little when the breeze drifted up the steep gullies on either side of us. I really wanted to be warmer, instead of always feeling on the edge of shivering. But it felt tremendous to be leaving the mountain, as I had a sense that we had been treated too kindly by 'the powers that be'.

Descending the pillar didn't start well. We abseiled 50 metres before realising we'd taken the wrong route. Sudden feelings hit us: anger; tiredness; frustration. But we soon began fixing the mistake, as we didn't want to get caught in the dark not knowing the way to abseil. I held one of the ropes while Athol jumared back up, then I jumared with the pack as Athol simultaneously hauled it up from the anchor. When I arrived I took the pack off and kicked it into the corner of the small ledge, then clipped it into the anchor, muttering what a bastard it was. I would have loved to have kicked the pack right off the edge, but felt too attached to what we had in it, a sense of belonging to those various, cold bits of metal.

Athol tied himself into an end of the rope as I belayed, and he probed out along the edge of a short, knife-edge granite ridge to make sure we had the correct line of descent this time. He found an abseil anchor and belayed me over. I remember standing there in the late afternoon shade, being relieved and exhausted all at once. The yellow granite was marked with scores of vertically running ribs, in between which were thin fissures. Our abseil anchor was a couple of disintegrating pitons laced with some old rope, whose faded sheath was disintegrating so that its core exploded through. We guessed they had been placed there by the late Casarotto. A poignant reminder of an historic ascent, the pitons looked simultaneously fragile and immovable, the oxides from their metal slowly returning to the rock.

There are only a few abseils before the Casarotto line drops away very steeply, straight down the pillar, like the entrance to a black hole. Clean lines make for a rapid descent, so we wore tired smiles as we linked abseil after abseil, scanning for the next station, conscious that there would be regular anchors. Often we found them, sometimes we didn't. At one point, about two-thirds down the pillar, having abseiled right to the end of the ropes I found myself five metres short of an anchor. The gear I currently had in wasn't adequate to make an anchor where I was, so there was nothing for it but to unclip from the ropes and down-climb to the good anchor. Facing in, I traversed and moved down to the good anchor along a narrow ledge, stressed but strangely accepting of it all. Athol then made another abseil from a slightly lower anchor to join me.

Looking back up at the corners on the pillar was amazing. I never grew tired of it. It was like a million trapdoors and false corners were opened up for inspection, so colossal was the scale. As dusk spread over the mountain, what we could see of the pillar from our position in the corner glowed, a soft light reflecting off the rock. The corners and curved arêtes furrowed into infinity as I eyed them while waiting on an anchor. A few more minutes passed, and the intensity of the ambient light grew. It was like being on the golden edge of everything: we were surrounded by a speckled, deep yellow colour, and thousands of shades in between – it was impossible to tell where the rock changed colour, yet it did. Five-minute patches of sleep helped as we got further down the pillar.

After a rope-stretching abseil I just managed to clip into a small wire I found in a 90° corner, the walls dead vertical. I had no suitable gear of the right size to back the wire up, which I remember regretting at the time. As I transferred my weight onto the wire the ropes left me in an elastic surge, and hung rather gently a few metres away. Again on the stretch, he was able to get very close to the single wire anchor. I held up a sling, which he clipped into, and pulled him in. Then, as soon as possible, after slowly and awkwardly transferring his weight onto the single wire I was already hanging by, we backed up the wire with another.

Soon we were on our way again, the light now gloomy. At 10 p.m. we decided to sit it out for the night on an angled ledge, even though we knew we weren't too far from the bottom col. We were a lot tireder than we realised at the time. In reality, we were shattered. There we were: at the end of an abseil with hardly a word we called it quits for the day with just enough light to climb back up the wall ten metres to free the stuck rope. We threw away pieces of ice and rock, trying to clear a place to sit. Ath mentioned to me after a few hours into the slow night between shivering convulsions that the single-wire anchor must have been the same one Pedrini and Locher had hung from in 1985 during their epic retreat. We had read about this in *Mountain* magazine. It was a warm feeling, hearing the lonely call of other alpinists who had been in the same situation years before. It is like a brother you never knew you had knocking on the door. Slumped on the angled ledge, with my head and helmet leaning against the tied-off rope, I could hear Ath's words again, that they'd hung there on the single wire just as we had, and I felt strangely at ease. High, thin cloud drifted overhead, perhaps a precursor to the inevitable bad weather.

We brewed up in the dark and at first light were off, like thieves escaping through the underground tunnels of a bank just robbed. Within the hour we were at the bottom col, chewing on a bar of nougat we'd left there on the way up, sweet and hard. We both nearly tore our teeth out trying to bite it. There was some reorganisation to do at the col, as we now had the gear we'd left there on the way up.

Getting from here down the 400 metre couloir to the ground felt like it would be a formality. But as soon as we moved the gravity of the situation became obvious: we were dangerously, almost overpoweringly, tired after three cold nights out with no sleep, and many pitches of climbing in between. Soon enough we were on the way, absolutely drained. I'm certain that if we were fresh it would have taken half as long. The warm sun was channelled into the couloir by the massive wall on the right and the expanse of the north pillar on the left. By the time we were halfway down we were very exposed to rockfall. We heard sounds of small rocks falling past us at terminal velocity – like the noise of artillery, the close sounds of sucking, rushing air magnified like sonic booms – but strangely didn't pay much attention to them. It felt as if we were waiting for the mountain to cease fire.

About 80 metres off the ground, Athol was abseiling about ten metres down from the anchor I was hanging on, when I noticed the piton moving. The only other component of the anchor was an old tied-off knot jammed in a groove. Ath said, 'It's probably just flexing ...' Half-asleep, I replied, 'I think it's *moving,* be careful ...' It was only later that I remembered I had a rack of wires on my harness, yet it didn't occur to me to get them out and quickly back the anchor up. Once Athol was down and I had the 'OK' call, I just clipped in and descended. Everything was a big effort. The sun, the claustrophobic helmet, the continual draining of sweat into the eyes, the entrapment of slings and the usual collection of gear over the shoulder preventing me from getting layers of clothing off easily. I put up with the immense discomfort of overheating and the anxiety, knowing we'd be on the ground very soon. The minutes ticked by yet we never looked at our watches, for time was irrelevant; all that mattered was getting onto the ground and what we knew would follow: relief, water, food, rest, sleep and space.

On the glacier, near the base of the coulior, was a snow cave; by the time we reached it we could barely move. Kennan and Topher had dug this cave weeks before. Small pieces of melting snow dropped clumsily from its opening, its roof drooped, it seemed as though everything was on the way out. We had been hounded from the mountain in a chaotic explosion of falling rock and ice, exhaustion, bad anchors, and now we contemplated the threatening collapse of the snow cave. After only five minutes in the cave I had to get out – I never have been one for close, tight spaces. Ath managed another half hour before he too had to leave it.

We were shattered with exhaustion and had to rest, to drink and eat. We also wanted to wait for the evening and colder temperatures, hoping the snow would have frozen over, making it easier and quicker walking. The heat from the sun was intense. I sat for hours slumped over, asleep on my knees, with a gaiter over my head. Even getting up to put more snow into the pot was an effort we could hardly be bothered with.

But we maintained some sense of discipline, no doubt motivated by thirst and hunger more than anything else. Keen to get to base camp, we packed all the gear and started walking across the glacier at dusk. The freeze we'd been hoping for didn't happen in time. We were too tired and hungry to wait any longer. I was busy plunging step after step into the soft snow as we walked toward the ridge that led towards base camp when Ath called out to stop. I looked into the sky and saw three UFO-shaped clouds travelling as if in a formation. I turned around to Athol and he had his camera out. I leant over on my ski poles and felt my lungs and chest rising and falling with each breath, my pack pulling on my shoulders.

We had barely been going for an hour before we had to rest in the snow. We sat there, laughing and joking about the climb, looking back up at the north pillar, silhouetted in profile by the setting sun. Athol flicked snow around with the tip of his ski pole, and it felt as though we were sitting beside a lake, throwing pebbles into the water. Standing up, we started walking again, focusing on the occasional crevasse and where the descent ran close to the tottering ridge edge. Otherwise we walked on 'low alert', conserving energy, in tune with each other's steps. At Lago de los Tres it was dark. We scrambled across a section of wet, slabby rock, each negotiating our own way though only a few metres apart, resigned to accepting the final, time-consuming hassles, every movement made hard work by the heavy pack and the desire to sit down at every step. Sweat poured from my head, my throat dry. The sound of water trickling into the lake was everywhere.

A quick stop on the hilltop above base camp before plunging into the final knee-smashing descent, ski poles straining under the load, the small yellow spots of light from our head torches guiding us home, until finally the silhouettes of the tents were in sight. People mingled around camp fires in the dark, the orange glow of the flames catching my eyes as we quietly made our way toward our tents. As we walked past the Americans' campsite we said hello to Kennan and Topher. We could just make out the glow of their eyes around the smoky fire. Kennan casually asked, 'Summit?' and we replied 'Yeah,' too tired to say much more. They both said well done, and we returned the compliment. As we took the first steps away from their camp, we both stopped and thanked them for clipping a bit of gear we had inadvertently left on a belay on to the pack at the bottom col.

My eyes stared through my open tent door where light was streaming in. I didn't have the energy to focus, so I let my head crash back on the pile of clothes I was using as a pillow. My body was in the sleeping bag, the earth feeling warm under the floor of the tent. The shadow of a bird moved across the tent fly. Athol was outside his tent lighting the cooker, sitting on the log, slowly looking around.

Soon I was too hot in the tent, the morning sunlight bringing a sweat on, yet my semi-comatose state was overpowering – sleep whacked me out time and again. When I finally awoke, drenched in sweat, I drank sweet tea under the shade of the trees that rose above our camp. Looking around I noticed the packs dropped next to our tents. 'It must have been around 11 p.m. last night we got back,' I said to Athol, yet I could barely remember. And then I saw empty chocolate bar wrappers and evidence of other food near our tents, yet I could scarcely make the connection between seeing these and eating the contents the night before.

Later that morning we talked with a Japanese alpinist who was preparing to solo climb the *American* route on Fitz Roy. We told him as much as we could about the approach. I was caught between feeling incredibly keen as I stood silent and motionless listening to his plans, and lethargically distant. Observing this man with his equipment spread out, his clothes that had obviously seen previous alpine epics, and his *personal motivation,* his intensely quiet demeanour, I suddenly felt the clarity of the early mornings up on the north pillar. After the exchange of 'Good luck', 'Thank you', shaken hands and slight bows, Athol and I strolled back to our camp. Sunlight broke through the leaves and branches of the trees as the wind rushed through.

The beautiful, almost mythical Cerro Torre, one of the most revered mountains in the world. In January 1994, Athol and I raced bad weather to climb the Maestri route (south-east pillar), which faces camera. Base camp is at bottom left of picture, next to Lago Torre. *David Neilson*.

Athol climbing the ice towers on Cerro Torre's Maestri route, the glacier far below. *Author.*

INTO THE WIND:

Cerro Torre, the Maestri route, south-east pillar

3128 metres
Patagonia, 1994

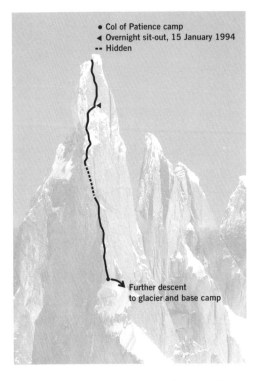

• Col of Patience camp
◄ Overnight sit-out, 15 January 1994
▪▪ Hidden

◄

● ➘ Further descent
to glacier and base camp

As WE WALKED along the soft, flat track from Fitz Roy base camp to Cerro Torre base camp, saw-tooth granite satellite peaks of these two mountains spread out before us: clouds stretched out by big winds, glacial streams gushing over logs caught by polished granite boulders, the wind lifting the rapids. Crossing the river along dead wood one afternoon, I noticed fine spray from some crests curling savagely in the wind, at least a metre above the surface. And even though I knew we'd never get bowled over by the continuous, lifting waves, the threat of the freezing water caused me to focus as the old grey log wobbled under my feet.

We stopped for a rest at the end of a lake in the cold wind and hot sun. Another hour toward Cerro Torre base camp it was drizzling and warm. As we turned a corner, emerging into a wide valley, Cerro Torre came into view. Fast-moving, low cloud swept past its sides, the Adela range hiding the weather approaching from the west. Clear sunlight high up turned very hazy as it reached through the swirling white cloud wrapped around the Torre's lower sections. We imagined how violent it would be up in the wind. The trees in the base camp for Cerro Torre were all bent away from the wind, and the Rio Fitz Roy, Fitz Roy River, flowed past; its icy waters were to be the source of numb fingers while water-fetching.

El Chalten was only two hours, or an hour and a half at a quick clip from our new camp, so we dropped in for *coca, cafe con leche, bun, jamon,* Miguel running vastly inaccurate tabs that sometimes worked in your favour, sometimes didn't. If one paid kind attention to his *guanaco,* like a cross between an alpaca and a llama, called Nau, and fed it chocolate, Miguel would drop the tab accordingly – perhaps. The postwoman was operating a fix, and almost without any guilt presumed we were all oblivious to it. Mining and petroleum trucks were rumbling down the gravel roads on preliminary exploration excursions and one of the drivers filled a kerosene bottle for us. He would have given us the entire 1000 gallons if we'd asked. It was as if everything added up to nothing, until the wads of cash came out, when US greenbacks were preferred.

El Chalten was on the cusp of development, new concrete kerbs waited for people to walk on them, local youths wandered and drove about: long black hair, oil-stained hands, diesel engines, rubbish wrapped around power poles and flattened along the fences, heads tilted perpetually into the wind. Running a continuous glucose and carbohydrate drip into our systems, we would sit there all day and saunter back to camp into a headwind. As we strode out one morning on our way into El Chalten for more supplies we saw a woman walking up the track toward us – it was Athol's mother, Ava. We could have been back in Rangiora, the Whimps' home town in New Zealand, so casually did we all greet. Ava had biked, bused and hitched down from Buenos Aires, spent Christmas with a Welsh family, and had now finally arrived at Cerro Torre base camp.

Under the beech trees, we pitched our tents on silky white and yellow granite sands. The wind funnelled down the river alongside the campsite, cracking the sheet of plastic between our tents all night like a flag beachside. It was a relief to see Cerro Torre consumed by storm most of the time while we got all the gear over from Fitz Roy base camp, a two-and-a-half-hour walk.

Halfway across the plateau one afternoon, walking in that strange mixture of overpowering heat from the sun and numbing cold from the Patagonian wind, we passed two Germans on their way to Fitz Roy base camp. We talked about what had been done, what was planned, what a bastard the wind was. A few times since when I have thought of these men I have felt almost ashamed at how fleeting my memory of one of them is. His death only several days after this cursory meeting shocked me. There was no personal friendship, it could have been anyone. But it had occurred on a mountain I had climbed, Fitz Roy, and in this was a link, however tenuous. When his memory comes to the fore tragic elements surface in me, like when one finds old photographs of lost friends, briefly being embarrassed for ever losing them. The impossibility of explaining such an accident is paramount in my mind: where to begin, where to draw the lines, and then, of course, that no one really knew *exactly* what happened, even those practised at the game.

On one of our forays into El Chalten to re-supply our bread and chocolate, we met two Australians, John Fantini and Simon Parsons. They had arrived to climb Cerro Torre and, they hoped, Fitz Roy. I hadn't seen Simon for some time – he'd been working in Canada, an intensive-care paediatrician. Athol and I walked out from the shelter of Miguel's Cafe and called out to Simon, whereupon we all gathered, shaking hands. I'd never met John, a veteran of the Australia/New Zealand alpine scene. He looked worn out and like he could walk a thousand miles all at once. They were keen to know what we'd done on Fitz Roy, the weather pattern, and other logistical details. As we talked, all of us leant into the wind to hear the words, and then stood straight again when the sentence was finished.

Simon seemed happy to be away from work in Canada for a while, escaping to Patagonia on his return to Australia. I was seventeen when I met Simon. Athol and I had been living in his house in

Melbourne, and had moved out the night before departing for South America. My brother and parents arrived on the verandah at 5 a.m. ready to take us to the airport while we were still busy running back and forth inside, stuffing last-minute, just-remembered, items into the kit bags. Athol detoured by a friend's house on the way to the airport and picked up a piece of gear to complete the climbing rack, and we were away. Sitting with my family before going behind the sliding doors into Customs were full of unspoken feeling. My mother's nervous, grappling eyes needed somewhere to rest. I could feel her looking deeply into me as I spoke to my father, yet she could find no solace. I was about to board the plane for Patagonia.

The plane's wings shuddered and we left the ground. I suddenly realised we were going on an *expedition*. The frantic past weeks seemed to evaporate; the insecurity of debt, of cancelling my university English thesis for the year, and of knowing that I would have to face it all once home, faded away. My mind was far away during our last weeks in Melbourne. Indeed, once committed to our Patagonian expedition, I had begun to feel dispirited about domestic detail, the plan for my thesis seemed to amount to nought as I stared at the computer screen. A small moment of awakening came as I turned out of the university gate one day and recalled the image of Fitz Roy in *Mountain* sitting on my desk at home. Soon we would be there – it was almost too much for me to comprehend.

We had a brief pause in Auckland, then onto Argentina in a labouring 747, skirting the Antarctic before flying across and north up the South American continent to Buenos Aires. A series of pictures of Pope John Paul II were stuck on the hotel reception's wall at just over head height. I really thought the hotel-keeper wanted to look *up* to the Pope. After he told us the hotel rates he looked at the little pictures and then back at us, saying in slow, broken English, 'For commercial business, he is a good man'. Argentina was re-incarnating its currency, the peso being pegged to the US dollar to curb inflation. Walking around the old bank end of town was like something out Borges' *Labyrinths*. The occasional evidence of the Galtieri regime of the early 1980s – such as police wearing wrong-sized, out-of-date riot gear for pedestrian patrols – put an extra spin on things. A few more days on the coast were the perfect relaxation, before heading south to Patagonia.

Cerro Torre stood like a giant needle at the head of the glacier, its sides stuck with wind-blown ice and snow. Even after climbing Fitz Roy, I felt a nervous thud in my heart as I stood sorting kit in base camp, a haze of cloud far overhead. On 12 January Athol and I carried a load each up to the Norwegian bivouac (otherwise known as the 'rock bivvy'), a small cave under a boulder, whose tightly packed stone walls had been made and maintained by climbers over the years. It was directly beneath the east pillar, the Maestri route, of Cerro Torre. The Italian alpinist Ermanno Salvaterra had informed us of the two approaches to its base from maps inside the hut he had built at base camp.

We had everything we needed to make an ascent on that load carry if need be. That didn't seem likely as, by the time we got close to the base, the Torre was in a massive storm, the winds incredible; driving rain, sleet and snow making progress hard work across the white ice. Leaning into the wind, goggles and windproofs on, we staggered on toward the rock bivvy. When the white ice finished, we found ourselves trudging over soft glacial silt and sporadic, strewn boulders, through a gradual narrowing of the glacier. We brewed up under a huge block out of the wind, the screaming rush of air a metre on either side causing us to raise our voices a lot to be heard.

Huge winds cracked on the rock walls like sonic booms, their reverberations pressing on our chests as we laboured on to the rock bivvy. By mid-afternoon we were ensconced there as the rain and sleet hammered down. I'd never seen anything like it – horizontal rain that accumulated in a vacuum-like frenzy at the cave's entrance. By 2.30 p.m. the following day we were getting wetter and wetter, water dripping in the back of the cave, and the wind hadn't let up.

It's always a hard call in the mountains – when to go down for some respite from the bad weather. This had all the signs of a set-in storm. And in Patagonia a storm could last for weeks. After packing the minimum we bolted, barely able to string more than a few steps together before being knocked down by the wind. I remember as we dropped into the gully that had been home to a trickle 24 hours previously we encountered a surging chaos of water. Once down on the white ice we made rapid progress, the wind behind us the accelerator to base camp.

Next morning dawned still, clear and calm. We had been punished for taking the soft option up at the rock bivvy and retreating to base camp. We ate breakfast slowly and ate up well, packed methodically, and were away by midday. We made good time to the rock bivvy, slight compensation for leaving the afternoon before. It was very hot walking on the glacier and, as we panted our way around the corner toward the rock bivvy, I wondered how I was going to keep the momentum going up the mountain.

It was already mid-afternoon when we arrived at the rock bivvy. Two Spanish teams were moving up the slope toward the initial buttress below the start of the south-east pillar proper. We sorted our gear, ate some more, and drank a lot. I walked over to a small stream to collect more water. As I manoeuvred around the side of a large boulder an older Spanish man nodded to me with a big smile from further down the moraine wall – he had been busy helping his 'lads' prepare for the Torre. Unshaven and proud, a veteran alpinist, father figure.

As Athol and I shouldered our packs to move out, John and Simon arrived. We said we might see them up there 'somewhere' – at that stage we had no idea how or where, and in the back of our minds there were visions of some strange meeting in an obscure place on the mountain. There was a rather tremendous feeling running through us as we made our way up the snow slopes below the Torre. It was as if we existed in a vacuum, and every movement and sound we made was accentuated by the stillness of the vacuum. We roped up through the grid-like crevasses and contoured around their gaping lips. Up ahead we could see six other climbers moving into the mixed terrain below the Col of Patience – yellow jackets illuminating their movements in the gloom of a shadowy dusk.

By halfway up the buttress we had caught them, keen to establish ourselves at the col with the benefit of first arrival. I remember talking in broken English to two of these men as we shared a belay and being struck by their politeness. They literally waved us through. One of them said to me, *'Compressero,'* meaning it as a question, and despite not taking it as thus, I simply said, 'Yes, Compressor route.'

In June 1970, the Italian mountaineer Cesare Maestri went to the south-east side of Cerro Torre and started one of the most dramatic and controversial sagas in mountaineering history. His team was equipped with a petrol-driven air compressor for drilling bolt holes. This was winched up the route as they climbed, and enabled them to place bolts to get higher. This was of particular use when they encountered smoother sections of wall, where regularly spaced bolts enabled them to transfer their weight from one bolt to the next, gradually moving higher. The compressor still hangs from the final headwall of Cerro Torre, stalactites of ice draped from its sides. Interestingly, Maestri chose to climb in the winter, when temperatures are extremely low (minus 20°Celsius would not be uncommon).

He and his team didn't reach the summit on that expedition, despite an effort that saw them climb the majority of the south-east ridge, so he returned in November the same year. They climbed back up to their high point, resurrected the air compressor drill, and eventually made it to the top, placing many bolts in the process. Placing bolts has always been a contentious issue in climbing, and some people saw this ascent of Maestri's as a desecration of Cerro Torre. Despite this, the 'Maestri' route is one of the most revered

Left: Athol shortly after leaving our bivouac at the Col of Patience, Cerro Torre, around 7 a.m., 15 January 1994. *Author.*

Below: Athol abseiling the summit headwall of Cerro Torre after our ascent. I am standing on Maestri's infamous compressor. *Author.*

Above: Playing the waiting game. Left to right: John Fantini, Athol Whimp and Simon Parsons at Cerro Torre base camp, January 1994. *Author*.

Below: A rare still morning on Cerro Torre, seen from base camp, as westerly cloud starts to roll in. *Author*.

climbs in the world, the definitive classic. Far from a 'desecration', his bolts gave Athol and me an amazing climbing experience. Maestri and co. elected not to ascend the summit ice mushroom of Cerro Torre, claiming that it wasn't really part of the mountain as it was constantly changing; there one season, gone the next.

When they abseiled from the top, as a final touch Maestri removed the highest section of bolts from the headwall – perhaps aimed at those who had cast serious doubt (due to a lack of hard evidence and inconsistencies in the account) over his claimed ascent of Cerro Torre, via the east face, back in 1959. But even now, despite the route's fame and the desire of many mountaineers to climb it (with relatively few successes), Maestri's ascent of the south-east ridge – the Maestri route – is seen by some as the ascent of a tormented man, driven to get to the summit of Cerro Torre 'at all costs', to prove to his detractors he really has, and could, climb it.

By the time Athol and I had reached the hard wind-packed snow of the Col of Patience we were on our own, and an almost warm breeze greeted us there in the darkness. There was still the faintest of faded pinks washed through the western horizon as we sided up to the crest of the col. The lip of the crest overhung by a mere few centimetres, all of it taking the crampons to half-depth. We each had one ice tool out, and rapidly side-stepped up and across toward the schrund (a crevasse-like break in a steep snow or ice slope) at the end of the col, right under the Maestri route. It was as if the whole place emanated a supernatural glow. It was beautiful and eerie at the same time. We cleared the schrund out as one would clear out the back seat of a cluttered car. Ath got inside and spread the icy debris evenly across the floor until we had something we could spread our sleeping mats out on and get the cooker going. It was a stunning situation: from our sleeping bags we could stare around the horizon's perimeter and hear the very faint tinkling of the Spanish climbers a few hundred feet below.

It wasn't until we had put the cooker out and were lying silently trying to sleep that the Spanish arrived. Athol still laughs when he remembers the sight of one of the Spanish men knocking down icicles hanging from the ceiling of the schrund. We thought he could have gone on all night like that, knocking little icicles down, much like people pop bubblewrap endlessly. In reality, he was waiting for his friends, killing time as it were. They stoically sat the night out without sleeping bags, much to our surprise. My heart was beating savagely; the thought of moving out in the morning was an almost overwhelming prospect, but something I couldn't wait to do. *Why wasn't it morning now*?!

At 5 a.m. we were brewing up. Ruthlessly, we left sleeping bags, mats, most of our food and a few other unneccessaries in the schrund. Leaving a lot of gear behind is luxurious, as if saying to ourselves as we ditched more and more, 'another ounce not on our backs ...'. The last minutes before leaving the bivvy dragged on. We were very keen to get on with the climb. As we made our final preparations we said to the Spanish, 'See you up there,' but they had decided to descend instead, not feeling quite ready, and too tired. At 6.30 a.m. we began climbing. I have a photo of Athol only two pitches up from the schrund in the soft light of the early morning, still low enough to hear the cracking of the glacier below. The top of El Mocho already sat below us, the stunted child of its stupendous parent, Cerro Torre. From the glacier, El Mocho is menacing enough for the new visitor to believe *it* is the Torre, if the cloud is sitting low.

There are approximately 27 pitches from the schrund to the summit, nowadays naïvely catalogued like supermarket aisles by some climbing magazines. The weather during the early part of 15 January was clear; however, the beginnings of high cloud were already appearing in the west. I remember thinking it wasn't too cold – summer mornings on Mt Cook can be far more frigid.

At the eleventh pitch we saw the first of Maestri's famous, if not notorious, bolts. Already I could feel the day moving on, but the sight of the bolt ladder cheered me so much I felt as though I had a cartoon dollar sign lit up on my head. After 20 metres or so I'd sorted out a good system on Maestri's apparatus *de luxe*. I anchored just over the lip of a sloping ledge and yelled for Ath to hit the jumars. On my immediate left I could peer around the arête, the ridge, and view the amazing south face, hanging as if in limbo, so massive was it. Sharp smears of ice hung from the face. It seemed strange to be standing on the ridge, leaning back in my harness, while only a metre away the south face stretched away and down on a huge scale, out of proportion to the rock and ice beneath my feet. Indeed, it felt as though things were off the scale.

When Athol arrived at the anchor he moved past me without hesitation, eyeing up the road above, where pathetic old ropes hung in disjointed fashion along the way. We were now on the way across and up toward the major crack that provides access to the celebrated ice towers, guardians of the headwall. I jumared up to Athol, trying to counter the ensuing swing after I released the tight rope from each clipped bolt, usually every sixth or seventh one. Grey clouds moved swiftly, high overhead. If the next time I'd looked up they'd covered the headwall, I would not have been surprised. The wind blew in occasional spirals amongst the ropes and ourselves, muffling our calls, reinforcing the potential of localised violence on the mountain.

We could hear faint, sporadic calls between John and Simon far below – it appeared as though they were going down after reaching several pitches above the schrund. From base camp, we had noticed the weather – the usual pattern was westerly, generally windy, with cloud forming and streaming from nearby summits. Up on the mountain the trick was to view the weather as if we were down on the ground (altogether a far more relaxing exercise), not so easy to do when the sound of the wind cracks like rifle shots on the walls and ice falls with alarming regularity against a backdrop of UFO-shaped grey clouds.

Near the major crack below the ice towers, Athol belayed outside the crack to avoid falling ice, and from my movements. Leading, I stemmed my feet on opposite walls and jammed my way up the crack, displaying the usual alpine desperation of trying to move faster than the terrain dictates – not resting for too long anywhere it would be easy to waste time. A calculator ticked over in my head, minutes added up to dark hours. The rack of gear around my chest scraped against the rough granite walls of the tight corner. The hard part was having faith in smearing my rock shoes on rough patches of granite that looked either wet, or wet *and* frozen. This resulted in holding on very hard with arms and fingers – an exercise all too stressful, but necessary. Eventually, like a beached whale I slumped onto the belay ledge, the remaining gear on the sling catching on chunks of ice scattered and sticking over the surface as I crawled over to a crack at the back of the ledge to make an anchor.

When Athol turned the lip of the ledge I was already getting cold. After a methodical swap of gear and a few words about our progress ('We're getting there') he headed up another bolt ladder to a smaller ledge. Deciding that from here on we were likely to be climbing on ice, we left our rock shoes here, put on plastic boots and crampons and quickly changed the rack over again. I put most of the rock protection in my pack, and clipped the ice screws on to my harness. I was immediately confronted with steep mixed ground, granite showing through smears of blue and white ice that shattered as soon as I gently kicked a crampon in. Soon I had broken through this terrain and was able to climb quickly up a shallow dish-like formation of 'plastic' ice, squeaky and secure. I saw an old sling anchor directly above, under a huge rock buttress, and headed for it. When Athol climbed up toward me he realised I should have gone further out to the right and belayed under a shield of ice. I remember being annoyed with myself for misjudging this – but I let the frustration go, and moved swiftly to better the situation. As soon as Ath was safe I traversed across the ice to him, rhythmically placing my ice tools and stabbing my crampons in. While we sorted some gear out at the belay and had a quick drink, we looked at the weather, the dark clouds arcing across the region very threateningly. As we hadn't been hit by a storm at that stage, we were optimistic that the weather might just go our way – the only problem was it was getting worse.

From where we hung we could see where the next two pitches went, so I began moving up the ice shield, striking my ice tools into perfect ice. I stepped left to ensure I could exit the ice shield in the right place and saw the ice occasionally went hollow right to the granite underneath. I belayed just over the lip of the ice shield, resting back on some granite protrusions in a shallow gully, trying to see where we needed to go.

While Athol climbed up I leant out and snapped a couple of photos of him. Far below, the glacier ran as if made of broken concrete strewn over a moonscape. From the belay Athol led up until he hit the base of the ice towers, the large walls guarding the summit headwall, connected to the headwall by a thin ridge of ice. We discussed which way to go. A quick sortie out right revealed nothing useful, so back left it was, around the toe of the ice towers to belay just up around their side. The temperature had dropped a good deal by the time we reached here, and as I followed Athol's lead to his belay I noticed we were climbing directly above the south face. Cold air drifted up from the colossal space beneath. We briefly hung on the belay, looking at the headwall looming overhead and the huge, overhanging ice mushrooms forming the summit.

The next pitch was a bolt ladder, but what should have been fast progress was slowed by having to chop the ice out from the bolts. As a result, I stood as high as I could in my aiders and only chopped the minimum amount of bolts out from the ice. I was immensely relieved to see an anchor hiding under the build-up of ice as I turned the crest of the vertical wall of ice and granite, but the show wasn't over until I'd spent ten minutes chopping ice out around it to make sure the anchor slings were OK. Blood dripped from my hands as Athol quickly jumared up to me, the heat in them rapidly fading away as the icy breeze from below floated past.

The headwall wasn't far away. Athol deftly manoeuvred himself through the belay, handed me the jumars and, with ice tools in hand, traversed around to the base of the headwall, about 20 metres away. He belayed from the headwall. I recall being impressed that he didn't merely belay when he hit the wall, but launched up it to get the rope out, and the distance in. I was relieved when I began climbing, as it was cold and very windy – we could barely hear one other – and slowly getting dark. But on we went. I was stunned by the ice traverse to the headwall from where I hung, how thin, how perfect, it was. Its final few metres narrowed down to barely a metre wide, dropping off very steeply on both sides of the 'ridge'. This spot was soon to be our 'seat' for the night.

By the time I'd joined Athol at his belay he'd sorted out the line to climb. Without much talk I headed up and through a series of flakes, some of them expanding and verglassed, pulling on intermittent bolts and wires placed behind the flakes. On one section on this pitch I saw there was a long gap between my position and where the bolts began again, so I climbed what I could and then moved on aiders, using wires behind the expanding flakes, their edges crumbling as I put weight on the wires and stepped up to make the next placement. When I'd crossed this section, Maestri's bolts went straight up, express. I kept going until Athol called out 'Two metres' – meaning he had only two metres of slack rope at his end and I would have to find an anchor – my ears only catching the middle of his words, the wind taking the rest. I was panting savagely, driven by the gloomy light and violent wind, and the unknown prospect of whether we'd reach the summit that night. Athol jumared up fast.

It must have been the quickest changeover on the route: within a minute and a half Ath was above the belay, swinging through, bolt after bolt. As I paid the rope out I watched the loops below my feet come level with my face as they were caught by gusts of wind. All around it was a desperate scene, even the green forests at base camp had disappeared in the darkness. We both knew we'd be digging hard to get out of this one.

Athol rigged the belay and I quickly got my head torch out; as I was connecting the wires the battery dropped out. 'Oh fuck,' I screamed out, loud enough for Athol to hear. Without giving myself time to get too angry with my clumsiness, I hit the jumars, channelling my anger into the line.

At the belay Ath calmly asked me, 'What was that about?'

'I dropped my battery as I was connecting it,' I said.

'Oh well.'

The wind was howling. We both calculated the options, and the consequences of whatever we chose to do. Two pitches remained to the top of the headwall. It must have been close to 11 p.m. at this point – we'd been climbing well into the dark, our eyes trying to adjust to the conditions. We both hung there, our feet pressed against the vertical wall. Climbing with one head torch between us would've been too chaotic and time-consuming in the dark and wind. As we scanned around the scene things grew slightly simpler in our minds. Neither of us wanted to start abseiling off the mountain, so sitting out the night in hope of some better weather with the morning seemed the answer to our predicament.

'We could fix the ropes, rap to the base of the headwall, and jumar them in the morning,' said Athol.

It wasn't just a good option, it was pretty much our only option if we wanted to keep going.

'It's worth it,' I said, vaguely aware that we wouldn't forgive ourselves for retreating from that point.

We perhaps would have only started retreating when it was almost too late. The weather seemed to be moving so rapidly it would have been easy to misjudge this. Such was our paradox. So with that we tied off one of the ropes to an anchor and abseiled. The wind was spinning the rope in circles, its end making huge sweeps across the wall, occasionally coming into vision when it was lifted a little closer by the violent updrafts. Once at the end of this rope, we tied the other rope to another anchor and abseiled again, leaving the higher rope tied in tight. We arrived at the tiny ice 'ridge' at the base of the wall with a few metres of rope to spare. By the time I got there, Ath had managed to get a piece of protection in, as well as being clipped into a jumar.

I stepped over Ath to the far side of the 'ridge'. The situation was nothing short of horrible. The top of the 'ridge' was so narrow and shallow it felt as though it might break like a fragile wine glass. We were hemmed into a cramped 70° gully. The wind was going like the clappers, as if some old man was shovelling coal into the furnace with God's helping hand. It took me 15 minutes to get an ice screw in by my side, as I was only able to use one hand, my axe in the other hand was holding me on. I was standing on my crampons' front points, calves aching, spindrift flying into my face and stinging like sand, the whole deal. Some bizarre, abstract part of my mind was waiting for the pain to end, even though I kept hacking away at the mountain. I became almost oblivious, for a few moments, to the maelstrom. It was really a luxury, my mind dropping out like that, pretending nothing was going on. There was no time or *consciousness* to complain, instead I was driven by a deeper-seated instinct for survival.

Once I was clipped to the screw we hacked into the iron-hard ice in a bid to get some sort of seat organised. The depressingly small chips of ice we dislodged just blew back into our faces. I could only use my right hand, as my left side was caged by the wall of the gully. It didn't take long to become breathless, for my arms to feel sloppy and uncoordinated – 'fucking wasted' were the only audible words coming from our mouths.

As I was putting the finishing touches to my side of the seat, Athol was busy getting his crampons off and his legs into his pack to try and get warmer, and at the same time trying to prevent slipping off the seat of ice. 'That'll fucking do it,' I said, and awkwardly turned around to lower my weight onto the newly fashioned seat. It was just like trying to sit on a sloping ice block. After another ten minutes I had my legs in my pack as well. It would have been laughable if it weren't so serious. We couldn't see it, but the glacier was nearly a thousand metres below. We put our goggles on to warm our faces. Again I experienced a momentary absence of the present-mind, some part of my brain looking for a way out.

'How's your seat?' asked Ath.

'It's working, just.'

'Same.'

We didn't have the energy to say much. Soon we needed a brew – our only sustenance since breakfast had been a few chocolate bars and about a litre of water each. Athol chopped out a tiny pod between us to place the cooker in. He didn't even hesitate to pick up his ice axe again to get the job done, belting the ice for 20 seconds or so, then gasping. Once the cooker was settled, we doused it with kerosene to prime it, then *woomph*! It was the perfect time for overkill. We added ice chips to the pot as the cooker roared. Athol opened the bore right out and pumped it again, and we sat there being careful not to move and knock the pot off its tenuous perch. We passed the pot back and forth, watching the liquid swish around and the hot drink was gone all too soon.

I couldn't believe how much my body ached. I hunched over, the rope pulling my harness around my waist to the side, and drifted off into intermittent sleep, being woken by the cold and wind, with saliva running from my mouth. We were almost too wasted to intellectualise about the weather – it was difficult to tell in the dark whether it was getting worse or gradually backing off.

At 4 a.m. the wind died down. We peeled our goggles off and looked around. As the dawn light gave way to the day, patches of blue sky appeared. With daylight it became much easier to get the cooker going and we ate some porridge. Athol began jumaring soon after. How amazing it was to feel my limbs moving again after a night of freezing immobility! My legs and arms hungrily ate up the hundred metres of jumaring to the top of the fixed line. I took the bottom line with me as I moved through.

It was my lead at the belay, and we hoped it would get us to the compressor. The only sound was the clipping of karabiners and heavy breathing – unclipping, weighting, unweighting, moving through, gaining height, every metre one more in the bag. Sometimes I needed to unholster an ice tool and belt off ice from around the bolts above head height: a rather unremarkable and brutal display of technique. The belay was directly underneath the line of my climbing, and thus in a plumb line for falling ice debris. Athol ducked as much as possible to avoid falling ice, partially relying on intuition, curling his shoulders inward, taking up less space.

Athol called out 'Two metres'. Immediately I knew I didn't have enough rope to reach the compressor. I climbed as high as possible, tied one of the ropes off, and yelled for Ath to start jumaring while keeping me on belay. I waited while the compressor sat silently only a few metres above my head. Ath called out again: 'You've got four metres ...' With that I stared at the compressor with renewed interest: massive stalactites of ice hung from its sides, blast-frozen to the wall by the wind, as water melted and refroze down the line of bolts.

After getting as high as possible in my aiders, I stepped out of them onto the rock. I thought I'd be able to reach down and grab them, but already my boots were slipping on the thin granite edges, my hands clamped onto thin expanding flakes – 'What a nightmare' was my immediate response. It must have been sickening to watch: not dissimilar to waiting for a lazy cat to get out of the way of an oncoming vehicle. My predicament had temporarily seized me. I kicked the ice that was stuck to one of my boots off – there could have been a terrier on the end of my leg – then put everything into a lunge for one thin flake, the toe of the boot forced into a crumbling flat edge. As I stood higher I moved faster, fear the accelerator. Another lunge and I had a hand wrapped around the compressor's base, but my feet were threatening to cut loose. With a serious drain on power, I managed to get a heel hooked up onto the compressor, eventually heaving the rest of myself up. The adrenalin slowly dropped back as Athol made his way up on the jumars.

Only one pitch of the headwall remained, and it was still before 10 a.m. The Maestri 'express', fast despite the missing bits covered in ice in between all the bolts, had now come to an end. The compressor hung like the last green bottle on the wall. Athol dealt with the Bridwell pitch at a good speed. The American Jim Bridwell, with Steve Brewer, made the first re-ascent of the Maestri route in 1978, after Maestri had smashed out his bolts from the top section of the headwall as he started descending.

It wasn't too cold; I belayed wearing a thin pair of gloves, a faint sweat breaking over my upper body – I was still wearing my down jacket and waterproof shell from the previous night. As Ath approached the anchor, he called down the moves he was making. Finally the call resonated peacefully within my mind – 'Safe'. I waited anxiously for Athol to call out 'OK, jumar!' then I hit the jumars like a whippet. Two bolts with a piece of tape threaded through made the anchor, and the balance of the pitch to the summit area consisted of a gentle slope. Out to our right, an ice mushroom overhung the headwall and formed the very highest tip of the mountain. We clipped our crampons on one-handed in an extremely cramped position. I was under Athol, my knees pressing on the vertical wall, taking things slow and steady while I contorted to place the toe bail first and then pull the heel plate of the crampon on. A delicate operation, to say the least.

Athol landed an ice tool in the ice overhead and pulled himself up. Within minutes he was embedded in a small crevasse on the edge of the ice mushroom, next to the gentle slope of the top area, belaying off a screw. It was too delicate to jumar, so I reached up and over, onto the ice, with my axe and made my way up to Athol.

The west face of Cerro Torre dropped away very steeply within spitting distance from where we sat. The summit area sloped away to the south very gently, a vast understatement of what lay beneath. From where we sat the summit ice mushroom rose up and out over the headwall, and we decided not to risk going up and out there. Seeing base camp below us, the hazy cover of beech trees on the ground, my mind turned inward, it all felt so simple. My eyes looked around, I accepted all that I saw. A faint warmth from the sun met the cold coming from the ice on which I sat and created a startling, sleepy equilibrium. I could hardly remember doing it, but I had hammered an ice tool in by my side and clipped myself in short to it, lest I fall asleep. I knew Athol was happy to be there as he handed me a hot drink, 'There you go,' he said. 'Get that down.' Sugary sweet and very hot, the drink burnt my throat.

The weather was slowly turning worse; it looked like we had been given just a few hours in which to top out and get down. We abseiled the whole route to the schrund at the bottom col, the Col of Patience, in seven and a half hours. It was astonishing how quickly the hard-won ground from the ascent disappeared as we abseiled down. The spine-tingling sensation of pulling the final metre of rope through the anchor, when gravity is about to take control, occurred time after time, but with each abseil there was always something new to watch out for.

Once down at the schrund it was as if we had turned the corner. We poured the remaining fuel into the cooker and made some porridge. Everything seemed so distinct and alive as we lay in our sleeping bags. We still had 500 metres of serious ground to go but it was manageable even in hostile weather conditions. Relative to base camp, this schrund was our home away from home: a roof over our heads, protecting us from the dark twilight that disguised nasty, approaching stormclouds. We were tired enough that we didn't care if the weather really turned bad.

My hand was cold. I pulled it back into the sleeping bag. I could hear the wind outside the schrund, clouds of spindrift bursting in at random. It was very quiet, despite the wind. Sitting up on my elbow, I peered out of the schrund. Gentle streams of snow filtered through the hazy focus of sunlight, a million snow crystals drifting all at once against a backdrop of the shadowed glacier underneath. Only 30 metres out I could see it wasn't snowing – what a beautiful scene, what a privilege it was to stay there a few more hours before plunging homeward.

We scampered carefully over to where the lower, initial buttress tops out and rigged an abseil, the wind slamming into us. No longer was our progress smooth: the ropes got caught on nearly every abseil. We swore angrily as we climbed back up time and again to free the centimetre of stuck end. Sitting on the anchor waiting to abseil I noticed snowflakes building up in the creases of my shell jacket. I brushed the snow off; I could have been picking dust off a dinner suit. Suddenly I thought of being on the ground. Within seconds this sensation resonated with a peace deep inside my heart, and I saw in my mind's eye the faint glow of the candle in my tent at night.

An outrageous storm was unfolding in front of our eyes, the Patagonian *grand finale*. Deathly black clouds, thin and wispy, passed rapidly over the col, bringing with them a freezing mass of air. The upper half of Cerro Torre was now covered in cloud, the foreground awash with falling snow. Every so often small areas of sunlight broke through, but never for very long. I can still clearly remember the sounds my crampons made on the rock as I repositioned my feet, that unmistakably dry, hollow pitch. A few tears came from my eyes, somehow everything felt so clean.

The glacier was a wet ordeal, and we had to rest every half hour. But we never felt miserable despite being wasted – quite the opposite. The wind drove the rain into our faces. The water ran down my neck and down my chest. Base camp was all too tempting compared to the dreary, damp confines of the rock bivvy so we hammered it out. We fell over at random as we scrambled down the moraine wall from the bivvy, our plastic boots smashing through the mess of ice and rock, sending larger rocks crashing down the wall. My ski poles were working overtime as I struggled to control all the forces – the wind, the slippery ground, the steepness – working against me. Ath had a Kylie Minogue song replaying through his mind, 'Better the devil you know, better the devil you know …'. Down on the glacier he held his ski poles together at waist height, out to the front, just like he would have carried his rifle back in Oman, and he didn't even realise it. I felt very proud to be with him.

As we walked, thoughts of when we had made it back to the rock bivvy and our supplies only a few hours before raced through my mind; of Ath searching through the gear saying 'Fuck it, where's the lighter?' as he was getting the cooker out, and me saying, 'Christ, where's some food?' Maestri had built a hut on the side of the glacier near our base hut. It was derelict now, but we got inside and sat down. It was as wet inside as out. Dead leaves were lying over the muddy earth. We put our runners on, cinched the plastic boots onto our packs and stumbled down toward base camp, ducking under the dripping trees.

The abundance of life was overwhelming. The rain eased off as we approached camp, and the wind moved in gentle pushes, as if sets of small summer waves. We walked with our ski poles tucked under arms, the glacial sand slipping underfoot. Suddenly I saw the glow of flames as we crested the bank beside our tents.

Ava was seated by the fire – she was calm but immensely pleased to see us. This was nothing new to her: her son had been running into the hills since he was ten years old. She pressed fresh bread rolls stuffed with cheese and jam into our hands until we couldn't eat any more. John Fantini and Simon Parsons shook our hands and, in the last light of the evening, I felt quietly and incredibly happy. It was as if we were still on the mountain – up in the schrund at the Col of Patience – but with the luxury of being in base camp. I fell asleep in front of the fire, little scattered drops of rain hissing on impact with the coals.

The whole area around base camp took on a new perspective when I woke up in the morning in my tent. Released from the mountain, I strolled around with hardly a care, didn't even look back at Cerro Torre. My friend Lisa was arriving in a few days. I walked into El Chalten and sat around in shorts and t-shirt. I leant against an old wooden fence-post and waited for her bus, relying on a vague hunch from a short conversation over the 747 radio a few days previously. The bus arrived and we both somehow missed one another in the throng, eventually seeing each other inside the wooden-floored ranger station, dust rising as we strode across the floor to meet.

Over the next few days, I stared vacantly around as she keenly observed the area. We had some good days walking around in the wind, but I was strangely unsettled. I was devoid of motivation, could barely be bothered walking. I just wanted to go home. 'You didn't even talk to me on the plane,' Lisa later told me.

Under an endless torrent of rain and wind Athol, Lisa and I walked into El Chalten for chocolate and coffee. We slumped in tiredness over our table, knocking empty chip packets to the floor. I tried calling Australia to no avail, until, eventually, Miguel – *bon enfant* – signalled me over to the radio, put me through to El Calafate and onto Australia. My father's voice sounded like my own echo, but I managed to get through 'On the ground, safe,' before the transmission ended.

Back in base camp the following morning, Athol and I shook hands, and he turned away and headed back up the glacier. He had talked to me earlier about staying on. I could sense then that he perhaps wasn't totally convinced about the idea – the risks involved. But as we stood there in the wind, the river sands blowing about our faces and the tents cracking in the wind, I knew he was comfortable. Despite this, I felt nervous for him. However, he knew the deal, and knew himself very well in the mountains. He was the right man for the job: attempting Cerro Torre solo. It felt very strange not to be going with him. This mountain had only ever been climbed solo once before, by Marco Pedrini.

Lisa and I said goodbye to Simon and John and wandered off along the track, down-river. They went on to climb Cerro Torre via the Maestri route, and another mountain, Aguja Poincenot.

Athol spent the best part of a month going up the glacier to the foot of Cerro Torre, waiting for good weather and all the feelings to be right before committing himself. Lisa and I walked out that day to El Chalten and the bus, and onto home via Rio Gallegos.

We sat in an old diesel Renault and made the trip to Rio Gallegos, a provincial town centre, the tight upholstered confines of the cab hazy with unfiltered Marlboro smoke from the aged driver. Wind-blown plastic sheets landed against the side of the taxi and all along the fence lines. Dust flowed freely through the air vents. The wipers scraped over a barely wet windscreen, fed by sporadic drizzle. We could barely hear the driver over the rushing wind outside. He was constantly correcting the steering. All I remember of him was his thin grey hair and nicotine-yellow hands on the steering wheel, and the final glance as he turned around as I got out, his wet, bloodshot eyes looking into me, as if he wanted to talk but had nothing to say. At the check-out desk, the 747's captain laughed when I asked him how long the flight would be, given all the wind. 'Always at God's speed,' he assured me in a clipped Argentine English as he walked off, the ink from the stamp still drying on his papers.

At home I walked across the paddocks of my parents' property with my sister and I wanted to be away again. I wondered what Athol was doing: was he back down from Cerro Torre, had he made the summit, was he safe? Then I got a phone call, breaking the silence of the room I sat in. We met in Melbourne the next day. He emerged from the river-bank weekend crowd and told me how he'd won, creases over his windburnt face.

The staggering 1500 metre north face of Thalay Sagar, Indian Himalaya. This was attempted many times by some strong teams through the 1980s and early 90s. Athol and I eventually succeeded in making the first ascent in 1997 (after a failed attempt in 1996). *Athol Whimp*.

On Thalay Sagar's north face, a new arena of harsh suffering. Athol and I (and the Americans trying another route) endured extreme cold and constant spindrift avalanching during this failed attempt. Here Athol is at 6000 metres, trying to forge a line up the ice. *Author.*

GREETINGS AND RETREAT:

attempting Thalay Sagar, north face

6904 metres
Indian Himalaya, 1996

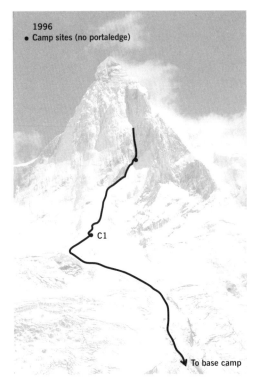

1996
• Camp sites (no portaledge)

C1

To base camp

A NEW ROUTE up Thalay Sagar's unclimbed north face, a spectacular 1500-metre wall. Athol had seen a photo of the north face – mostly cold and dark, late sun highlighting an immeasurable beauty – in a magazine ten years previously. It had made a big impact on him, and he filed away the potential for a major new route, a goal to be filled later on when it felt right. My own impressions of the face were from torn-out magazine photos, supplemented by my imagination of how cold it would be.

Athol talked to me in 1995 about the possibility of climbing the face, and we soon began developing a plan. Thalay Sagar, in India's Himalaya, became the canvas on which we projected our ambition. The short trips we took to Mt Cook from Melbourne provided perfect opportunities to realise that the Himalaya, and Thalay Sagar in particular, was the right direction to be taking.

We worked through all the regulations, ticking every Indian bureaucratic box – money, permits, lists, bio-data – *ad infinitum*. Piles of gear were packed and air-freighted to Delhi, and in time the harsh late winter Australian light gave way to a subcontinent swathed in soft colours like rose petals. The day after arriving we taxied out to the Indian Mountaineering Foundation for official duties. We entered the wide-doored, hilltop stone building under a dripping, cloudy sky – the monsoon was in full swing, but would end within the next month.

Old black-and-white photographs of bygone days hung from the walls in the boardroom as we waited for the director to enter. Soon enough he strode in, followed by a woman who was finishing a sentence with 'sir'. Small cups of hot, sweet *chai* got the conversation going. 'This is your liaison officer, Rajvinder Kaur,' the director said, beaming. Then, turning to Rajvinder he pronounced, 'She is representing India.' None of us missed his paternal tone. He talked some more about Rajvinder's role as liaison officer (LO) being an honour and duty, and that Rajvinder was a graduate of the Indian Mountaineering Institute. Every climbing expedition approved by the Indian authorities is obliged to take an LO with them. As we walked back out into the afternoon heat and haze, we arranged to meet Rajvinder in a few days to begin our journey north.

The sweat poured off us as we accumulated stamp after stamp at the Delhi Customs import building where we had to undertake the arduous task of retrieving our gear. The Assistant Commissioner sat at his desk in an office within a labyrinth of corridors, with three phones on the go all at once, Hindi and fluent English gushing into each mouthpiece. Another scribbled signature in another little carbon-copied box, and we doubled back to Terminal 2 at the airport, feeling we were caught in a vague Indian version of Kafka. We escaped with our barrels and a sheaf of paperwork requiring at least a hundred signatures.

The road into the Himalaya was a boyhood discovery trip, the unexpected breakdown of our Mercedes-powered truck giving us licence to explore surrounding grass flats and single lane, mud-brick built villages. While the truck's driver and his assistant hailed a motorbike to go in search of some new drive shaft bearings,

Athol and I walked down a dirt road. The road and the houses all merged into one colour, a faded sand yellow. Invited into the garage of the local landowner, we inspected his 1960s Massey tractor, its nipples recently greased. Before long we were ushered into the tight, hot confines of a bedroom/guardhouse. Sweet *chai* followed the customary enquires of our origin in rapid waves of Hindi. With nothing understood we – us two and eight of them – resorted to drawing maps and writing place names, complete with an arrow and cartoon 747 jet from Australia. There was slight tension as we stood to leave and then we were gently welcomed for more *chai* and conversation, eye contact forcing us back into our seats. To break the stare I glanced around at the posters of half-naked women sitting erect on motorbikes, the hopeless fantasies of our forty-year-old host.

Our second attempt to depart was assisted by Almas, our local logistics man until Uttar Kashi, at the foot of the Himalaya. Athol and I had silently communicated to one another that we had to get out, and as we began standing Almas called out from the street, providing the much-needed excuse to stand and leave. Our host politely escorted us from the dark room, past his tractor and outside, where we were hit by the heat of the sun. Any tension had dissipated and we shook hands before walking back toward the main road. Almas then issued us with a warning about civil unrest and the potential danger for tourists: 'Much trouble in the region lately, OK?'

The Mercedes was repaired without an underground pit or lift, by a roadside mechanic who had his knees up to his ears for at least an hour under the chassis. He emerged, still with sunglasses on, indifferent to our amazement at his rapid job. 'But wait, there's more,' assured Almas. Our mechanic had to go back under and house the bearings securely before we could continue. We were invited in for *chai* at a small house only a few metres away, a child leading us in as he twirled a rock on a string around his head.

Rajvinder, our eloquent liaison officer and a quietly spoken inter-
preter from the Brahmin caste, followed, giving us instant credi-
bility. Inside, we were put on display for the Sikh family, who
appeared sporadically with beaming smiles, little kids who ran
away giggling. An elderly woman gracefully said hello in Hindi.
Rajvinder offered her our respect and thanks for her hospitality.
Old black-and-white photographs leant against the whitewashed
walls. The woman saw us looking and asked one of her sons to
pass them over. Then tears came forth from her soft old eyes, and
I felt sweat drop from the back of my head.

Rajvinder translated to the effect that her husband, a dentist
and local politician, had been executed by 'secret police' 15 years
ago, during Indira Gandhi's emergency period. A framed photograph was passed to us, almost out of despair, her grasp weakening
as I took hold of it. While I looked at her deceased husband's
image the widow took hold of Rajvinder and cried even harder.
Her sons, daughters and grandchildren surrounded her, one of
them relieving us of the weight of the dead husband's photo.

Our departure was punctuated with a respectful *namaste,* a
spoken wish of goodwill. We backed out of the doorway, and only
turned once well outside. Our driver was waiting, tapping the
steering wheel with grease-stained fingers. Insects crashed into the
windscreen as we headed off into the dull, hot evening. We took a
smaller road to avoid traffic through the cooler night air. My
excitement escalated when I thought of where the road was leading, the purpose of our journey rising above Kedar Tal, the lake-
side base camp for Thalay Sagar's north face. Air rushed over my
face and sleep came sporadically, worse than a plane flight.

The road had taken us higher by the time we got to Uttar
Kashi, the truck being funnelled into narrow ravines and roads
that undercut collapsing granite cliffs. Arriving in Uttar Kashi,
the final big town and the end of any flat ground, we stumbled out
of the Merc amid the evening end of business flurries. The last

half-kilometre into town was on a slithering slide of grey mud, the
driver gearing the truck down to first, desperately trying to control
its back end beside the inviting yawn of the River Ganga's gorge.
Light grey clouds moved in front of a black monsoon stormcloud
backdrop, the streets were wet with a just-passed hailstorm, and
my ears crackled with the small increase in altitude as we ascended
to the Indian Mountaineering Institute.

While Rajvinder inquired at the Institute regarding our official
appointment with its director, Athol and I strolled the campus
grounds, the air swelling with alpine cool and the scent of bloom-
ing rose bushes. Curiosity got the better of us as we sauntered past
a 1960s hand-painted 'No Access' sign, in Hindi and English to
hallways and gymnastics room, where the students go through
routines complete with a bizarre set of ritualistic, mantra-like say-
ings about bravery, courage and the difference between life and
death on a mountain.

Raj emerged from the labyrinth-like building and cheerfully
announced that we needed to climb to the temple for a blessing. 'I
think the director, he is also there,' she softly said. We wound up
through pine trees on concrete steps, all the while guided by a
faded, light-blue handrail. At the temple, chanting emanated mys-
teriously; smiling, Raj nudged us into the small white shelter and
into kneeling positions. Respectful of the traditions I was so
naïvely stumbling over, I eyed Raj for approval, so she would
anticipate the next move for me. Soon some brown sugar, sporadically decorated with brightly coloured pieces, was squashed into
my palm, and the eating ceremony began. Athol and I were lined
up, heads bowed, before the transfixed main man, the Institute's
director and his children looking on. Between calls of the mantra
through the loudspeaker, I could hear the wind outside rushing
through the pines, a little bit of calm in this overwhelming reli-
gious experience. I dared not look up, but soon I felt it – the *tikka*
daubed onto my forehead, local goodwill for the upward journey

ahead. It felt right in there, under the authority of the holy man, but once out in the world again I washed the *tikka* from my brow with a mixture of respect and self-consciousness.

As we walked from the temple I saw the mighty Ganga tumbling through the Uttar Kashi valley at least a thousand feet below, and specks that were people working into the dusk. Crossing the gutter outside the hotel was akin to leaping from ship to shore, a trio of pigs rooting around in the trench. Upstairs in our room we wrote expedition thank-you postcards to people and companies back home who'd helped us with equipment and food. We penned them under the sombre yellow electric buzz of a swinging, naked bulb, the exercise fuelled by *chai* and greasy chocolate. Around midnight, I squatted in the corner of the bathroom like a cowering prisoner and washed myself in freezing river water, a self-proclaimed Himalayan baptism.

Negotiations for the porters we needed started at 8 a.m. next day inside the office of a trekking agent. Porters are controlled out of Uttar Kashi, even though they only begin walking from Gangotri, 2400 metres and a long day's bus journey above. The porters were pretty much union-organised and had us over a logistical barrel from the start. We had to pay for their bus fares to Gangotri and six porter stages (six days), despite the fact that they were up to the base camp and down again in three.

Soft-faced, curious porter men (it's an exclusively male domain) idled around the scene inspecting Athol and myself, the Western mountain specimens. Posters from previous expeditions to Shivling and Thalay Sagar's north face were positioned *ad hoc* across the walls. A Korean Thalay Sagar north face expedition poster from the early 90s had individual team mugshots, all looking very serious. *Chai* and cigarettes were offered to begin the discussion. As we took the first sips of the hot, sweet drink, I sensed Athol tensing. I knew that as soon as the head man behind the desk evaded a precise cost for porter delivery and pick-up, he was

after more money – more than was laid down by the bureaucracy.
We pulled out the calculator and all was surprisingly settled in a
few minutes, bar a few hazy peripheral requirements such as possible food resupplies, our head man sensing an opportunity to
pack in a bit more profit. Hands were shaken and heads bowed
and we boarded the Merc once more, destination Gangotri.

The road was cut halfway to Gangotri by a wet landslide and the
Merc could go no further. Sadly, we unloaded the white beast and
began walking loads across the landslide to buses – the ubiquitous
Tatas – on the other side. Also stuck, they had no option but to turn
around and take our load on to Gangotri. The porters' work had
thus begun early but only a few were prepared to begin slogging it
through the slippery, boulder-strewn mud. An Indian Army officer,
decked out in polished black boots, puttee gaiters and other parade-
ground attire, was supervising the clearing, one arm supporting an
umbrella, the other arm a whistle, with his eyes on the threatening,
slithering scree slope above. While we plied a passage across the
slide to the waiting buses and back again, a score of local men
scraped away at the mess in a vain attempt to clear it. Every time a
trickle of slithering rock and mud came down the officer blew the
whistle and all and sundry bolted, giggles aplenty. It wasn't until
three more army fellows eventually cranked up a sleeping yellow
bulldozer that things happened. By that time we were loaded and
away, soaked and steaming in the thick of another monsoon storm.

At least 50 people, plus our expedition's worth of food and
equipment, were loaded into the bus. Progress was a worrisome
exercise as we drove through the mid-monsoon downpour with a
drop of a couple of thousand sheer feet on one side. The bus
stopped wherever it was flagged down, passengers boarding while
the driver rode the clutch, the bus slowly slurring forward up the
steep hill.

After darkness covered the valley and we'd ascended another
thousand metres, the porters staged their strike. The bus slid to a

stop. It all came down to more money, over and above what we'd already negotiated with the agent. They thought our hands were tied, that we needed them more than they needed us. Hindi was rapidly being spoken by the *sirdar*, the porters' head man on the ground, once he realised we weren't going along with the plan. Raj, the only female on the bus, and barely five foot tall, stood on a pack in the aisle and laid down the rules, as discussed with us. We told the porters we didn't care how long we waited – that we'd happily sit there all night – but we weren't paying any more than had been arranged in Uttar Kashi. Raj then said this in Hindi for the benefit of the porters and was greeted with laughter all round. Athol and I laughed bloody hard as well, just to show we didn't care. Ten minutes of stony, tobacco-perfumed silence followed before the *sirdar* offered a brief, muted utterance, the driver crunched the gears and we slipped off again through the mud. It was later revealed, after the porters' immediate loss of face had dissolved, that they were 'trying the strike on', just to see how far our wallets could go. Athol and I laughed once more at the thought of this – the whole expedition had been put together on a very minimal budget. As the bus rocked ceaselessly into the night, almost leering over the abyss at times, we slowly climbed up to the holy village of Gangotri through seemingly endless switchback turns.

Swathed in curling clouds of tobacco, we stumbled from the bus at midnight – a clear sky with just a little glitter of starlight – and began unloading the gear. The cooling air brushed over my arms as I stepped onto the granite-gravel road. Athol, Bell our cook, Raj and I tried to keep all the gear together, while the porters were keen to shoulder the best-looking loads and move off to their sleeping place. Raucous shouting and fingerless whistling from Bell kept it in hand, his capped figure moving about the throng, his waving arms emphasising the point. The porters slowly surrendered their loads, sharp red dots of burning cigarettes illuminating their gaunt faces in the darkness.

The Ganga River surged through a chasm at one side, pushing misty cold air through the hotel. I stumbled into our unlit room and crashed on a bed. As I lay there waiting for sleep, I could smell mist and pine trees, and the damp concrete that was the floor. I awoke with a tender head – the altitude was taking effect. A weak, dusty light filled the room. Athol shook off his sleeping bag and stood at the door, peering out at the pines on the other side of the gorge. He sterilised two litres of water, flavoured it orange, and handed me a litre. After waiting a while, I began drinking, even though I wasn't thirsty and all I felt like was a strong coffee. But it is essential to drink plenty of liquid if one is to acclimatise to high altitude. The concrete was wet on my bare feet that morning.

Seven a.m. and the porters were already milling about, keen to shoulder their loads. Bell, Athol and I sorted them into 25 kilogram piles and the porters tied these into loads, carrying them using a band around their foreheads. I stayed on the concrete porch, to bring up the rear of our caravan, and watched Athol and Bell merge into the fog as they crossed the gorge on a footbridge. Bell, holding the stereo to his chest, was playing Hindi tinsel-rock, a sort of Madonna-esque Hindi disco. Young local boys pushed their way into the crowd of porters, their sweatshirts emblazoned with mis-spelt Western logos. The footbridge seemed to shake under the porters' feet, but it was only an illusion produced by the white storm of rushing water underneath.

The porters clumped together down the steps but spread out as soon as the uphill began, exiting Gangotri as quickly as they could. As they emerged from the fog and entered the forest, I had the sensation that our expedition had generated some sort of momentum; people were acting of their own accord. I spied Raj's small frame stepping up the initial steep hill, a few porters watching her as she approached their resting spot on the side of a switchback turn. The differences between them, determined by caste and job, were too much to be dissolved by walking together: Raj passed them slowly, without interruption, the men glancing groundward, then at one another.

A Czech expedition to Brigupanth, a lower mountain next to Thalay Sagar, was walking in at the same time as us. Their main man and the only one who spoke English, Karel Sykora, was the isolated diplomat for their expedition. I recalled seeing him trudging around the Delhi Customs terminal at the airport, a weighty sheaf of paperwork under his arm. As I waited for the final porters to leave, I watched Karel pass across the highest point I could see from my little concrete porch, his legs lurching as he tipped the short downhill side. By the time I arrived at the same place, the clouds had dropped and we walked through a warm, thick fog. I accompanied Raj, who was grateful I was knocking all the water off the plants so she didn't get as wet.

At Kedar Kerac, the meadow between the initial gorge of the valley and the glacier, the peepul trees became less frequent, their papery bark now lying sporadically over the wet ground. Huge black walls reared above us on the right, scores of tiny streams cascading down their reaches. As I crested a small rise and the end of the peepul forest, I walked into a group of our porters brewing up under a rock, out of the rain. It was hard to tell the smoke from the fog and cloud. Moisture hung in little droplets from the porters' woollen sweaters. I didn't realise how wet I was until I felt water running down my face and legs. The *sirdar* called it camp for the day, and the rain fell faster, sometimes as hail. The white water of the Ganga River rushed past and below our camp, the water on its periphery washing out loose granite scree from between the huge boulders. We could vaguely make out the funnel of a valley above us and descending clouds hanging over the final green belt before the moraine desert.

Edging up the hill in soft rain next morning, I could see Athol moving along with some of the porters, the various bright colours forming an artificial rainbow upon the misty scene. Higher, we caught up with the Czech expedition – a few of them had descended due to altitude problems, having ventured too high too quick. Karel greeted us at their camp, a few tents on the meadow bristling with moraine stone. Athol and I downed our packs and talked shop with Karel, who informed us they would be at Kedar Tal, base camp, the next day. Athol and I both felt no effect from the altitude besides being short of breath, and because the porters were very keen to get their loads into base camp and get back out again, we followed suit.

We sauntered around base camp under falling snow while the *sirdar* guided his men in, then hurriedly urged them back down the hill. The silty earth between the moraine debris was dry beneath the snow-covered surface. I passed a few letters to the *sirdar* with some money for postage, and he casually slipped them into an inside coat pocket, pulling his neck into his shoulders to avoid the wet snow. Vision was down to a mere hundred metres; fog hung around, and only seldom did a short breeze stir the scene, brushing the surface of the lake, Kedar Tal.

Athol and I cleared platforms for our tents, but every downward bend we made produced a pulsating headache. Our dry-throated breathing was eased by much water and our daily dose of Diamox (a drug that aids acclimatisation by enabling the body to expire more carbon dioxide and increase alveolar oxygen pressure). We knew we hadn't walked in slowly enough, and hoped we wouldn't have any problems as a result. Still no sight of Thalay Sagar. It was as if we were at sea in a deep fog, drifting, about to hit land at any moment.

The first glimpse of the mountain was through a fog-bound halo at dusk. Slowly, as if simultaneously with the darkening of the day, the clouds began to break apart, and for a few brief minutes we were welcomed by an astounding view. Yellow light graced the summit pyramid, framed by a circle of dense cloud and twilight. Thalay Sagar's notorious shale band was cloaked in fresh snow, while the steeper sections appeared ominous and black. Further down, the face was drenched in the dark, shadowed light of evening. It was a spine-tingling sight and I felt a little fear in the pit of my stomach. The difference between the photographs in our folder and seeing Thalay Sagar in front of us for the first time was vast. Remembered photos still hung around in my head as I tried to sleep, giving the strange sensation I was being watched by the mountain.

That night Athol left base camp with a massive headache, very much the result of going too high too fast. Dropping altitude from the base camp wasn't easy, however; he first needed to go across the moraine, which was at the same altitude as the camp, for close to an hour. I woke to find him gone – 'Athol boss going down, big headache,' Bell told me as he cranked the kerosene cookers inside the mess tent. I poured a mug of tea down my throat, grabbed some energy bars, a couple of litres of water, painkillers, and went across and down the moraine to find him. My head thudded with every step. At a small glacial pond Athol sat with head in hands, his eyes bloodshot. We joked about the great start, how we'd 'blitzed' the mountain and were on our way home. It was too difficult to think too far ahead.

By mid-morning the overnight snow had melted. When I stepped across the boulders little watery traces of snow slid off to the frozen earth, chased by the sun. The tiring effect of the altitude was amplified by the early afternoon heat. Light travelled everywhere around the Kedar valley at God's speed.

The scale of the mountain and the glacier slowly fell into perspective. As we carried loads up to the glacier over the next week we talked about our attempt on the north face. Plans always change once the objective is sitting a kilometre away. Thalay Sagar's north face hung with blank yellow shadows. From the edge of the glacier we moved up a well-defined moraine ridge that led towards a small plateau at the foot of the face. We dumped our

loads at a small rocky platform on the snow line and headed back
down to base.

We established camp one slightly above some Americans, keeping to ourselves, simultaneously offering space to them. Kitty
Calhoun and Jay Smith were attempting the central line on the
north face, the scene of Kitty's somewhat famous 1986 attempt
and eventual retreat from 6400 metres. After eight days sitting out
a storm in their portaledge (a platform with a stormfly that can be
anchored to the mountain) she and Andy Selters abseiled, eventually making it to base camp.

The scale of Thalay Sagar was exacerbated at dawn and dusk. At
camp one, it was as if the delicate light at these times held the
mountain without any change for a few minutes, enough for us to
get a feeling for how serious it was. After several days acclimatising at camp one, we initially made sorties up the slopes, soft and
loaded, ready to avalanche, toward the beginning of steeper terrain. The afternoons were monsoon storm-saturated, with snowfall that swirled up into the nostrils while the sun's heat pierced
through the zero visibility. Up at the base of the huge rock buttresses, above the initial snow slopes, we had to move a long way
to the right, looking for a place to start climbing the really steep
ground. Our ice tools went into occasional good ice, usually into
cruddy mess. Our crampons sliced through crust-protected powder. Staying in one place long enough to get some protection in
entailed repositioning my crampons at least half a dozen times.

We soon decided to head for a narrow, shaded couloir on the
right of the central buttress. Moving up the side of the massive
buttress toward it was slow and tedious, as though our boots were
continually being grabbed by shifting sands. Solid belays relieved
some of the stress. On one pitch I felt like I was drowning in the
school butterfly swimming race, but what surprised me more than
anything was the steepness. Getting our tools and crampons' front
points into the ice was slow work. The other option, plunging the

shafts of our ice tools into the loose snow, was precarious but faster. We were always balancing options with rasping, dry throats and under threat from the inevitable afternoon monsoon snow-show. The snow, after accumulating up high, would reach break-ing point and free-fall toward the initial slopes – in continuous, violent, cascading formations.

We fixed 300 metres of rope up and around the base of the cen-tral buttress, looting a few 'old attempt' karabiners and pins as we went. It was mid-September and we were waiting for the mon-soon to end. After nearly reaching the start of the couloir at 6150 metres, we descended in a flurry of icy gravity-driven missiles, cutting the crust of the snow slope on impact. We abseiled back down the lines, through the raging torrents of falling spindrift. Clumps of snow tumbled down the slope as we faced into the mountain and down-climbed over the schrund and the lower slab zones, into camp one.

Camp one, our highest camp, was at approximately 5600 metres: it consisted of a lightweight single-skin tent and snow cave. During the days between our movements up the face we rested and attempted to stay on top of continual dehydration. Athol managed to sleep for long periods in the tent, but I was driven into the snow cave out of boredom. Once, as he woke from a long slumber, I excitedly began brewing up – any excuse to get the cookers roaring again, the sound of their droning jets surprisingly therapeutic. We had piles of chocolate to eat through, and we polished them off from worst to best, saving the *de luxe* bars for the face. It seemed almost untenable at times that Athol and I, just the two of us, might be able to make a mark on Thalay Sagar – and it was not the size of the face that caused this nervous shudder, it was also the thin air. Even 'Cheyne Stokes' breathing (after breathing increasingly faster and more deeply for a period, one breathes more shallowly until breathing stops, and the cycle repeats) kept fairytale sleeping at bay.

We took another lot of food, fuel and equipment up our fixed line. Reaching the beginning of the fixed line was always a slight concern: the potential for a major avalanche was ever present. I felt my lack of experience at altitude, having to adjust to a different rhythm, feeling the compounding logistical problems all the way into the lungs – less oxygen and deeper cold meant more water had to be drunk, therefore more fuel needed to be carried, and so on. It was hard not to feel the thinner air was a real hindrance, rather than living in it as we would in the Alps.

The morning was bitter. Our watches hung from small loops of cord inside the tent and our simultaneous alarm sounds were the call for a 'quick march': get up and get dressed. Leaving the sleeping bag was like being kidnapped from the cradle. As our head torch beams swung around inside the tent I noticed frozen sheets of condensation stuck to the fabric. Eventually I staggered onto the packed, frozen ground outside the tent and wandered off to relieve a near-bursting bladder. Down at the Americans' camp I could see a few yellow head torch beams sweeping around the insides of their tents. I heard the spluttering gasps of the cooker's primed fuel lines: Athol was at work in the snow cave. It was porridge and coffee for breakfast, all washed down with a litre of warm electrolyte drink – hard work to prepare at 5 a.m. with the temperature sitting at minus 15° Celsius. With still no sign of dawn, we shouldered our packs and began climbing the avalanche slopes to the beginning of our fixed line. After some time spent moving directly up, we traversed right to where our first rope was situated.

Our hands and feet flushed alternately with heat and cold as we desperately attempted to stimulate constant warmth at our peripheries. We noticed Jay and Kitty jumaring up their fixed line a couple of hundred metres to our left; they appeared as hazy, dark blue figures against a slowly brightening day. Jay had their portaledge strapped to his pack, and Kitty, about 20 metres below him, seemed to have a heavy pack as well.

Above: Athol jumaring on the north face of Thalay Sagar, 1996. *Author.*

Below: Americans Kitty Calhoun and Jay Smith climb down over the debris of the huge avalanche they were caught in the night before as they descended the final part of the north face of Thalay Sagar, after their long and final effort in 1996. *Author.*

Above: A storm rages high on Thalay Sagar while base camp has just received another dump of snow, typical of the weather that made progress on the mountain extremely difficult in 1996. *Athol Whimp.*

Right: Looking homeward: the day prior to walking out (with very sore toes), Thalay Sagar base camp, 1996. *Athol Whimp.*

'See you guys at Arapiles,' yelled Athol.

'I hope so ...' came the reply from Jay. Even over that distance we felt Jay's humour, his ability to wonder what the hell we were doing up there, while all the time being quite focused.

As soon as Athol had reached the rock he called out, 'OK'. The snow dropped out from my legs as I starting jumaring and tried to get over the schrund. I briefly paused, looked up at the enormous north face and noticed that way up on the north-east pillar, across the edge of the shale band, the sun was projecting its radiance like a photographic spotlight on the edge of a diamond. It was as if the ice lit by the sun on the north-east arête was transparent and a wand of yellow dawn light breached the gloom around us. As I focused on moving upward again, I saw Athol transferring onto the next rope, beginning to move up and around the central rock buttress. Arriving at the anchor gave me an excuse to rest for a few minutes, but it wasn't long enough. The rest passed as if I was sitting in a plane waiting for it to take off, with everything shuddering – there is neither time to relax nor the ability to take off.

The air was eating away at my nose and cheeks. My fingers, wrapped around the jumars like those of a baby, operated on a mixture of instinct and sensory delivery from my hands. My breathing gradually steadied, my pulse tried to fall into a normal pattern. Then conscious thought – that the only way to stay warm was to keep moving – overrode the desire to have a rest, for warm sleep. Just a little piece of space opened in my mind, enough to let me visualise myself higher up. I clipped into the next rope and stepped across to the right, landing my crampons in the soft snow and feeling them slip a little before seating enough for me to weight them fully.

At the beginning of the couloir proper – and the end of the steep snow slope – we stared at the problem: the apparently wide couloir was in fact a series of ice runnels, with no easy option. From base camp this couloir had looked nearly as broad as a runway, but once at its entry point the climbing narrowed down to about two metres, and even then very intricate route-detecting was involved, tracing little threads of ice until termination, *finis*. Then a tedious process ensued, of crossing tricky ground to get into another shallow system of ice. We were also graced by the first spindrift avalanches, falling powerfully, headlong, for the ground. They tumbled over us, never too hard, but soon enough the entire scene was a white-coated mess, snow working its way into every crease and crinkle of our shell clothing and equipment.

Athol led off from the belay and was immediately at work with thin ice over the speckled yellow granite, hood up against the cascading spindrift. The afternoon cloudscape had turned nasty yet again, and let loose its weight of snow. It was around September 25 and snow had fallen on all but three days. Crystals fell slowly, pushed up by little fronts of wind. Then, as visibility became drenched in grey and black, the spindrift avalanches began again. Time dragged while we held ground, waiting for the avalanches to cease. The spindrift was like crushed chalk, like heavy fire-hose water. We could see no further than perhaps two pitches above us; the scale was hard to comprehend, it was as if we had made no progress.

Time began moving quickly, the day being sucked into long shadows across the granite pillars. As the monsoon clouds evaporated, the avalanches became less frequent. Behind us the last minutes of strobe-like orange sun-streams made their way onto the upper sections of the face. We were left in minus 30° Celsius twilight and Athol's bright yellow wind-suited figure was slowly assimilated into the gloom; soon we would have to find somewhere to spend the night.

Inch-thick cruddy ice stuck to the sand-coloured granite until I tapped and it went end over end into the abyss and we heard the little, faint crashing tinkle of the ice as it hit some rock below. Athol was trying to establish some sort of tenure on the face before darkness held us prisoner. I was shivering on the belay; reawakening my feet by wriggling my toes gave me something to focus on, the sporadic tingling of nerves and blood a sign of life. Being so close to the wall held its disadvantages: we couldn't see that much, our vision around the immediate area being restricted by the large and close features. After working higher into a narrow, bulging couloir Athol tied the rope off, then abseiled down and across toward the very tip of the snowface, directly beneath the centre of the couloir. He kept moving on an angle by keeping his crampons in well and transferring his weight from leg to leg in a sideways direction rather smoothly. Once there, he called out I could climb across and up to his chosen site.

The chill of evaporating sweat ran around my skin as I moved away from my little stance; it felt as though I were losing all my body heat from my neck. A small flurry of snow crystals, invisible against the snow and ice, blew down my neck and melted instantly, trickling down my chest. It felt as though they'd fallen all the way to my toes, whose deadened sensation was only exacerbated as the temperature dropped with the night. At the site we began chopping a ledge to put our small tent on. It took a lot of effort to *keep chopping*. Clumps of snow dropped away from the slowly forming ledge and gained momentum until we lost sight of them, gravity an ever-threatening presence. We kept hacking inwards until we were scraping our ice tools against the granite wall. Our hoods were up to guard against sporadic, avalanching spindrift. The single-skin tent, a prototype fabric on loan, went up quickly, instinctively hurried by the failing light.

Inside the tent was incredibly cramped, like a car boot. Loose powder snow covered everything, and toppled down from above at the slightest hint of movement; the small space between the tent and the wall soon bulged with packed, taut snow. Out into the dark we went, taking turns to unload this burden before the tent collapsed. We kept our helmets on and tried to remain still while the hanging stove did its best. Athol tried to induce it to burn a little hotter, a little harder, by adjusting the fuel control. Eventually we had half bowls of orange drink, and intermittently passed out, being woken by tinkling ice showers. I saw my helmet squashed in the corner of the tent, its fabric being held tight by our knees, bent into half-sitting positions. Athol was asleep, his head resting on a knee. My feet had been cold all that day and still were. The unmistakable sounds of sucking air came from high above us, like a distant wind, before being amplified into a fast-forward helicopter noise and then, like a stone into a still pond, a falling ice missile buried itself into the slope by the tent. My stomach groaned with weakness and I soon felt all my recently consumed food and drink rising toward my mouth. Just as I got the tent door down the vomit tumbled out, the loss of hydration nearly bringing tears to my eyes. I slumped back into a foetal position, knees scrunched up, wishing it was daylight.

Dawn was frigid and dull, our north-facing position no help in giving us any warmth. Loose powder snow got into everything. We rolled up the tent and loaded up our packs. As I removed the anchor, Athol began jumaring up the fixed rope; it became tight and slid across the wall, into the line of gravity. At the high point Athol called out and I stepped the weight onto my jumars and began my own ascent. My fingers and toes were still numb after my body had become flushed with heat, the first sweat of the day. I stopped at the anchor and beat my hands together, feeling stinging, nauseating pain through to my stomach. Memories of riding my bike around wintry Melbourne as a boy rushed through my mind, of being unable to open the front gate with my frozen Sunday morning fingers.

From the high point, where we'd left the rack of gear, we needed to get across and right, back into the line of the couloir. Athol was ready to climb when I arrived at the belay. Hanging in my harness from two ice screws, I sorted the rope out, cold fingers working to get a grip on things. The front points of Athol's crampons were driven into the ice just above my head, his arms reaching high over the blue ice. Soon he climbed out of my sight, around a large bulge off to the right. All I heard was an occasional whisper of falling ice as it was funnelled down the couloir, out of sight, and a corresponding movement of rope through my belay device. After Athol's call, I removed the anchor and began weighting the jumars. Higher up, on the way to Athol's belay, I took out his protection, a few wires and the odd screw – marginal security.

I took the pack off, hung it on the belay and felt thirsty. It was late morning but the monsoon clouds were already forming, turning over themselves, carrying black undersides, moving toward us. Athol handed me the rack and I headed away, directly up on squeaky plastic ice until I met a shield of rock. From there, the line went right and up again. Athol called out some directions from the belay as the temperature dropped, sharp pushes of cold air coming from below. After the next, short upward section, I traversed right to the base of a vertical granite pillar covered in shattered ice.

The rope went taut and I could tell Athol was on his way. I looked out at the glacier, all the way to base camp. The disparity between our position on the wall and the ground felt surreal.

During the next pitch, Athol's crampons only just seemed to be getting a hold in the shattered ice and rock. The rope looped from me to a single piece he had clipped in three metres below his feet. Spindrift began sluicing down the face. Soon Ath was caught in a much heavier amount of spindrift but fortunately had just reached some higher, decent ice. I lost sight of him as the spindrift tumbled down. Jumaring the pitch was completed through continuing spindrift avalanches, the freezing snow suffocating my face every time I looked up to see what was happening. At the belay we decided we would make no progress in this weather, to abseil back to the bivvy site, and jumar the fixed line next morning.

I carefully pushed the rope through my belay device to abseil, and clipped it through the karabiner. The rope felt too thin under my gloved hands, my fingers were numb from hanging so long while belaying. Looking down was just like a dizzying camera shot, individual snowflakes drifting past my face then disappearing into a greater white mass. The rope was a black line cutting into the windless air below me. A few metres down Athol reminded me not to abseil off the end of the rope as we hadn't tied the end to an anchor, his voice sounding soft and clear. He hung from the anchor, evidence of the avalanches all over him, loose powder snow hugging all the folds of his shell layer and sticking to the rack by his side.

We joined the rope onto the rope already fixed from our bivvy site and zoomed down the near-vertical wall to the disintegrating ledge we'd chopped the night before. Under the torrent of more spindrift avalanches we began kicking and chopping the ledge out again, trying to get its back wall deeper into the slope. The front edge kept falling away as it became dark, time passing without our awareness, our minds driven by instinct for shelter. My feet were numb, my chest and arms warm. It was minus 20° Celsius as we crawled into the tent, keeping our packs by each entrance so we could get at the food and fuel.

We had to take turns when taking our shell clothing off, so cramped was it. I leant against a back corner, trying not to press on the outside wall of the tent in case it tore. We carefully got into our sleeping bags – if only up to our waists. Ice and more spindrift tore down the wall, frequently hitting the tent. Again snow built up between the tent and the rock wall. It seemed as though we were fighting more than the usual amount of trouble. Within minutes of one of us getting out to dig the build-up away from between the tent and the rock, a long period of avalanching started. Halfway through this 'session' it seemed as though the tent was about to collapse. One of the poles broke and the tent roof slumped accordingly. 'I hope this shit stops soon,' was about all we said. Athol wasn't too downhearted, his energy being put into producing a brilliant bowl of hot orange drink. The sweet glucose taste swirled luxuriously inside my mouth. Chronically dehydrated, I struggled to finish my drink, overcome with an apathy for food and drink. Sometime through the night I noticed my toes were still numb and, only half-awake, I tried in vain to warm them by rubbing my feet together.

We packed up in the dark, slowly preparing for our day on the face. We slurped down hot orange drink and some porridge, the tiny space of the tent lit by the cooker flame and the white strobes of our head torches. Our hands became cold very quickly cinching down straps and buckles as we stood on the snow ledge. The one-minute job rapidly crippled the fingers, requiring a 20-minute recovery.

Athol started jumaring under a clear sky, the faint glow of dawn, an iridescent pink, stretching over the mountainous horizon. The weight of the pack pulling back on my shoulders was debilitating, the struggle feeding an anger I could only re-direct back into the task at hand. My crampons scraped over the vertical rock and bit well into the threads of ice. I looked up and saw Athol about halfway up the next section, could hear an occasional sound from his scraping crampons.

I reached the ice screw that the first rope was tied through and waited for Athol to reach his anchor before I changed onto his rope. I stared at the clove hitch through the karabiner in front of me, my eyes zooming in on individual snow crystals, then drawing back to my black gloves. As though I wasn't quite aware of what I was doing, my black gloves gently brushed the loose snow off the head of the ice screw. I brought a small scraping of snow up to my mouth and drew the moisture from it, my lips turning wet and cold.

Athol led off from the high point, hunting down the line. My toes still felt numb, the only sensations of life in my feet being a residual warmth around my heels. Strangely, I wasn't alarmed, only telling myself to deal with this properly that night. The rope inched through my belay device as Athol forged a passage up the wall. The grey clouds had moved in again without me noticing, their slow, low creep up the west ridge bringing with them a colder mass of air and snow. Without warning, we suddenly became surrounded by swirling snowfall. I lost sight of Athol – but soon I felt three slow pulls on the rope, our signal for the second to proceed. A slightly denser shade of grey and white was spreading out across my line of upward vision as I began jumaring – the spindrift avalanches had begun. I had time for a few more steps on the jumars before the first wave hit. Within seconds the air was heavy with rushing snow, millions of snowflakes a second making headlong for the ground. Ath and I were in private worlds, waiting for the avalanches to cease. My hood was up, I could feel my warm breath pass my lips and then instantly condense.

At the first break in the onslaught, I looked up and saw another wave of spindrift ripping down toward us, as if in slow motion, billowing outward as it impacted with the wall. I shivered as I brushed the inch-thick layer of snow off my jacket layer, the clouds and air lightening a little. As I moved upward I saw a little slope of granite in sunlight – small, wet crystals reflecting light into my eyes. On our right was a massive rock rampart, the obvious feature of the right-hand side of the north face from base camp. We moved against it, like a slow-moving whale breaking the icy surface of a southern ocean. At the belay I felt drained, my eyes sunken. Athol's head seemed to be sitting a long way back under his hood, and I could see snowflakes drift past his face, silhouetted against the shadowed background of his face.

From our hanging belay we could see the route as we had envisioned from photos and at camp one. Higher up, the vertical prows gave way to more ice – the area where we'd move left onto the mixed buttress that led to the shale headwall. The clouds of snow appeared to have backed off a bit as Athol racked some gear for another pitch. I could feel the back of my throat catching on words, devoid of moisture. The spindrift began cascading down the face yet again and Athol was hidden in the mess. He was about 50 metres up. The rope paused and moved, corresponding with the beginning and ending of the avalanches.

I watched Athol carefully during the steepest section as visibility opened out again. He torqued one of his ice tools into a crack and pulled himself up, reaching higher and further with the other tool, eventually landing it in some good ice. I could hear some muffled panting from Athol, like a wretched dog driven by instinct. Then ten minutes passed and the rope didn't move, communication swallowed by the weight and noise of the cold and the continuous, storming snow.

By mid-afternoon I still couldn't feel my toes, and images of the scratchy black-and-white footage I'd seen as a child of the Russian soldiers under snow in the Second World War projected somewhere onto my mind. Athol was taking more and more rope. I had now climbed above my belay, with not an inch of rope left to give him, and he still needed another two metres. I heard his voice but couldn't make out the words very well; however, the timing of his yell meant he wanted only one thing – another metre. I hesitated to let the rope go on such steep terrain – to be unroped in this situation was theoretically crazy but quite straightforward at the time. He yelled again. Athol was 100 metres above me. His reality was more important than what I thought was going on, so I let the rope pass through my belay device. It stopped a metre above me, followed by a faint 'Safe'.

'You wouldn't fucking believe it up there,' Athol said as he arrived back at my belay, shaking his head. He'd scraped around for half an hour, tracing thin fissures into a frustrating blankness instead of thin cracks that would enable a quick anchor. Eventually he secured a piton and abseiled under incessant waves of spindrift.

He had to abseil back to me as we had to take two packs up.

We hung on the belay and the weight of our situation was felt by both of us. A few final rays of sunlight reached us during a break in the storm, the shallow heat only just piercing the layer of cold on my face. We had two hours of light remaining, and were unsure about chopping a tent site out – ice lay underneath a thin veneer of snow at the high point Athol had reached. Chaotic emotions were sparking about between us, and it suddenly felt unlikely that we would make it back up, especially if the bad weather continued. It was as though we had been forced into a corner.

I could feel Athol was desperately upset, acutely aware of our impending decision. For an hour and a half we hung at the belay, trapped between up and down, the massive scale of the face narrowed down to the few metres immediately about us. I noticed tiny frozen crystals sitting only 30 centimetres from my face, oblivious to our struggle. I was shivering from standing and hanging still for so long, the cold in my feet reaching back to the heels. We both knew that as we had nowhere we could put our little tent up where we were, we *had* to descend. As dusk smouldered on the horizon, burnt colours of autumn light filtering through bulbous clouds, the temperature dropped again, approaching minus 30° Celsius. My memory quite suddenly shot back to our time in Delhi a month before, 35° Celsius the other way. We tied all the technical gear and food to the anchor and abseiled into the fast-approaching darkness.

At 6 p.m. we arrived at the bivvy site, the snow ledge now a disintegrated, collapsed mess. We had no rope, so could abseil no further. We talked a little about the cold and our tiredness, ensuring each of us was all right. I paused to get my head torch set up on my helmet, the elastic straps slipping under of my numb fingertips. When I looked down I saw Athol making headway into the gloom. Everything seemed steeper in the dark, the buttress overhead felt as though it were leaning over us and the cold was reaching deeper into me. Loose snow stuck to hard ice, tumbling away once we put our full weight on it. Still my toes were numb, and kicking in my crampons became awkward and increasingly insecure. I paused again, slightly lower, to clear some slings away from my chest and noticed how quiet the evening had become. The glistening black sky felt infinitely distant, while Athol's movements below me only just broke through the blackness to make an impression on my eyes. I could see his arms lifting the shafts of his ice tools out of the snow and driving them in again. At the fixed rope I shone my light for Athol to rig his head torch and we continued. As he abseiled and became more distant, and I could only hear the faint tinkle of his movements, I felt a strange loneliness pressing onto me. Perhaps I was worried about my toes.

After abseiling around the buttress we down-climbed the slopes into camp one, deep steps breaking away the slope in every direction. Every 50 metres we would stop and take a short rest, prodding the slope with our ice tools, knocking snow off our legs. It was very quiet. Once down-climbing again, I could hear the sound of clinking metal from Athol, as he cleared the snow build-up on his crampons with ice tools. And then, between these sounds, was the soft brushing of the snow against our shell layers.

Not far from camp one we heard a faint voice drifting toward us from below. We stopped.

'Are you guys OK?' The words were spaced and deliberate, making up for the sound-deadening effect of the snow. It was Kitty Calhoun, calling out from the Americans' camp.

'Yes,' called Ath, his voice fading with tiredness. I was so exhausted I could barely open my cracked, dry mouth.

'Good job,' said Kitty, my mind placing her face on the voice from the darkness.

'Nearly halfway,' replied Athol.

'That's a good job,' she continued.

Then just the sound of our breathing against the silent, night-time backdrop. From ten metres away I heard Athol knock one of the cookers as he leant into the snow cave. I was sitting on the edge of our camp, waiting a few moments to make the final steps.

Sleep was the immediate, peaceful reward for our freezing descent. I got into my sleeping bag, rubbing my feet together before I was asleep. I woke up in the middle of the night – it was as though I had woken in a large room, my eyes unable to see the ceiling, perhaps as if I was sleeping outside, but protected by the strong walls of the room. I could hear nothing as I lay there – even Athol breathed as if he were in a coma. Then, after a minute or so a small slip of snow slid down the slope, just down from the tent.

The tent was warmer when we woke, covered in sunshine. I pulled the socks from my feet outside in the sun. My two big toes were stained a mottled blue and black, while the other toes and the balls of my feet were blanched stark white. Yet it was barely shocking. I was too exhausted to be anxious. Instead, it seemed to reinforce, in a slow-motion logic, that we'd made the right decision in coming down. Another contributing factor in our defeat.

We didn't say much. The north face stretched far over our heads, entering my consciousness every time I saw it, the vision producing immediate, cold memories, memories not even a day old.

Base camp was a warm(er), blessed retreat. Thalay Sagar, in the background, was consumed angrily by storm again. Arriving there in the dark was similar to a jet-lagged arrival home. A Czech doctor looked at my feet, administered vaso-dilators and told me to sit down. A few minutes later I was hit by a rush of blood to my peripheries, my toes flushing with heat, my face sent fridge-white. Athol steadied my balance as I felt the full effect of the drug, the steam from a hot bowl of tea rising into my nose, inducing nausea. The wind shook the mess tent's walls, little streams of snow pushing under the ground flaps. All the Czechs were in the tent, passing 80 per cent proof pink brandy around the huddling circuit of chairs and people, Bell in the middle cutting the cake, a post-celebratory birthday moment for Athol and me. I'd had my birthday while we were up at camp one, and now it was Athol's turn. There was a few centimetres of snow over the frozen ground. I stared toward Thalay Sagar in the dark, washed with a pink brandy nausea hue, relieved of some of my disappointment.

Another inspection by the doctor revealed that circulation had returned to my toes again – pink but numb to the touch. He urged me to see a specialist as soon as we arrived home as I was likely to have damaged the nerves. Kitty Calhoun and Jay Smith were still up on the north face, trying to last out the storm in their porta-ledge. After several days, Athol and I left base camp to retrieve our gear from camp one. We met them on acres of avalanche debris on the slopes below camp one, the late sun providing scant warmth over the desolate scene. We shook hands. Fire burned in their eyes, the residue of their ride in an avalanche, sparked when they were abseiling the end of their fixed line down the snow slopes above camp one. They were worried, and warned us about the avalanches still lying in wait.

Athol and I continued up and over the debris toward our camp one. The daylight was dying, shallow creases of cloud layered over the western horizon, obscuring the sun. We made our way up the apex of the snow slope toward our camp under a large serac, a pillar of ice. The wind made it hard to develop a rhythm on the slope, plugging knee-deep into the fresh snow. My fingers were going cold, wrapped around the handles of my ski poles. With our hoods up, it was difficult to hear and see what was happening. Then suddenly the surface level of the immediate area dropped and a cracking sound like thunder followed soon after, deep and resounding. Our hearts raced, I pulled my hood down and looked at Athol. We undid our pack straps, took our hands out of our ski poles' wrist loops, and stood still. I noticed how still it all felt, only hearing the squeaking of snow under the tips of my ski poles. Athol was just off to my right, silhouetted by burning filtered light. Then it sounded again, along with a rippling vibration we felt underfoot. We moved quietly, like cats, toward the camp. Soon the slope's surface was stretched as tight as a drum and our crampons only bit to half-depth.

The camp had been destroyed by the avalanche of the previous day, the one that Jay and Kitty had been caught in. After probing and digging we uncovered the entrance to the snow cave, like a lost tomb. The cookers, food and gear sat just as we had left them, the cave still perfectly formed. We joked that the cave would have been the place to dive had we been caught by an avalanche, yet diving in with the *feeling* that we would have been diving into our tomb. I was staggered by the density of the avalanche deposition – we dug with the snow shovel through at least two metres of hard snow, eventually revealing the flattened white tent.

There was an amazing feeling that night, so much seemed to have changed since we descended from our attempt on the face. The cold was far more shocking than any time before. The wind was sweeping ribbons of spindrift around in the gloom, the light and warmth from the sun having receded an hour before. Looking down the slope as I got into our resurrected tent, I saw the frozen surface of the avalanche zone, a massive spent energy, yet still retaining a volatile feeling. Staggering over it quickly the next morning was like walking through a cemetery with no purpose. That night I could barely sleep, a nervous beat coming from my heart. I wrapped my feet in extra insulation, Athol providing me with a hot water bottle. Leaving at first light was done quickly, with scarcely a glance up at the face. Dressed in all we had, the cold still stung into our bones. We cut a quicker line through the potential avalanche area, dropped onto and across the plateau area and then down to the glacier, crunching over the snow-covered moraine.

While waiting for the porters I thought about going home. In the mornings I watched the sun glint off Kedar Tal, the glacier-fed lake. At home so many decisions needed to be made, relationships with people renewed. For a short few days we had fine weather; drying gear and talking shop with Jay, Kitty and their friends Steve Gerbeding and Scott Backes. The Czechs departed under heavy snowfall and incredible cold, the porters huddling in disparate groups, looking unsure. Karel shrugged his shoulders, prodding a rock with a ski pole. 'I will write once I have somewhere to live,' he laughed.

Our final dinner in base camp was a grand affair, the Americans' cook and Bell joining forces to produce a melting pot of mountain fare, *à la carte*. Jay passed the whisky around, Raj uncomfortably baulking at the Western impurity. 'Well, we got three out of four,' drawled Scott – everyone had heard it before except Athol and me. Kitty continued, 'Come back alive, come back as friends, come back with all your fingers and toes, come back with a summit – in that order.' When the cold had moved everyone into bed, I went into our mess tent and got the kerosene cooker going to warm my feet. Athol came in and we watched the cooker flame for a while, rifling through the dwindling food piles for some chocolate or biscuits. Snow leaked into the tent from all sides, the entrance canvas cracking in the wind.

Athol was already in for a return the next year, his feeling stemming from a strong, calm resolution about his mountaineering. He could see a similar feeling in me, yet I felt nervous about returning, unable to put my finger on it. I was frustrated and somewhat ashamed I'd let my toes get damaged by the cold, and my mind went into a self-preservation mode by denying any possibilities of returning. I was sure Athol could see this in me, and we just talked quietly as the wind shook the walls of the tent. I wrapped my arms around my scrunched knees, my eyes staring at the gasping blue flame of the cooker.

Dropping into the heat of Delhi made my feet swell, any knock caused searing pain, the nerves constantly burning as if caught too long in front of a fire. I got on the phone to Gigi in Melbourne, her face zooming into focus once her voice sounded. I was afraid of returning to what might or might not be. My confusion, among other things, fed the straightforward exit from my advertising career.

One snowfall-ridden night just before we began walking out, as I returned to my candle-lit yellow ethereal shell from the mess tent, I suddenly realised something about what was happening to me, the days rolling over, the freezing nights, it all made alarming sense, but a sense I had no hope of articulating.

Back again: stormy weather on Thalay Sagar as base camp receives the first sunlight of the day, shortly after I arrived, August 1997. Patricia Galanopoulos is at right. *Athol Whimp.*

Above: At the top of the icefields, north face of Thalay Sagar, at 6000 metres. From here we had much hard climbing in bad weather to go. *Athol Whimp.*

Below: Life in the portaledge: desperate at the best of times. Showing the strain at the 6450 metre site as we waited out another storm. *Athol Whimp.*

HIDDEN BY STORMS:

the first ascent of Thalay Sagar, north face

6904 metres
Indian Himalaya, 1997

1997
● Portaledge camps

C2

C1

To base camp

AS WE WALKED out on 28 September 1997 I turned around to see Thalay Sagar and its north face one more time, but it was gone under another storm. Nature had provided the final curtain call for our departure. The further we descended down the Kedar valley, the more it felt as though everything was being lifted from my mind. I was happy to be leaving, yet I felt like I was moving into some sort of vacuum.

Passing through the boulder field, Kedar Kerac, the grass was wet from fresh snow melt that morning. I sat against a boulder and waited for the others. Thoughts of home flooded my mind, like a dam wall waiting to burst. I could see Bell walking fast down the end of the moraine, moving through, picking up the tail of the porter parade. He was very happy to be going home, 48 hours by bus from Delhi to Nepal and then into his village, Pokhara. I still didn't understand what he thought of our show but as Bell approached me I realised how much I appreciated him. *Ad lib* comedian extraordinaire, he made us laugh at the drop of a hat. The tired, serious look on his face as he put his pack down emphasised it all the more, the grimace an uncontrolled lapse of his normally comic demeanour.

As we descended we witnessed the changing of the seasons. Everyone could sense it, the hurried footsteps of the porters being filled shortly after by flurries of snow. The walls of snow drifting down the valley made me immensely happy; the distance across the gorge was hard to ascertain, but ramparts of rock rose up from our feet into the clouds. I nervously watched Prem, a 12-year-old porter, clamber around a wet granite buttress, a full load on his back. I quickly moved underneath him to guide his feet, the snow landing in my eyes, young Prem's feet sliding out of his plastic shoes. Back on the track, he rapidly regained his composure and moved off, displaying a pride and strength way beyond his years. Of course he was too young for the job. But he wanted it desperately. We were assured he received the pay of an adult porter – but didn't believe it.

That evening we arrived back in Gangotri. The wind was warmer. A day passed. As I lay on the pine needles in my sleeping bag I could hear diesel engines droning across the Kedar Ganga, and the soft voices of my companions asking for coffee. I realised I wanted to get home, yet I hardly wanted to move. I just wanted to sleep.

2 August 1997. The glow from millions of under-powered lights soaked through the black haze of the Delhi night, the double-layered 747 window giving the scene a focus as if seen through a bubble. An engine catches fire, stewards panic, time stands still. Hydraulics clunk and wheeze and we shudder into a holding pattern, the engine immediately to our left a molten mass, streaming sparks and meteor-like flames. The present slowed into eternity until the eventual landing, being guided off the plane with 'Just a spark, just a spark, have a nice day ...'

It was the fiftieth anniversary of India's independence. Prime Minister Gughral orated from behind a bullet-proof screen, complete with supersonic jet stream fly-by. The late, hot sunlight of the day gave the laneway wall opposite my room a rose colour; *DOWRY IS HELL* was painted there in red. Stuck in Delhi for ten days waiting for vital clothing and equipment to get into port, every day I was drawn into a 35° Celsius, 100 per cent humidity bureaucratic labyrinth, the populace seemingly drunk on nostalgia and debates about the meaning and validity of the Indian nation.

Athol and Patricia had gone ahead to take care of official duties on the road up, paying courtesies to the magistrate and the Mountaineering Institute in Uttar Kashi. Every hour walking around the streets I was crushed by a thousand and one colours, by rapid sideways glances from women and the drawn-out stares of men, under the glaze of the hot sun. In the city wind is rare and kids fly kites over the exhaust fans of multi-storey buildings, laughing harder the higher the kite flies. I was too tired to bother drinking enough water, but it was everywhere the monsoon: the wet road, steam rising from lime-pasted corn, neat deserted piles of betel nuts, all punctuated by the short hiss of raindrops landing on roadside coals.

I walked beside Ombrakesh, an import agent. As we approached the Customs office he said, 'Don't tell him you're going to, just give him the money.' I did as he said and we rushed away with the cargo before it was too late. I tried to slow the pace a bit, calm things down, so I could tick the boxes off and ensure it was all there. At the downtown Delhi bus terminal things were going ballistic, sparse English was spoken faster than Hindi, and I self-consciously staggered between buses looking for clues through a black diesel fog. A sari-adorned saviour, an elegant, spectacled woman, walked from the shadows, took my hand with warmth and landed me and the crammed haul bag on the right bus, destination Rishikish.

Hillside townships announced themselves with little yellow and black signs – names like Tehri and Deridun. The vehicle lumbered through these Himalayan foothill townships, trading points for thousands of people terraced farms on slopes so steep you nearly have to climb to get up them, the colossal scale of the lush hills almost hiding the occasional spots of human density, the townships. In Rishikish each shop was cashed up and counting the notes for the night. Three hundred and fifty rupees bought me a 3 a.m. front seat in an 'official' paper delivery vehicle out of Rishikesh: a 'PRESS'-stamped Ambassador, a 1950s British sedan still made in India. Departure was late but there were still about 20 keen young men to help me tie the haul bag down to the roof.

It had been raining all night on the road from Delhi, and as I stepped out of the mud into the Ambassador an explosion went off and pushed me into the door. The reverberations made my hair stand on end and my ears ring like an electronic alarm. Driver and friends delivered nervous smiles before all realised with embarrassment it was no more than a massive clap of thunder, originating only metres away, somewhere in the wet, black night.

Part of the deal of getting my front-seat ride in the PRESS Ambassador was throwing bundled papers out at the right place at the right time – this followed the driver's calculations, and he reached down into the footwell to make the count, eyeing the road far less than he should've, all the time pushing the runt of a vehicle at devil's speed. I asked him to slow down and he laughed – we had the 'right of rapid transit'. I couldn't help liking him, despite the fact he nearly drove us close to death on numerous occasions. Finally, we made another death-defying descent over another ridge and into the Uttar Kashi valley, the re-treads finally stripping as he ground the vehicle through the last corner above 700 metres of slithering shingle wall.

The PRESS ride was over, so I organised another vehicle to get to Gangotri, the end of the road. It felt like I was leaving the ground as the diesel 4WD changed gear up the hills out of Uttar Kashi, the gentle wheeze of the turbo cutting into the gradient. Goats hid in long grass, mountain children wore woollen caps, and men were grouping around smoky pots of *chai* where small streams marked the green gullies. The driver established we were the same age, the link providing the medium of under-standing amid cross-cultural silence. We turned yet another bend at close to 3000 metres and the sun cast its late light upon the silent hills, the engine running hard in second gear. 'Very beautiful,' the driver said to me, and for the first time I understood him. We have passed the layered confusions of language and judgement, dollars and rubber stamps. We pulled into Gangotri, holy village, several hours later: 8 p.m., 3050 metres. My heart started beating a little faster from the sudden rise in altitude. It was time to start drinking more water, wandering through the village and the cooler air.

A *saddhu* waved me through his garden from behind the exhaust of his electric generator, chilled out enough to sit there in the noise for hours. Stands of marijuana were watered by the wind wash of the Kedar Ganga, and as I crossed the footbridge to the other side of the river gorge, I could see tiny droplets of water in the darkness illuminated by the light on the edge of his garden.

I sat on the concrete steps scattered with pine needles and looked at the mountains still a very long way above me, spend-ing a day acclimatising, watching the sun-faded coloured prayer flags along the track from my hut. I picked up a few things left by Athol and Patricia in a lock-up: cooker, shell gear and other essentials. Patricia had come with Athol to the Himalaya, after recently visiting the mountains for the first time at Mt Cook. She was also the expedition doctor. I read Athol's letter, and I could tell he was happy to be in the mountains again. 'It will be good to have the team together again ...' Our team: so small, yet sorted and calm.

The gear was all over the terrace after the great escape from Delhi and I began arranging it for the two porters whom I would walk in with. It all seemed so unlikely – to be lying there on the grass while cotton-clad *saddhus* sauntered past, giving me strange looks. I tied the loops on the portaledge bag and felt something akin to the first numb fingers of a brisk alpine morning at Mt Cook, the delicious snap of cold as we make the first hundred metres away from the hut.

Conversations with English Diana, a medical student on a three-week holiday from England, accentuated my purpose; her talk of day-walks and sun cream ironically brought our north face mission into incredible focus. She seemed a little thrown when I told her what I was doing, the portaledge lying in a mess over the scattered pine needles. Suddenly I was thrown into a relaxed world, of gently spoken English-accented words, and I thought of swimming pools and summer at home, of people luxuriously oblivious to climbing. As Diana wandered off after dark, lifting her legs a little clumsily up the steep granite steps, I thought how good it would be just to go for a walk, not to feel the compulsion of the mountains.

On the way to base camp the boulders sat like discarded bombers, American B-52 graveyard style. I went for a walk over the undulating alpine meadow, seeing my tent in the distance, a mere thousand headache-inducing metres away. I pulled the camera out between rainstorms and listened to the mechanical rhythm of the shutter. The two porters had already delivered their cargo to base camp. They paused for a few minutes on their way down and handed me a note from Patricia – all was safe and well up there. Despite having walked up to 3800 metres slowly over two days, my head was growing tender. At 10 p.m. I woke in a panic with a severe altitude headache, and under cold drizzle I ran down the hill, forgetting my head torch but clutching my sleeping bag. I was too scared to go back and get the torch and I needed to lose height very quickly – the pain was really hurting. Within metres I lost the track and stumbled headlong into the rain, feeling hard for a drop in the slope. 'Don't break your ankle, wanker,' I told myself. Two hundred metres down the slope I collapsed behind a rock, wet and panting. I waited for the savage beat in my brain to die away. The rain fell in little patches on my face as the headache faded, and I dreamt of Gigi's mother holding my arm a few months before as I lay in a food-poisoning sweat. With these sweet thoughts I slept again, waking under a hanging fog, a new dawn.

I moved very slowly up the beginnings of the moraine, dehydrated and tired from the bad night. I kept scanning the skyline for any sign of Athol or Patricia. They had carried a load up to the glacier, so I wasn't sure when they might appear. I figured I had about an hour to base camp when I sat, my head going like the clappers again. I heard Athol's unmistakable call and as I looked up he was moving down the moraine wall very fast, evidence of a week or so up at 4500 metres. We talked quietly and very happily, actually rather ecstatic to see each other with Thalay Sagar standing over our shoulders, nearly a year after we had walked out. Ath took my pack and I slowly put in the distance to base camp. I was ready to vomit from altitude-exacerbated dehydration as Ath and Patricia sat me down in the mess tent. Patricia administered a few tablets along with a couple of litres of water over the next half-hour, enough to allow a long sleep and clear-headed awakening.

Back in camp with the crew, my friends: a sterling situation. I shook hands with Bell, our cook, friend, translator and industrial relations spokesman. Within minutes Ath and I were lining up the north face with the binoculars, scanning the central line. We could have been at Mt Cook, Thalay Sagar looked so close on that clear still day. But the altitude and corresponding cold signalled that things were different here, requiring different strategies. With t-shirts and shorts on, we drank *chai* by our stone benches and table. Tools, hardware and clothing were all out for inspection, simplification and modification. Ath helped me sort the foundations for my tent, a neat little flat stone platform, the doors running east-west, my yellow capsule sitting on it like an alpine flower.

Our liaison officer this time was Paul Singh, fresh and green from the sheltered environs of the Punjab establishment. His ex-army colonel father had wanted a meeting with me in Delhi before I left, no doubt to shoot the breeze in the 'how' and 'what-to-do' stakes travelling to the mountains, and to explain that his son was running the expedition *à la* the Indian regs. Fearful of losing days sipping Pimm's, I declined. However, things were rapidly getting out of hand with Paul and at one point he threatened to cancel the expedition over a petty argument about the standard of the equipment supplied to him by us. In Delhi, the expedition had begun with Paul in a shop-front argument with Athol on the steps of the Indian Mountaineering Foundation re his 'unusable' gear. It was a very difficult situation.

Carrying the first load up the glacier, 15 kilograms on the back, stones shifted underfoot and slid down the moraine wall. We moved up the moraine ridge on the glacier's edge a few metres apart, little signals of the year before rushed forward faster than my steps. At the corner, where we cut across the glacier, last year's Czech tent-stamped impressions still lay in the

dried glacial silt, preserved fossil-like. We rose and dropped over
the glacier ridges, marking the high ground with cairns for the
future, stormy, trip over the glacier. At the other side, after an
hour and a half of up and down walking, it was snowing, and we
put on our jackets for another hour and a half up to the stash. I
could see the fluorescent tag on a bamboo wand at the stash
hanging in the white-out gloom, flickering in and out of focus
through falling snow flakes in the foreground.

As we moved up the moraine ridge toward the stash, where
we would later pitch camp one, it was snowing hard. It wasn't
really that cold but we still weren't wearing much. I looked
down the slope to see Ath had on Patricia's thick, woven cotton
hat from Bali, something we all liked to wear. Once level with
the stash I traversed around to it, probing the gaps between the
boulders with my ski poles, dropping out tiny, hollow bridges of
snow. Snow was being driven by the wind across the roof of the
boulder we had chosen for the stash so we ducked under the lip.
Patricia was giggling at us: the boys were into the chocolate at the
first legitimate excuse and guzzling energy drink like alcoholics
on metho. I felt very happy to be alongside my friends as snow
came piling in at our feet, grey clouds churning over the glacier.
With empty packs we scampered down the ridge and back across
the ice, Bell's dinner the motivating force. Crossing the flat to
base camp I could see a soft warm glow from the kerosene
lantern in Bell's kitchen tent and hear the pregnant hiss of the
pressure cooker.

We had 600 metres of rope to fix on the north face if we
wanted, enough to reach into the central couloir. Of course we
would rather fix nothing, but with the altitude and its compounding logistical problems, plus the fact that we didn't know
the route, we had to devise a flexible but rigorous plan. Last year's
attempt had taught us how difficult a climb it was going to be.

Our idea for the fixed line was to use it as a springboard for the top two-thirds of the route. Within that plan, however, there were seemingly a thousand options – how high to fix the rope, when to fix it, in what order? At what point should we launch with the portaledge? If patience is a virtue, we may have earned a few stripes. Our time in 1996 had been a storm-drenched nightmare: the nauseating cold leading to vomiting at the tent door and con-vulsions while on belay. I will never forget the haunting silence of the spindrift avalanches – slow-motion until they hit, then a massive rush of liquid weight on us. Perhaps one day a team will find our stash up there at 6000 metres, anchored to the wall, one of Athol's ice tools still hanging at the high point ...

But this was 1997. On September 1 we pitched a tent at 5100 metres: camp one. It was a small flat platform just above the moraine and 200 kilograms of food and equipment sat next to us at the stash. We began 'Operation Ferry', transporting it all to the site for camp two, at 5400 metres. Ath and I roped up for the first run up the hill, a 'post-holing' affair, our legs going into the snow up to our knees for most of the way. We panted hard up the snowy slope, altitude restricting our efforts. We marked out the route with bamboo wands, tagged with fluorescent ribbons purchased three weeks previously in Singapore. We crested a plateau, strolled to the flat, kicking through the soft snow, and lay back in the mid-morning sun. After three more days of early starts from camp one to avoid the sun while we laboured up the slope, all the kit was up, plus the three of us. Camp two, launch pad.

The amphitheatre at camp two was a grand affair, spread out as if the stage for an opera. We were in the only safe place, about 70 metres from the main avalanche zone, the area where Jay and Kitty had been avalanched in '96, protected by the drop-off to camp one.

Our first morning on the face began with a false start. Within minutes of leaving camp we were deluged with snowfall. Sitting

in the snow only 100 metres from the tents we laughed about
our first 'attempt'. We groggily walked back and crawled into the
tent, sleeping bags still faintly warm. Patricia brewed fresh coffee
and we chatted aimlessly and listened to the snow slide off the
tent fly, our early-morning talk show. Within an hour it was time
for take two – we plugged up the gradually steepening slope,
staying on a vague crest, moving toward a schrund. It was stressful work and hard to find a rhythm in the deep, loose snow. The
rationale was simply to get up and get down without any dramas.
The weather became stormy again as we approached the
schrund. We quickly negotiated it, got an anchor in the edge of a
rock band and made another stash. We descended the avalanche
slopes in heavy snowfall, lifting our legs out of holes we sank
into. My hands were hot and out of my gloves. With relief we
faced in to the slope for a few metres to descend around the large
schrund. Soon the angle eased off, and we picked up our ski
poles and stumbled into camp two. The snow was very soft and
seemed to be falling down everywhere. It was hard to move fast.

Patricia's eyes watered with laughter when I recalled the
Greek swear words I was taught by friends in primary school.
Inside the tent over the next three days we talked with great
energy: stories from 'the good old days', fondly recalling child-
hood, fishing in mountain streams, tree-planting exercises on
the farm. Athol cleaned his camera like a rifle: stripped it down,
re-assembled, checked a few parts again. I loved the sound of the
camera's mechanics. He turned on his elbow and took a shot of
Patricia and me 11 hours into the next day, still smiling. We had
a lot of room, even for the three of us. Brewed coffee, dried fruit,
chocolate and Capote's *In Cold Blood* kept us going. I watched
Patricia's eyes as she made invisible calculations while the
stethoscope sat on my chest. I tried to breathe normally, but it
was hard. Patricia's Walkman was the *de luxe* ride to freedom, for

some reason Sinead O'Connor the tape of the moment. I listened to it again and again, then took off the headphones in a sweat, as if I had woken up on the couch at 3 a.m. with the television playing *Hawaii Five-O* repeats.

Heavy loads were the go for the next sortie up the face. From the schrund we fixed 120 metres of rope, getting us to the end of the snowfields and the beginning of the icefield, protected by an initial rock shield. It was mid-morning when I began climbing the rock shield; loose snow and ice dislodged at the slightest knock with an ice tool. At times the whole shallow corner system I was in felt like it was about to drop out from under my legs. I must have been taking some time as I could hear Ath asking, 'How's it going up there ...?' Finally I broke over the lip of the near-vertical wall and sought our path. Sunlight had begun reflecting off the sheet-white wall, heat flushed out from my chest, and little patches of granite were being turned dark by glistening icy wetness. While Athol still shivered in the shadows, I managed to find an anchor. With gloves off I rested my head on the tied-off rope running to the anchor and gave Ath the call to jumar.

The sight of what lay ahead didn't impress us: thin, sugary ice coated everything. We needed to navigate by a sort of x-ray and braille, feeling for where 'the line' was under the rubbish on top. It was a tiresome task, one for true believers. From my anchor Ath led up and left to position us within a pitch or so of being able to head straight up to the central couloir. The sun greedily sucked the water from our bodies, and by 3 p.m. we were well wasted. We turned around at our high point and watched camp two through the filters of swirling monsoon cloud, just like being in an aeroplane, circling the landing strip with water streaming across the window in little dots.

Into camp two, another assignment through the avalanche

zone completed as we descended from the face. Clouds began dissipating as the evening crept in. Our two cookers belted out dinner as we stood around the tents, and sunset over the Jogin peaks lit up the top of the face with incredible effect. Like a ship on fire while anchored in the harbour, Thalay Sagar refused to move, announcing its sunset presence by releasing the occasional icy salvo from the headwall. The sun withdrew; night began to take hold. Shades of grey covered the snow slopes, and soon everything took on a black and white appearance. In the morning it was snowing: we slept in, then had coffee courtesy of Athol. We talked about the face, well aware the next step was setting out with the portaledge. It was September 9, and we were ready to give it a big effort. All we needed was a little rest.

As the snow kept piling up outside we felt concerned. What if it kept snowing like it had in 1996? Confidence stemmed from knowing the snow was merely monsoonal – anything else would have been far colder. 'We've still got some time up our sleeves,' said Athol. Both of us were thinking of the beginning of October, the artificial cut-off point, marker of the changing seasons, when the already serious cold here accelerates into nightmare proportions.

We sat around for another day, all good acclimatisation, waiting for the weather to clear. Hour after hour we lay back in our sleeping bags, interrupted by an occasional toilet sortie or rush to the supply tent for chocolate, daily medicine, dried fruit and nuts. A weather report from the person outside was obligatory, a function of boredom more than anything. On the evening of September 10 it was still snowing, although darkness fed our hope that it might soon clear. By 9.30 a.m. next day we were descending in wind and snow, covered in white as we crossed the glacier to the moraine ridge, on the express run to base camp.

Evening brought the clearing of the storm, and the bright light atop of Thalay Sagar was astounding. There was no rush. We relished our last evening in base camp with Patricia and Bell. That afternoon a bad argument with our LO, Paul, had erupted. The current system for Himalayan expeditions in India (most specifically the supposed role of the LO) is riddled with problems, and self-protection by excluding the LO from 'the team' is sadly the best solution. It's like an experienced racing-car driver trying to explain to someone who's just got their licence that he or she isn't quite ready for the circuit, and the rookie (seriously) doesn't believe him. Eventually it was sorted, Ath the meat in the negotiating sandwich, myself kept on the outer by Paul, enough to get me about the angriest I'd ever been. An hour later I was relieved to see Paul head up the glacier on a camping trip with Seetal, the LO for a Korean expedition attempting the original route, the north-west couloir and west ridge. We shook hands as they walked off, and I felt relieved we had resolved the situation, at least on a diplomatic level.

I wrote a letter by candlelight, wondering what was happening at home. My brother, my sisters, my parents; I have never really been able to explain any of this to them. Everything in the tent took on more significance on that last night in base camp; it felt especially warm. My pens and paper, envelopes with ink smudged from the Delhi heat, frantic last-minute items thrown into supermarket bags, lay strewn over my floor. Tapes, Gigi's Walkman, clothes for my pillow formed the hearth for restoration. The inside of my tent had been like a bombsite since I arrived, the relapse from keeping a tight kit on the hill.

We ate breakfast and packed all at once, using the opportunity of another trip up to camp two to take a few more luxuries. Bell walked out to the sun deck with last calls for omelettes and coffee, oblivious to the task that we faced. By 9.30 a.m. we were out of camp, with clear warm light on our faces. At the corner where we had left the moraine ridge on the initial load-carries we paused for a rest and drink. Within the space of ten minutes I sensed the situation had escalated: our time up at camp two acclimatising and fixing rope felt remote, somewhere in the past. After half an hour of lying in the sun I sat up, and Ath simultaneously offered: 'Well, guess we'd better head up ...' It was another replay for us, securely familiar, yet it had a power I had never felt so strongly.

Patricia, who had accompanied us here, seemed to be searching for reassurance in Athol; something that would guarantee our return, our safety. I think she knew the deal, but I was worried for her. I hugged her goodbye, voicing confidence, at least. 'See you in a week or so,' I heard Athol say softly to her as I wandered away toward the glacier. I could hear Patricia talking, but her words were too faint, gradually blending into the quiet tap of Athol's approaching ski poles.

On the glacier we moved fast; gone were the heavy load-carrying packs. As we walked we could see the evidence of an avalanche above camp one, a pale blue icy scar next to the soft snow slope. At the Koreans' advance base camp Paul offered us sweet Korean cake. We all knew where we stood and tension dissipated as we got on with the show. There was even a vague sense of understanding between us and Paul as we shouldered our packs and kept moving. As Athol said, he was probably relieved to finally know he wasn't part of the 'working team', able to relinquish his pride in an honourable fashion by doing his own thing with the Korean LO, Seetal.

As we arrived at camp one the avalanche damage was crudely displayed. We speculated about 'If it ripped now, where would you run?' and pulled our plastic boots from under the camp's rock shelter. Before long we were away again, crampons on and

The portaledge at 6450 metres, anchored on two ice screws. We spent two nights here, in the fall-line of constant spindrift avalanching. *Athol Whimp.*

Right: Nearing the summit of Thalay Sagar, I slump over to get my breath as snow begins to fall. *Athol Whimp.*

Below: Athol on the summit of Thalay Sagar, 6.15 p.m., 19 September 1997. We then descended in the dark to our portaledge 400 metres below. *Author.*

side-stepping up the avalanche scar. The sun was moving through its mid-morning sweep, the reflected warmth from the snow gradually increasing. As we crested the plateau we hit a good stride, crossed the few crevasses with accustomed care, and zigzagged up the final hill to camp two.

'We smoked that,' said Ath as we pulled into camp two non-stop from the boot change-over down at camp one. I had brought up a book from base camp that Athol had found earlier sitting in the nook of a boulder, near where the Americans and us had stashed gear in '96. There were two bookmarks in it: one for Kitty, one for Jay. We both reckoned it was Kitty who was further in. We took a load up to the end of the '120' (the fixed rope between the schrund stash and the rock shield) early the following morning, and were back in camp two for breakfast, all up a three-and-a-half-hour sortie. All that then remained was to head up with the portaledge, destination summit.

Athol was in fits of laughter reading Samuel Beckett under the shade of the tent; outside in the sun it was unbearably hot. As evening drew near we prepared the last supper, a large feast. Soon after, in the dark, we collapsed the tents. As Athol put away his point-and-shoot camera, he lined me up and pressed the button, the flash's light bursting around my head, shoulders framed square. I took the camera and shot his portrait, cold face, glowing eyes, shoulder straps of the pack indicative of the journey to come. As he put the camera away in the folds of the storage tent, we bleakly laughed about the pictures, 'At least if we get the chop there'll be some happy snaps ...'.

The brittle crunching cold had already set in as we followed our trail up the ever-steepening slope – our last time up the dangerously loaded avalanche zone. The altitude had begun to feel relatively normal – we were so used to panting our guts out we'd forgotten what sea level was like. As Ath jumared the

'120' I was still warm from dinner. I turned my head torch off and watched the barely visible snow crystals tumble down the edge of the rock where I was anchored, symbols of Athol's upward progress.

The excitement was phenomenal. So was the breadth and beauty of the massive north face. Fifteen hundred metres, all of it desperate work. It was 10 p.m. when we clambered into the portaledge at the base of the rock shield, the '120' dropping out underneath us. Inside the portaledge it was a nightmare. Cups, the hanging stove, clothing, energy bars, our sleeping bags – they were all lost and found as we slowly got organised. Then everything was quiet and clear, save for the occasional salvo of ice tearing down. Large pieces had usually shattered into a myriad tiny fragments by the time they impacted on the ledge.

It took about three hours to get from waking to a point where we were ready to climb. The drill began at 3 a.m., melting ice for hot energy drinks, then filling the water bottles – our own little hydro scheme. We jumared to the top of the fixed line at first light. Our project for the day was fixing rope as high as we could, most likely finishing somewhere around the beginning of the couloir. Five metres out from the previous day's high-point anchor I was already panting. Everywhere I looked, huge granite walls hung over me, a perfect confidence crusher. I had too much energy going into mental 'damage control'. I had no protection in at this point, the dense blue ice sat under a thin crust of snow, my crampons' front points scraped through and only bit securely on a second kick. A thin shred of faded orange rope revealed itself at the beginning of a steepening, remnant of the '96 American fixed line. For what it was worth, I chopped a section free from the ice, tied off a loop and used it as protection. A shallow corner began to form in front of me as I climbed higher, at least 70 metres above the belay, with nothing but distance and the slow release of adrenalin to show for it. Soon I got the 'Five metres ...' call from Athol – not much rope left, so time to look for an anchor. 'It's all shit,' I muttered to myself, scraping around, burning calorie after precious calorie. Finally a piton and a wire did the job, and Athol was on his way up.

The next pitch took Athol to the end of this very shallow corner, to exit up a steep ramp, ice glued over dark granite, just taking the blows from his ice tools without completely shattering. By the time I jumared the pitch my front points were peeling plate-sized sections off, sending them discus-style to the distant deck. Ath had carved out a small icy hollow which housed his anchor, the ropes exiting as if lines from a parachute rig. We leant back on the anchor and took a quick drink; I tried to mix the liquid with the chocolate energy bar scraping around inside my mouth. Athol took a photo of me about to gulp from my bottle, a swollen red cut below my left eye evidence of an ice-inflicted blow only minutes before.

The only protection I got leading the next pitch was a pathetic tied-off ice screw midway. At least 60 metres above the anchor I tracked through a thin section of better ice. Naturally, it soon ended and I was back on the sugary snow veneer, which was guaranteed to give way if one rested too long in one place. Worse still, the ice under the snow split and slipped over a harder layer – the right medicine to keep climbing. It was a relief when I encountered the wall that guarded entry into the couloir, 95 metres from the last belay. Brief spindrift flurries danced down the wall above me, an immense glittering yellow blankness. I pulled my hood up over my helmet, and proceeded to search for an anchor. Long run-outs between protection and tedious anchor finding had become the name of the game.

The day was drawing on and from my semi-hanging belay I leant back and waited in the long shadows for Athol. My anchor was no more than a piton in a tapered slot, bounded by a fracture in the rock, plus my ice tools. My watchful eyes observed the tightening of the clove hitch on the anchor as Athol, jumaring below, transferred his weight to the line. The spindrift kept showering down in random sessions. The monsoon build-up was mainly cosmetic – we seemed to be getting a bit of a run at things.

From this little chopped-out stance Athol followed the toe of the wall up and left. I snapped a few photos, Brigupanth entering the frame. Athol swore in frustration at a few minutes spent on trying to place a useless piton before clipping it back on his harness and moving up again. It was a long way before he found anywhere to place protection – everything depended on my belay. On the first steep bulge Ath wound in a solid ice screw. Ten more metres, another locked-down screw, and the rope was tied off, altitude 6200 metres. We abseiled quickly down the fixed line to the portaledge, small clumps of ice flying off as the rope fed into our descenders.

Next morning, body weight was nervously thrown onto the anchors – the show was on the road. While one of us jumared, the other hauled the haul bag and portaledge, which was packed away. Either way, we felt wasted. As I jumared across and up to Athol at the high point, I began to feel very tired. I didn't know what it was, but fatigue was creeping through my whole system. I thought I hadn't recovered from the effort of the previous day. I felt frustrated, yet couldn't move any faster. My legs were struggling. A big rack of protection picked up from a pitch below hung from my shoulders and pressed on my chest, my gasping lungs. Ath urged me on as I approached the anchor. I could tell he was anxious to get higher before dark. He talked quietly as we sorted things out at the belay, encouraging me to have a good breather. Before long I was shivering, and just wanted to curl up and hibernate.

Like scouts we looked for a good site for the portaledge. The eventual site, a freezing steep run-off from the upper couloir, was christened Camp Nothing. The thin crust of fractured snow over the ice was sprinkled with stony debris, impact points of all that let go from the upper section of the face. Darkness happened quickly, and with it the cold. Nothing could be done with bare hands, let alone a thin thermal layer. Every part of our bodies needed insulation. Only when we had our hanging stove purring later that night could we switch off. Encapsulated in a yellow glow, with no mountain visible, I slept in 20-minute spells, waking with half-chewed food in my mouth and a rapidly cooling brew in my hands. 'More ice,' said Athol as he checked the stove. I carefully twisted in my sleeping bag and unzipped the portaledge door, frozen condensation falling throughout the 'ledge, instantly melting and running off into the mass of stuff sacs, lost energy bars, spoons, fuel canisters, chaos *ad nauseam*. Within a minute my hands were frozen but fortunately the stuff sac was full of ice chips, and we eventually got another hot drink.

Never had the contradiction between staying warm in the sleeping bag and needing to move higher been so strong. Thankfully it was a horrid portaledge site, and we struck camp hungry for height and for somewhere else to sleep. Already, by 10 a.m., the massing cloud was sending snow down. Athol was dealing with the ice ribbon, a stunning smear of vertical ice. He was pulling rabbits out of a hat: tied-off ice-screws, camming devices, sideways wires, pitons, but there was still a long way between each piece of protection. And all under a minus 20° Celsius reign of violent spindrift avalanche storms.

I tried to get a head start on the haul bag as I jumared under the horrific strain of the now constant avalanches, but had to descend to free it. Athol's red figure, hanging on the thinnest section of the ribbon, had now disappeared. I couldn't look up as the spindrift was tearing down with massive speed, almost a suf-focating force. If it hadn't been so steep we would have been in trouble from the weight of falling snow. I placed an ice tool and clipped into it to release tension from a camming device. As I released the tension, I was catapulted across right in line with the anchor, immediately frightened I'd smash my legs or feet on the face. It was happening faster than my brain could take it in. Motion eventually steadied, and the line of gravity stabilised yet again. The spindrift didn't let up. Indeed, it became normal.

Athol was pleased to see me when I arrived at the anchor. All our weight was on our harnesses, front points of crampons painfully stabbing in, attempting to take some of the weight. We spent two hours hanging in pain, unable to continue due to the ongoing spindrift avalanching. Cold feet, cold hands, severe stomach cramps – we both needed to go to the toilet. It was a bizarre situation. We were well and truly castaways, beyond any rescue, yet we placed faith in the idea that the storm would eventually stop.

We received a couple of hours' grace as the afternoon waned, just enough time to complete another hard pitch and set the portaledge up. Athol climbed up and around a huge overhanging rock pillar, frozen drips of ice hanging from its underside. The ice was polished as if straight off the press in a steel plant. The portaledge hung from two ice screws at 6450 metres. The ice was close to vertical, and everything bar crampons slipped straight off it. As darkness folded over us the avalanching started again, and we struggled to get inside the 'ledge and sorted. Every task took a long time, and when we finally zipped the portaledge doors up it felt more cramped than it had before. We were practically oblivious to the frighteningly persistent storm now hammering the portaledge. We stared at the fly, listening to the wind created by impacting avalanches. We silently prayed nothing would tear the fly. Half-sitting, we drank hot orange drink, falling asleep as the cooker did its job.

Time drifted. Our alarms were set for 3, 4, and finally 6 a.m. – all to no avail. It was still snowing. However, the avalanching now only occurred every ten or so minutes, a reassuring sign from above. We kept sleeping, and managed to get another couple of brews down. Even when we woke to drink, we were falling asleep within minutes. At 3 p.m. we got out of the porta-ledge, taking a chance on still conditions. About 20 metres above the belay Athol turned around and took a shot of me hanging on the anchor, the entire scope of the wall dropping out beneath me. Watching the yellow light from the sun change to shades of orange as it streamed into the face, I realised it was late in the day. We were at the end of the couloir; the thin ribbon of ice had merged into a fierce ice shield, guarding entry onto the shale headwall. Small plates of ice peeled off and fell freely as Ath removed his ice tools and crampons in turn and moved higher.

Smooth granite buttresses reared away from the line of the ice shield and led us into the 'Y', where the ice shield finished and the mixed ground began. After an hour I heard Athol's voice. It was very faint, a good sign. At least 90 metres above me he had an anchor. As I began to jumar, floating snowflakes crashed into my face, and the buttresses above and on the right disappeared in the cloud. I was able to put in 20 movements at a time before a brief pause, leaning my head against the rope. The wind was pushing the snow upwards and around in gentle movements as I closed in on the anchor, and within seconds I could sense the scene changing. Soon I could see Athol's red figure leaning back on the anchor, illuminated by the setting sun.

At the anchor we watched the show of gentle wind and light, of cold and snow. The entire shale headwall was spread out before us, lit up in intimate detail by the evening sun. A thin frozen veneer, almost luminescent, was stretched over the headwall's incredibly complex expanse. We had no time or light to move the portaledge up, so we abseiled back down for the night. Athol endured an epic going to the toilet; when it was my turn, the spindrift was streaming down the face like sand down a funnel. My hands became unusable in the deep cold, and I couldn't even get toilet paper from a pouch in the haul bag. It soon became impossible to do anything, let alone hang and wait for things to calm down. I could feel myself becoming hypothermic, losing co-ordination, but denying this to myself. Athol urged me to get into the 'ledge before I began losing a grip on the situation. The pain from my stomach cramps were horrific, but eventually I managed to do the job from the portaledge door, balancing right on its edge. Athol was cowering from the scene, and from the fresh waves of spindrift blowing into the 'ledge. With no toilet paper, a spare thermal glove was used and sacrificed to the wind. Clothing and door were zipped up, the operation completed.

As we lay in the portaledge the sky began to clear – it seemed as though we were going to get the green light come morning. A merely occasional tinkle of falling ice on the fly was as soothing as ankle-lapping warm waves on the beach. It was 8 a.m. when we begin jumaring. Athol was up at the anchor hauling while I moved with the haul bag and portaledge, still set up. Inside the portaledge at the anchor we both remarked how 'fucking cold' it was, hanging around in a minus 20° Celsius freezer trying to get some sleep. More importantly, we had to brew up. As the sun arced through the sky, gradually closing in on our position, we enjoyed our best brew session yet, complete with pre-warmed energy bars. While I was outside sorting some of the rack, a falling rock hit Athol in the leg, entering the portaledge through one of the open doors. As he battled with the pain, I had flashing visions of a fractured leg, an epic retreat – something we didn't need.

Our 'camp' was situated at the head of the ice shield. Base camp sat 2000 metres below, in clear light, and we could just make out a square of blue, the tarp over the cooking tent. We wondered what the others were doing as we sat back and felt the warmth from the sun, now shining straight at us. Patricia might have been able to make us out with her zoom lens, but we were unsure, thinking we might just blend in with the rock and ice. At 3 p.m. we jumared 50 metres of rope we had fixed earlier up a steep snow ramp above the portaledge. From the anchor I headed up and slightly left towards a massive 'hanging' granite tower. Our plan was to ascend the left side of this tower, then begin climbing the shale band. Soft, unconsolidated snow sat over iron-hard ice. Ice tool placements were insecure but I was somewhat relieved by the warmth from the sun; it was easier to think without the constant spindrift barrages. I noticed a vertical gully and tracked toward it, crossing patches of overhead rock with my tools. My legs were capturing as much distance as possible with each step, crampons biting on angles, acting out the judgement of between speed and security.

The vertical gully ice was old and peeled off with each blow; I wedged my tools in some cracks after I'd shattered out the ice, bridging the angles with my feet to move higher. Where the gully topped out I wasted time trying to get an anchor that was good enough; the day was rapidly closing. A knifeblade and wire did the job. As Athol jumared I felt every available receptor in my system analysing the options ahead, and a shiver crept out of my one-piece suit. As I hung from the anchor I noticed the glacier two kilometres below spread out in the twilight. But our day was still going, if only just.

A polished blue strip of ice ran straight up to the left side of the tower, and from there we moved in under the right of the tower, and hoped it would get us up and out onto the shale band.

By climbing the left side ramp of the 'hanging tower,' we hoped we would be able to get higher faster than on the right side, and it seemed unlikely we would be able to stand on top of the hanging tower from the right and launch up the shale headwall. Also, the left-side option kept us on the good granite for longer.

I could hear Ath calling, 'Step right, step right, then you'll be in line,' as I turned a bulge in the ice. Thankfully he was keeping me in check as I was simultaneously moving and assessing the best way in the twilight, feeling utterly exhausted. A shallow wave of snow crystals tumbled toward me above the surface, a halo looking for somewhere to rest. I moved through it, needing to reach somewhere on the tower we could begin climbing the shale from in the morning. The corner of the tower was plastered with brittle, hanging snow and thin transparent ice – 'The stuff you find in the freezer,' the American alpinist Marc Twight aptly described this sort of thing. The left wall of the corner I was in was overhanging, confining my movements even more. As I stepped higher, my left arm straight up with the tool torqued in the corner crack, the front points of my right crampon threaten to skate off. Icy debris fell in my face and into my neck. Nausea rolled through me. I literally could not remember where I had placed my last bit of protection, and I was amazed I hadn't come off. 'Slow it down, Andy,' I muttered to myself. There was nothing for it but to stand high on my right leg, hoping I'd laid the foundations well. At mid-step I moved my right tool up, a little hop that made the difference.

The squeak of the planted ice pick on my right tool sounded like a sharp bird call, and I laboured up the gradually easing ramp until I could stand. Out to my left I plugged two camming devices in a horizontal break on top of the last granite buttress, tied the rope off and abseiled into the night. The yellow dot of Athol's head torch was suddenly hidden by a buttress as I descended toward the next anchor. I remained clipped to the top anchor until I heard his 'OK' call from below, the signal he was on the final line to the portaledge camp at 6450 metres.

Inside the portaledge we sorted everything out for a quick get-away at 7 a.m. The cooker ran softly in the background as we discussed the approaching day. We knew that once we were on the summit, every step would be a homeward one. We were surprisingly mercenary, a coping mechanism driven by a deeper knowledge of what we had to do to succeed. 'Once we've topped out, we'll rap the fuck off this face, get into camp two, and it's a done deal,' I said. 'Too right,' replied Ath, busy stripping back another energy bar. 'Chocolate or banana?' he asked me. I could barely hold my sleepy laughter – it was day five living on energy bars, and relishing every one.

Once again I noticed my gloves were lying out in the mess covering our sleeping bags; evidence of passed time. They were beginning to freeze over. I was annoyed at myself for not keeping tabs on gear that needed to be ready to go at all times. I thrust them into my sleeping bag. Our alarms sounded, one ten seconds after the other. It was 4 a.m. Ath checked I was awake, and together we put off the first arm movements out of our sleeping bags. It felt just like a bitter 2 a.m. winter start at Mt Cook. As usual, keenness got the better of us, a certain recognition that the day could easily escape – 'There was a reason we set the alarms for 4 a.m.' – and soon the cooker was gasping out its first blue flames. It was clear and cold as we began jumaring the fixed rope at 7.30. Hands surged hot and cold, the numbing salute to the new day. When I arrived at the anchor I'd set the previous night, Athol was ready to go, banging his gloves together, his eyes gently closed.

He began climbing with his crampons on a small granite stance, and his gloved hands on loose shale. The sound of the sliding layers of shale was disconcerting, broken pieces of ice falling out as the layers moved apart; it was as if sandwiches of ice held the headwall together. Within minutes on the belay I started shivering, all part of the deal of early morning when one is unable to walk around and warm up. The temperature was sitting around minus 20° Celsius; even with chemical warmers in our boots and gloves we were succumbing to the cold. Facing the wall, a blue expanse gathered on my peripheral vision and I realised it was the sky, below, above, all around. I turned to the right, looking for cloud. The light was as even as moonlight. Colours were appearing as black and white, as if the glacier was reflecting its grey-scale image upon the rising walls along its flanks.

Athol had decided on the final corner we needed to reach and was crossing towards its line – delicate manoeuvring over rotten stone that crumbled and broke with the readiness of ancient bones. There was no wind. Athol was climbing with the concentration of an archaeologist on the verge of some sort of discovery, delicate and fierce all at once, small salvos of ice from his moving crampons dropping into free-fall like the tick of a clock in a quiet room.

The belay sat under a horizontal overhang, a 'roof'. I lashed in there after jumaring and Athol began moving to the left, traversing along a vertical section of shale, one move with a tool working dry on the rock, the next move with hands. Again he needed to move a few metres leftward, causing horrific rope drag. Ath asked for more slack, but the rope could only move painfully slowly through the protection. It was a stressful situation. Ath was under the hammer – the only way out was up, and I was literally attempting to push the rope through the runners. All of this was a sickly warm-up for the crux section. Moving into it, Ath underclung and balanced around a loose block, shifting tiles of slate under his crampons, reaching high and torquing his right tool in a small corner crack and slowly pulling himself higher. With feet over the block, he continued through the vertical toward a large sloping basin, and found a solid belay on the right wall, 100 metres above me. I heard a faint call, 'Safe!'

I pulled out the belay, tensioned the jumars and swung into the line, my crampons scratching on the rock, dislodging layers. The snow cap sat just above me, and I moved as fast as I could toward where I knew Athol would be eyeing up the final section to the summit, over the sight of rope cut deeply in several places, just like the cliché in the movies. As I glanced up a snowflake hit me on the face; I could feel its sharpness melting on my cheek. Clouds were pushing themselves onto the massive black ramparts rising to my sides, condensing on impact. There was a storm developing, yet it remained eerily calm. Occasionally I even got a glimpse of the glacier, like a satellite photograph. The clouds tumbled into us, dispensing thousands and thousands of snow crystals, each one a perfect white form.

I pushed my top jumar over the final lip in extreme oxygen debt – as though I was in a perpetual 400 metre sprint. I ran the jumars along the rope to Athol at the anchor, my lungs heaving like never before – as Athol would say, I'd 'given them a good reaming'. I wondered momentarily if the blood I saw on the snow before me was my own, but then I saw Ath's bleeding knuckles wrapped around the rope. We had one more pitch before negotiating the summit snow cap. My heartbeat hadn't subsided when Ath was away up the final corner: clean vertical rock, edges dusted with snow. He turned halfway up and took a photograph – 'we're not coming back here ...'

We climbed the summit snow cap, and it felt very much the natural conclusion to all the upward metres. The clouds had moved in again, snow was sliding down in loose sheets. The cap's vague snow flutings that appeared so vivid from base camp were subtle creases in the slope. In places the snow seemed bottomless, sometimes there was a crunch as we hit some rock underneath. We had both tools with their shafts into their hilts and still they had no security. The slope could have avalanched, but with dark coming in fast, and being so close to the top, we had become distanced from an acute awareness of these conditions – our minds had already outweighed the risks. We were on auto-pilot, moving hard, yet brilliantly calm. Only 20 metres from the summit, I was absolutely stunned by the incredible situation we were in, the whole thing an uncontrollable line between being in tune with one another and our environment, and the impossibility that we had reached the summit. Athol took my hand as I stood on top, and I felt an immense love and respect for him. We barely had the energy to smile, and took photographs as the Himalaya was lit by storm-drenched streams of pink sunlight, atomic-like bulbous clouds swirling over themselves. A few flakes of snow fell on me and I couldn't tell where they had come from.

I wound my camera on and suddenly realised the film had been free of the spool since I had loaded it on our third day of the route. I quickly reloaded film and snapped away, my brain trying to calculate apertures and speed, hoping I was holding the camera still enough in the final moments of the twilight. We left a snow stake and five rupees each on top, an offering of sorts. We could have sat and gone to sleep, but it was time to go. At 6.30 p.m., with fresh chemical hand warmers and insulated jackets on, we turned face-in to the slope and dropped into the night.

The cold was very intense. Everything was further than I remembered. I had to adjust angle several times, even to stay on our existing upward steps! We were pushing the balance of speed, co-ordination and what the slope would allow, an amazing thing to be controlling. Loose, balling snow tumbled into the abyss as we moved down and I was surprised the slope didn't zip off. Athol moved very efficiently. At the top anchor we put on our head torches, fumbling around in the top lids of our packs for their shapes. Ath clipped in and abseiled. I followed soon after, trying to give the ropes a clean run over the edge so they didn't jam.

The next abseil dropped over the headwall. As we pulled the rope 90 metres below to free it, we prayed it wouldn't stick on the lip. As the end of the rope cut free from its anchor, we both faced the wall and covered our heads in case loose rock came with it. It took a few minutes to gauge the best line of descent for the next abseil. Surrounded by the black night, we looked for clues with the small yellow dots of our head torches. Soon we landed right on the steep ramp that led to the hanging tower, like coins down a slot. We took turns pulling the rope down, the effort draining our bodies, taxing their reserve tanks. After another long, angled abseil, we were only 50 metres from the portaledge. As I changed ropes I caught myself neglecting to clip in to the anchor by my side, and didn't bother anyway, tiredness running with the quicker options. My crampon front points were in the ice, one leg straight, the other knee-up, my arm resting on it, clipping into the final run to the portaledge.

Once there the relief was immense. My legs were cramping as I got out of my one-piece suit and into the sleeping bag, Dustings of snow dropped into my lap, the head torch still on my helmet lighting a corner of the portaledge. 'What a job,' said Ath, with much relief. We were giggling like kids and swearing, all the symptoms of getting away with it. It was 10.30 p.m. and we were too exhausted to eat. Around midnight Ath pulled a couple of warm energy bars out of his sleeping bag. It seemed easier to eat and drink after some time had passed, and thoughts of descending were beginning to take shape in our minds.

Sleeping in was the reward for the previous day's effort. Weather checks revealed a clear, still sky, a gift soon to be taken away. I jumared the rope above the portaledge and pulled the higher rope down. Athol was packing the portaledge and haul bag, and when I returned we jettisoned the food that we hadn't eaten – dried potato, noodles – in an effort to lighten the load. It wasn't until late morning that we were ready to go and, as we stripped the anchor back a little to keep gear available for anchors lower down, we noticed the beginnings of an approaching storm. Athol abseiled first and secured the anchor 100 metres below. I watched the ropes and saw the tension ease off, his weight transferring onto his anchor, the rope going free. We couldn't hear each other, the wind had begun to pick up in small, upward, spiralling gusts. I began lowering the haul bag and portaledge, keeping the bag clipped to one of the abseil lines so Athol could reach them at the anchor. The weight of the haul bag eased off and I paid out more slack, thinking Athol had it clipped to his anchor. But Athol was watching the haul bag and portaledge hang from an ice protrusion, with 5 metres of rope looping below them. He was yelling out, I was yelling out – we both wanted to know what was happening, but the only sounds to be heard came from the approaching roar of the storm.

Our voices mixed and disappeared under the shadow of the massive black clouds now about to hit us. Athol took cover as best he could as the haul bag and portaledge broke free and free-fell 10 metres, coming to a sudden, static stop. I felt no change in the lowering rope. We both operated on an unspoken understanding everything was sorted, and after another ten minutes I cleared the lines to abseil. I descended, the ropes running through my lightweight descender with ridiculous ease, my eyes picking out our crampon marks from the ascent two days ago. As we began pulling the ropes they twisted and jammed. It started snowing, ripples of spindrift began cascading down the vertical ice; the nightmare was beginning again. We cautiously hadn't let go of the ends of the ropes and quickly decided we needed to jumar up and free the jam. Athol tied one end off to himself and I jumared on the other line. The storm was now in full force. I managed to put in 20 steps on the jumars at a time, give myself ten resting breaths, then moved again. Snow rushed into my face, and the clouds were black and dropping onto Thalay with great speed. I tried to fix the mess from 10 metres below the anchor but of course it didn't work – 'Fuck you,' I angrily yelled to myself, I fiercely gunned it to the anchor.

It took ten minutes of untwisting to free the tangled mess – 'We don't *need* this shit,' I muttered. I abseiled again and we pulled the rope out successfully this time, 100 metres closer to our release. It was avalanching with awesome ferocity, the temperature was dropping and we prepared ourselves for a long day – we would have to fight every inch to camp two. As we descended each abseil had its own problems. When I lowered the haul bag and porta-ledge I would sense them closing in on the anchor, and slow their descent to centimetres at a time. I could almost feel Athol grab them with his hands and guide them into the waiting karabiner on the anchor. Then, with huge relief, he would clip it in – the spaceship was docked. At the base of the steepest section of the couloir, we weren't convinced the anchor would take the combined loads of the two of us, the haul bag and portaledge. Athol abseiled a further 10 metres lower in the falling vortex of spindrift to two pitons we had left in on the way up, marked with a piece of fluorescent tape. We somehow transferred every-thing over amid the confusion of snow and flurries of wind and continued.

I could feel the chemical warmers' spot of warmth in each hand as I abseiled, and I pulled my camera out and shot five frames of Athol, hoping at least one would turn out. With great relief we arrived at the fixed line and rigged another rope so we could abseil, then pull down and retrieve the fixed rope. As Athol abseiled onto the lower icefield, he yelled out to me, and I could detect happiness in his call. He had seen my ice axe, one that had fallen when a gear loop it was clipped to tore under the load of a diagonally loaded rope halfway up the route. When I abseiled he guided me into its location – it had obviously stabbed itself in as if having left the hand of a knife-thrower. I plucked it from the slope and traversed to Athol, who was waiting at the next anchor. We pulled all the fixed line as we descended, the sun occasionally breaking through. We could hear the storm battering the mountain above us and I could see the strain of the descent on Athol's face, his bloodshot eyes running on empty.

Silhouettes of clouds formed patterned movements across the icefield as evening was brought on by a cold, falling sun. Near the first rock shield the haul bag and portaledge became caught between Athol and myself. I abseiled and freed the mess, dropping a glove in the process. In the twilight I couldn't see how everything – the loops of rope, haul bag and portaledge – had become ensnared in such a mess. My brain felt like it was working at half-speed, yet I ruthlessly dealt with the situation, literally kicking the haul bag free, its weight rapidly dropping onto the anchor 10 metres above me. I let the haul bag and portaledge serve as a counter-weight, and front-pointed up the slope to the anchor.

The next abseil brought us to the top of the avalanche-prone slopes in the dark, with only a couple of hours to camp two. I was swapping my one glove between both hands: the exposed hand always getting too cold but holding the chemical warmer over a thermal layer just kept the hand from freezing. Athol abseiled the fixed line and I lowered the haul bag, soon losing sight of it. All I could make out below was a small yellow dot, Ath's head torch. Our calls were suffocated by the magnitude and expanse of the snowfields. Somehow we managed to get the haul bag onto Athol's anchor by a combination of extending the line it was on with a spare few metres of rope looped around the anchor and Athol wrestling it into place. It would have been easy to cut it all free, but our perseverance won over, the knowledge that we were only a short distance from camp two and flat ground feeding the momentum.

At the schrund we were off all the ropes, and a mess of ropes lay half-buried in the slope around us. 'Let's clear it up and keep moving,' said Athol. We decided to let the haul bag go, hoping to retrieve it somewhere on the snow basin below. He ran the haul bag and portaledge out on one of the ropes and released it. Facing in, knees pressed into the slope, we pulled in the ropes, icy and frozen. The realisation that we were in the middle of the avalanche zone made us move quickly, collecting energy I never thought I had. The night had become very still, very cold, stars dotting the vast black expanse above us, and clumps of snow and ice tumbled from our fresh steps as we descended. The storm had moved off the mountain.

Athol collected the haul bag and portaledge and began dragging it over to camp two while I collected our ski poles, one last grunt up a snow ramp. Only 10 metres from our collapsed tents I paused and watched Athol release the rope he was dragging the haul bag and 'ledge with, dropping it and walking a few more seemingly aimless steps. I could hear the crunch of the frozen ground under his crampons as he moved. I began to move again, I screamed out hoarsely, feeling like a shadow of my real self. Athol was swearing as he stumbled around the camp. I sat down

on the haul bag and pulled my knees to my chest, a second-
nature reaction to the cold.

We poured mug after mug of hot energy drink down our
throats, the cookers dialled to full bore, and ate whatever we
could without cooking – we were too tired. We put the tent up
under the black, clear sky. We threw our sleeping bags in – they
were cold and clammy from the time on the mountain. Once we'd
been still for a while I felt how cold it was as I held my hands over
the cooker, my sweat trying to evaporate. Inside the tent, I
knocked away the little clumps of ice stuck to my bag, sending
them flying into the corner. 'Here we are,' said Athol, nestling his
camera away. 'This tent is huge,' I said, 'like a King's castle.'

We were like children in a tree-house. I left my door open a little so I could see outside. Involuntary laughter came from both of
us. We started talking about times on the mountain, like when we
both hung from an anchor together, hoping a storm would ease,
shivering and in pain from stomach cramps. As we talked, it was
as if we perhaps didn't quite understand those parts of us: the shivering, the pain. 'It just seemed to go on forever, hanging on that
anchor, waiting for the storm to ease, like a watched kettle,' I said.

Then we started laughing, shaking our heads. We kept talking,
animated, alive, in-tune … I woke and it was morning, the sun
shining on the tent. We brewed up outside, feeling the warmth.
We searched through everything for more food, peeling back
frozen bags, looking for the good food we'd forgotten about, 'it's
got to be here somewhere ...' The next day, we made a midday
departure to base camp, carrying light packs, our wasted bodies
moving across the rise and fall of the glacier. We paused to rest
quite often. Already the weather had changed; the mountains were
under the darkness of another violent storm. A few sporadic
snow-showers moved around the glacier, the temperature dropping. We both wondered where Patricia might be, and whether

Tristram, Athol's brother, and Erik, a friend from Melbourne, had arrived. Erik had walked into our base camp, via other parts of India, on his way home from Europe.

Patricia was there to meet us where we said goodbye ten days ago, her voice a welcoming reassurance. It started snowing heavily and we stopped to put our jackets on. I snapped a photo of Ath and Patricia on the moraine, the air cold and grey, their cameras sitting on a flat rock. For the next hour we walked toward base camp, the wind and snow chasing us down the moraine ridge. I thought of warmth and home, of the people I loved so dearly. It brought a few tears to my eyes, but before they had a chance to dry, the wind had picked them up and carried them away. I felt tired, my knees sore with each downward step.

Patricia told us about walks she had been on while we had been up on the face, looking through the telephoto lens and only occasionally spotting us – most of the time we were hidden by storms. I was struck with how satisfying it felt to be walking down to base camp, an indescribable weight lifting from our shoulders, an amazing sense of freedom. Erik shook and hugged us with all his might as we self-consciously stood around the mess tent in the falling snow, ski poles in hand, oblivious to the packs still on our backs. I was overwhelmed by everything, bewildered by the sudden human presence and energy around us. I looked at Ath and saw the same reaction in him. As the snow fell, we all got inside the kitchen tent and Athol and I started talking to the others. It felt like we hadn't seen them for a very long time.

For the next week we sat around, Erik staging *petanque* championships on the flat ground beside the tents. Bell became the undisputed champion. I had the energy for only a few games before getting bored; I found more peace sitting and staring around at the scene, my companions, and back at Thalay. The view was the same, but everything else had changed. We had one last gear collection trip to camp two, and after a lazy start we eventually made it back to base camp late that night, leaving all the gear on the glacier at the foot of the moraine ridge below camp one. Descending from camp two in the early evening Athol carried the overloaded haul bag and I carried an overloaded pack, and Patricia shouldered too much as well. Too lazy to put my crampons back on through a short, steeper, section cut with steps from our upward journey, a boot slipped on an iced-up step and I rocketed away, the weight of my pack rapidly accelerating me. I heard Athol yell out to me as the cold slope screamed past my face, like rushing toward infinity. I halted with anti-climactic energy, the result of a second nature self-arrest: I dug my ice axe pick into the surface, held on and came to rest with my chest centre weighted over the axe. I wasn't the only casualty: Ath was lowering the haul bag on a rope not as long as he remembered when it shot off down the slope into the moraine, tumbling end over end. We stood and laughed – at least it no longer needed to be carried down. In the gloom of dusk we got all the gear under a large boulder on the glacier and with light packs, made our way towards the base camp, stumbling over the moraine.

The days that followed collecting all this gear from the end of the glacier were beautifully calm, complete with *chai* stops at the glacier corner with an Indian Army expedition to the Jogin peaks, followed by a portaledge demonstration on our return. Their doctor had been in Oman in the mid-80s when Athol had served there with the Oman Reconnaissance Force; now, ten years on, they met at the end of a Himalayan glacier and talked shop about Oman, and the politics of a nation once their home. We walked, almost drifted, across the glacier, the only deadline to meet was the porters' arrival in base camp on 27 September, and to walk out on the 28th.

I think we were both happy to finally leave. As Athol said, 'I can get on with my life.' I am certain we didn't realise the extent to which the valley had a hold on us. We walked a hundred or so metres apart, Walkmans on, sometimes under sunlight, otherwise through sporadic snow-showers, meeting every hour or so to have a drink, sit and talk. Paul left early, on track for admission into an MBA in Delhi.

The evening before our final gear collection, a porter carrying Tristram's pack arrived in base camp. 'New Zealand man coming,' he said, lighting a cigarette. Tristram had made it, with a day to spare! Ath walked down the moraine in search of his brother. We all waited for Tristram to keel over with altitude sickness – he had walked up from Gangotri in one day. 'If I drink any more water I'm going to vomit,' he said. The porters gathered round their fire in the cold evening while I packed my kit bags. As soon as it began snowing, I zipped them up and crawled into my tent again, listening to the snow land on the fly and slide off. The morning brought delayed packing, Bell cooking omelettes out in the open in the clear warm sun, the ground still frozen. Tristram and I took turns trying to do tricks on a yo-yo while the porters cooked chapatis on their fire. A few hours later, after the porters had left with their loads, I picked up my pack and was immediately touched with a faint regret, strangely not wanting to let go of our time on the mountain. I slung my camera across my shoulder and took a ski pole in each hand.

Small wisps of white cloud drifted toward the Thalay Sagar's north face, colouring in white the patches of rock low down on its north-western side. A storm was on its way, bleak and dark. Without premeditation, my eyes looked at our route, at the depths of cold and shadow, and at the fine, disappearing lines of sunlight gracing the north-east pillar. A strong spark ignited inside my heart, the recognition of what ran true inside me,

that I had learnt a lot about standing up in the mountains. I had
been pushed toward my limit, and this had affected me in ways
I will perhaps never realise. Further down the valley, I saw Athol
walking toward me, oblivious to my thoughts, and I felt very
privileged to have shared such a time with him. I turned around
and with relief stumbled down the hill with cold ears, the sunlight hidden under the fresh, falling snow.

Returning from the summit of Jannu, along its intricate east summit ridge, after being caught in an electrical storm and shivering the night away at 7600 metres. *Athol Whimp.*

Above: Looking up the massive north face direct of Jannu, scene of our failed attempt. Here Athol hauls to the site where our portaledge was destroyed by a rock and ice avalanche the following morning. *Author*.

Below: Athol at camp two (5450 metres) on Jannu. *Author*.

SHADOWS AND LIGHT:

Jannu, north face

7710 metres
Nepal Himalaya, 2000

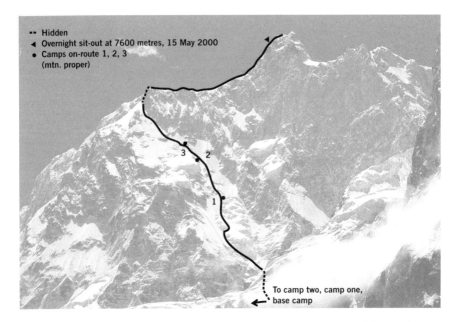

IT WAS A different sound. Without talking, we both felt violence was approaching rapidly. It felt hard. Not snow. Not another spindrift avalanche. Immediately, I felt a sickness in my empty stomach. I was just about to exit our portaledge, having got my full clothing, boots and helmet on. Ath was sitting up, but in his sleeping bag without his helmet on, when we were hit.

Total helplessness overwhelmed us as rocks and ice tore through the 'ledge's storm-fly and exited the other side, near the floor. There was nothing we could do. We hunched into ourselves as the onslaught continued, an incredible vortex of spinning snow, rocks and ice, blue and hard. Black and grey rocks streaked through like a shark's shadow underwater. It was impossible to see anything, to visually decipher what was happening.

Within a few seconds we began to expect that anything could happen. We weren't tied in independently from the 'ledge to another anchor. If the 'ledge's anchor rope was cut it was all over. Curtains. I had a vision of my anchor rope lying under this latest avalanche mess outside, waiting for my frantic, numb hands to burrow in, grasping for the safety it promised.

I found myself staring in disbelief at Athol's helmet, only inches from my face. It seemed to take forever for my mind to realise *it wasn't on his head.* The overpowering noise made it very difficult to think. What was coming next? Perhaps all this was merely a warm-up for the big rocks teetering on their edges a few hundred metres up the mountain. The terror came from a sub-conscious recognition of what the noise meant, of how very close we were to being killed by the rockfall.

My mind fumbled, imagining rocks hitting Ath's head. I saw his eyes searching for *something* to put over his head. Then nano-seconds later I thought, 'What if he's already been hit?' I tried to unclip his helmet but my fingers moved too fast, uncoordinated. To my relief, I saw Ath's hands reach out and grab the pot from the hanging stove, and place that on his head. Soon he had the helmet.

The careful and tedious effort of keeping our sleeping bags, brew gear, food and other personal kit organised had now been rendered a white, frozen waste. As the thunder of the rock and ice abated, we found ourselves staring at the inside of the 'ledge, and at each other. 'Are you OK?' It sounded so glib, like we had just tripped over a gutter, or stubbed a toe. We were both trying to comprehend what had occurred, as if we disbelieved it. Light shot in through the shredded storm-fly in rods, and in the side of the 'ledge behind Athol. He turned back to me after inspect-ing the damage, his face ashen.

He picked up a rock from the debris, and it reinforced our amazement that we had not been hit. I literally felt sick as I looked around, exasperation nearly bringing tears to the surface. 'I've got to get out,' I said, and cautiously began unzipping the door. I knocked the heavy snow build-up away as I struggled to slide the frozen zips down. The snow was packed like concrete, pressing in the shredded fly like a yacht's spinnaker under full sail.

With the remains of snow from the avalanche on my face melting and running down my neck, I reached out and into the snow, scraping it away, pawing like a pathetic mouse. I was trying to get one of the anchor ropes. After a few minutes I had it, clipped a jumar in, and awkwardly clambered out. I still didn't have my crampons on, but was able to stand on the heavily packed snow while I snapped them on, my hands turned very cold and numb from the metal; fingers sticking like a tongue to ice. I thrust them into my armpits for a few minutes, and waited for the slow return of warmth. I told myself that I had always enjoyed that painful re-warming process, the feeling of rushing, then creeping blood struggling to make its way to the extremities as the fingers hung limp and useless.

Stepping into the clear light was an enormous relief, the massive space and height offering an escape from our near-tomb. The sky was a pale blue over the northern horizon, already washed of the richer dawn colours. I stood carefully on a small, sloping stance, just big enough. I reached into my pockets and threw out old chocolate wrappers, watching them fall down the steep, hard ice. They were lifted by the soft breeze, and fell again. Like watching butterflies. The claustrophobic confines of the 'ledge kept returning to my mind despite the calm morning. It felt all the more shocking when outside, starting to receive the first warmth from the sunlight. Such a large space – the mountain, the Himalaya – but we had nowhere to run, even move. It had become so quiet during the minutes after the avalanche, like nothing had ever happened.

Athol was sorting out the destruction inside the 'ledge, or better said, on the 'ledge. I could hear his solemn voice, 'This is fucking outrageous in here, I can't believe it.' I turned and watched the shredded fly gently flapping as small amounts of spindrift slid over the cliff above and dropped in. We both became absorbed in our own thoughts about what we were going to do. I climbed down a few metres to untangle a rope as Ath began making repairs with some tape. For an hour we both worked away under the lukewarm sunshine. There wasn't any wind, just small, short breezes that ceased as soon as we felt them. I never made any progress on the rope. I needed to pull one end right through, but kept looking for shortcuts. My bare hands melted the snow and thin ice stuck to the rope. Pulling the endless loops and knots through one another was exhausting work. I could hear Ath working quietly away, the sharp sound of his teeth ripping tape penetrating the awesome mountain silence.

I stared out to the horizon and down onto the Jannu glacier where we had carried our loads across from base camp so many times during the last month. Base camp was out of view, hidden by the thousand-metre rock buttress we had climbed to get from the glacier to camp two. Dark clouds were already churning with anger and lifting higher toward us. We knew we didn't have a lot of time before it would be snowing and we'd be tortured by the spindrift avalanches again.

We talked about what options we had. It was very stressful. We both felt exhausted and slightly shattered by what had happened. The upper part of the mountain was already clouding over, taking the sun away to leave us with a sullen sky, the temperature rapidly dropping. Snowfall was imminent. Ath said we could try shifting the 'ledge higher, to a more protected site. I admired his optimism but was very doubtful about this, knowing the 'ledge was finished, and also sceptical about getting a better site. We talked the idea through. Tiny, isolated flecks of snow began to drift around us. I felt stunned that after so much effort we were faced with making a decision in such difficult circumstances. My head was buried deep in my hood as tears fell over my face. I fought very hard to keep them away. I watched the snowflakes passing my eyes. I looked at Ath – his eyes were watery and red and he looked back at me. Right then I felt like we were little boys, brothers, who had run outside, confused and shocked by the sights and sounds of our parents fighting. We searched for words that would offer our impending retreat some dignity. The shock of nearly being killed an hour ago was coming to the surface, to the edge.

But the thought of descending brought on most of the anguish. It was not about the 'summit at all costs', or other associated clichés. We were absorbed deeply in the mountain, in the route. It was taking shape. We were moving, the only living things on Jannu. We had 14 days worth of food and fuel, and a large rack of gear to deal with the massive headwall of the route. I recognised the hurdles: the feeling of wanting to crawl under a rock or bed when faced with the seemingly insurmountable, then turning about and walking headlong into it all, grinning.

It was very quiet. There was a faint rush of wind across the headwall, like a wind across the other side of a wide lake, pushing the trees. It looked deathly, black streaking clouds like scars across the sky. Our effort had hit silence. It took some time for both of us to finally say to ourselves and to each other, 'Fuck it, that's it, it's over.' We began moving gear, slowly but certainly.

Our decision was probably inevitable, as I write here with the benefit of hindsight. The 'ledge couldn't have sustained any bad weather, and as we found out, it would have received loads.

We both dearly wanted to climb the mountain. We were trying a new, direct route up the north face, but with this attempt rendered a failure, instinctively we decided to climb the *Wall of Shadows,* a route up the left-hand icefields and rock barriers of the north face.

The snowfall became denser, we knew the spindrift avalanches would soon be upon us. Ath passed our sleeping bags out of the 'ledge along with shards of blue ice and clumps of snow from the avalanche. It was incredibly depressing. I stuffed the bags into our packs and warmed my hands up with exhaled air. Soon I would have to put my gloves on, but I tried to do as much as possible without them as it was faster, less cumbersome. We quickly packed everything, some of it into the packs and the rest into the haul bag. All the gear was frozen and sticky with cold, like *rigor mortis.*

All of a sudden I hated the 'ledge; that which had protected us so much, had made life possible on the route. We pulled it apart: it felt like a skeleton, clacking and folding like dry bones might. It made an awkward bundle. We rammed it into its long black bag, clumps of ice sticking to its side. I neatly tied the top of the bag and clipped it to the underside of the haul bag. We were ready to go. Small rivers of snow from above broke over our legs, below the knees. I had put my goggles on but tore them off in frustration when they became coated with snow and ice. I stuffed them inside my down suit, and struggled to get the zips back up to my neck as more and more spindrift hurtled down.

We started abseiling. I went first. Athol disappeared from sight within a few metres, so heavy was the snowfall and cascading spindrift. I heard him yell: 'Watch out!' I glanced upward and met a rapidly expanding cloud of avalanching spindrift with my eyes. Like a downward-exploding atomic cloud, grey and violent. It passed after ten seconds, leaving the rope vibrating like a plucked violin string. It left me spitting melted snow from my lips, white like a snow-covered pine tree.

The entire descent occurred as if in slow motion. It was a series of abseils, repeating the same process: I would abseil first as Athol simultaneously lowered the haul bag alongside me. I pushed (or often just kicked) it free when it became stuck on some ice or rock. Sometimes it was like trying to move a dead animal. It was incredible what the haul bag became stuck on (a small loop of webbing would catch on a little spike of insignificant granite in a near-vertical section, for example). It was always surprising how quickly the haul bag took off once I'd dislodged it. At the end of my rope, I'd make an anchor (one ice screw), clip myself and the haul bag into it. I would then disconnect myself from the abseil rope. 'OK!' I would yell, projecting my voice upward, hoping Athol could hear me. Our voices always seemed to be absorbed by the immensity of the mountain, to evaporate. Ath would then abseil and once he had arrived at the new anchor, we'd pull the abseil ropes down and begin again.

Soon the avalanches started again, pushing against me like a swelling wave. I turned my head into the snow and muttered 'Fuck off.' It probably sounded like there was actually someone there to talk to. As the avalanches fell lower, they spread out, like a sheet falling, wave-like, over a bed. Cold air rushing aimlessly, pushing against our faces, trying to get into our suits.

From the other side, the north-west, the clouds had grown and were closing in on us. We could feel the air growing colder and colder. Almost snap-freezing. My feet were getting cold. *They're not freezing, so just ignore it.* We laboriously kept abseiling. The lower we went, the more features or rock and fins of ice we recognised. By late afternoon we were on the névé, the flat. Safe. We trudged a couple of hundred metres out and away from the wall as the bad weather simultaneously lifted. 'That'd be right,' said Athol softly. We were oblivious to the time that had passed. Early sunset colours reached through the pulsing clouds. We pulled the ropes into where we stood. Our shoulders drooped. I sat down on my pack after letting it fall carelessly from my shoulders. We sat there, too tired to say much. I wanted to go to sleep. The previous 36 hours, culminating with the rock avalanche and getting off the face, seemed to have caught up. Light snowfall drifted past. We stood and began to walk back to camp two, keen for food and sleep.

Athol took some photos as we made our way back. I stopped every 20 steps and leant over on my knees to rest. I couldn't understand why I felt so tired. I was even too shattered to take my pack off, let alone get my camera out like Ath had. I realised I was probably severely dehydrated. The muscles in my legs were burning, twitching with thirst. My throat was unbelievably dry, catching on words. At the point on the névé where we did a sharp turn down to camp two, the soft light radiated all around and I felt a lot warmer. Ath asked me to pause so he could get a shot and I looked forward to hearing him pressing the shutter again. We trudged across the undulating, slightly downward, névé into the increasing darkness. We had never roped together through this area other than the first time. I remembered where the few crevasses were and stepped carefully around them, half-asleep. Ath was about 50 metres ahead, still turning around and getting photos. The last light was like old, faded neon.

I was in Kuala Lumpur. The bus driver was dragging on his final cigarette before the drive to Singapore. Gigi and I didn't really know what to say. I was booked on the 8 p.m. bus. All day I had worried about changing it to the 11 p.m., thinking about what we could do in those final hours, wandering around town, sitting under big green tropical leaves, moisture in the air. *We all have to say goodbye, sometime.* Gigi and I held each other, and I could feel a small wave of terror inside my stomach, an intangible anxiety that said I hoped I would be back to see her again.

As the bus drove away and I lost sight of her, I knew she would be hailing a taxi and heading home. I hid my tears, even though there was only one other on the bus. I and the Singaporean businessman stared out of our respective windows as the bus steamed along the freeway toward Singapore.

I staggered up to the arrival gate at Singapore Airport to wait for Athol's plane after a four-hour sleep on a stone bench inside the terminal, waking up shivering from the cold. He emerged from the white tunnel and we walked to find some coffee. It was 6 a.m. We sat down and drank 'instant real' coffee then did a quick tour of the gadget shops, looking for some good gear for base camp. Ath got a shortwave radio and I some speakers for the CD player. We had tried to get hold of a satellite phone and laptop computer at home, but it wasn't to be, the till was empty.

The final weeks before leaving had been frantic, waiting for gear to arrive from around the world, the usual story of holding off in the hope of getting some more money, and then not managing to arrange it, so borrowing again to get by. I had left for Malaysia before it had all arrived, and Athol, with his brother Tristram and my brother Rob, drove our gear to the airport and freighted it all to Kathmandu. Ath had just returned from working on a movie in New Zealand, so we only had a few days together in Melbourne sorting gear out before I left for Malaysia.

As I packed I wondered deeply about my family and close friends, the colossal differences that lay between us. So much was never said. One evening as my father was leaving his office, I wanted to stop him. I was to fly out in two days. I needed to tell him something about not worrying. I felt so guilty. But as he got closer to his car, I turned away, already with regret. I should have said something that would help him understand in case anything ever happened in the mountains, like an accident. What had taught me to hide this from them? To hide what most desperately needed to be said? That look in my mother's eyes when I went to the mountains frightened me so much. I knew how an accident – dying – would affect her and my father. I was scared to show this knowledge to my parents, for I wanted to protect them from the fear that had been etched into me.

Dad drove past and I could only just see his face as the street-lights played on the windscreen. He waved a wave that said 'see you tomorrow'.

At the airport check-in I had the usual problem with excess baggage (a curse for mountaineers everywhere), but after enough smiling and joking with undertones of diplomatic seriousness, and finally grimacing a desperately broke (true) look, the bags all slipped through. On the plane I listened to the soft whining of the engines. It was dark outside. I had been dispatched. I tried to imagine my parents talking as they drove home, the radio barely audible, the dark roads lit in streams by headlights. I felt sad and relieved all at once.

We were spending more and more money. I grimaced with pain as I filled out the credit card cash advance form in the Kathmandu bank, my sweating fingers constantly slipping on the pen. I hit-up my card for all I thought it could handle. It was obscenely embarrassing, the thought of the bank at home monitoring my transaction. I imagined some stunted office guy drumming his fingers on his plastic desk, waiting for my details to come through from the database. And then, as he scrolled the cursor up and down, calling out to his friends, laughing. Some people just never learn.

I was called forward from the queue to hear my request was denied. Fuck. Feeling totally sick, I re-sent the request, for a trifle less than the first request. I waited again. It was insanely humid inside the bank despite the air-conditioning. The request went through. The teller piled up the rupee notes on the counter and we did the usual double note-checking before I thanked him and wrapped the notes in rubber bands. 'Expeditions very expensive,' he said with a wisp of sympathy. I wanted to leave the bank before someone inside a computer changed their mind. Athol and Patricia got cashed up as well, and we swung the door and left.

'I hate expeditions,' I said to Athol.

'Bullshit.'

'I know.'

Athol and I had been to the Ministry of Tourism, Mountaineering Section, sorting out details of the expedition with our assigned liaison officer, and finalising the peak fee. Our correspondence with the Ministry before we left had informed us there was a $US3000 peak fee. Now we were told we had to pay another $US1000. There was no way round it: to progress the expedition any further we had to pay the difference. It was very easy to slide into anger. We were already immensely frustrated and short of money – we had decided to pay off the liaison officer not to come with us, to stay in Kathmandu. We didn't want him draining our energy and resources through the trip.

The day Patricia arrived was bright with late winter sunshine. While Athol went to the airport to collect her, I walked to a store with our cook, Dudh, arriving back at the hotel a few hours later with a couple of rickshawloads of pots, pans, baskets, etc. It was good to have Patricia with us again.

Athol had organised a vehicle to transport us and our gear to the roadhead at Taplejung, far away in north-eastern Nepal. The dollars were agreed on – all we needed to do was pay a deposit, load up the bus, and go. But that night, after we had paid the deposit and loaded close to 20 cycle rickshaws with our equipment (the bus couldn't get down the narrow streets to the hotel), the deal was off. Suddenly the bus owner wanted more money than had been agreed. It was midnight. We'd had enough. We took the deposit back after a tense argument. Fortunately the locals and hotel staff thought it was a big joke.

'Everything off,' we shouted, and started carrying all the gear back into the hotel yard. The rickshaw men were pissing themselves. We graciously paid them out for loading and unloading their rickshaws. They asked for more money, but started laughing every time their spokesman tried to get serious.

Another night in Kathmandu. Sleep came slowly, my mind rewinding and playing back the days since our arrival. We imagined the bus owner would return in the morning with a revised offer. And he did. But we kept to our decision, reinforcing we already had a deal. Taplejung or bust. So at midday we loaded all the gear onto a smaller bus and drove out to the main bus terminal. There we waited again while Dudh and his assistant Mima went searching for our bus.

Local teenage boys with slicked hair and combs in back pockets asked us, 'Where are you going, man?'

'Kumbhakarna,' whoever was asked would reply, 'Jannu.'

'Aaahhh, Jannu.' Glaring, darting eyes of recognition. Smiling. Then talking like they were arguing about where Jannu was. We stood around, us and the teenagers, taking the piss as if we were cowboys, our arms crossed over our chests, exchanging short sentences. The teenagers wore big leather boots. We just had runners.

The bus moved up the hills out of Kathmandu slow and powerful, like an elephant. Passing trucks pushed diesel fumes and the noises of their roof-top passengers in through our open windows. Every time Dudh or one of the owner's workers cracked a joke, the driver would laugh and keep laughing, turning around to continue the conversation at the same time. It was nerve-wracking. The steering wheel was about two feet wide. The driver leant his entire body into turning it through the hairpin bends, the tyres flicking the loose gravel over the thousand-foot drops. But we all drifted off to sleep before long.

On the plains below Kathmandu it was a little warmer. We drove past the ochre-orange sunset, along the edge of the Chitwan National Park. I hadn't seen the driver yawn at all. The glare of oncoming headlights kept me awake. The driver drove like he was taking us across an ocean, as if we'd sink if we stopped. 'Doesn't he want a sleep?' we'd ask. The answer was just a comically waved hand, as if to say 'don't be stupid'. At midnight we stopped for *chiyaa,* tea. The temperature had dropped.

The locals stood around in t-shirts with Western movie names printed on them, staring at us and the gear filling the bus. Then the driver began to race the engine, the signal to get aboard. Another multi-hour session into the graveyard end of the night, blurry sleep, empty Coke bottles rolling and crashing around on the floor in time with the changing gears.

The next time my eyes were open we were creeping over the crest of a ridge-top, mist running over the road, through the trees. The first dim daylight filled the bus. The driver was the only other person awake, smoothly gearing through the downhill corners. A few of the others woke up, then everyone. The bus owner became very excited when he saw Ilam across the valley. He planned to hire another vehicle cheaply here to take us to Taplejung, and return to Kathmandu in his vehicle. But when we reached Ilam the owner started sulking – another vehicle was going to cost far too much. He was with us until Taplejung, so long as the bus could make it. He kept turning around in his seat, giving us looks to make us feel that his bus, and he, was being hard done by, that the drive into Taplejung was too much for the bus. But he gave it away by smirking too much.

About two hours after leaving Ilam, a short while after the sealed road ended, we saw Jannu for the first time. It was far bigger than I had imagined it would be from a distance. Kangchenjunga seemed smaller, further back – even at 8595 metres. The driver shuddered the bus to a stop and we all got out, pacing up and down on the dewy grass, trying to peer through the early morning haze onto Jannu's summit snows. Patricia, Athol and I took photos, struggling to focus on the mountain itself as the haze was so bad. We stood in amazement, like children might at the bow of a massive ship. It was symmetrical. A seemingly horizontal summit ridge dropped off on each side to broader shoulders a few hundred metres below.

At 1 a.m. we pulled up at a ridge-top village called Gopitar. Finally, the engine of the bus was turned off. The driver stumbled out and started drinking *chiyaa* again. Everyone else fell asleep in their seats. We were at 2000 metres and, still being winter, it was cold. Even my feet turned numb. I clambered over stacks of gear to find my kit bags and pulled out warmer clothes – my feet ended up inside my down mitts. Dogs yapped all night. At 6 a.m. we stamped our feet, wandering the length of the village. I sat in a smoky hut drinking *chiyaa,* waiting for the sun. I asked Dudh why the driver wouldn't have a decent sleep (he talked most of the five hours in Gopitar), so Dudh asked the driver in Nepali. 'He was a driver in the Army for 40 years' was the reply, as if it made him immune from the need to sleep. He had the engine roaring again, so we threw out what remained in our cups, and jumped on.

2.30 p.m. The road was over for the bus. We unloaded all the equipment as the locals gathered around. We were at Banande, on a bend in the muddy road, halfway up a long hill and an hour and a half's walk below Taplejung, the normal roadhead. Dudh and Mima went off searching for porters in Mima's village, about a day's walk away. We hauled all our gear into a chicken yard beside the house where we arranged to stay, sweating under the afternoon sun. A porter who had come with us from Kathmandu, Yam, stood around and guarded it all. I felt embarrassed. He said he was going to sleep next to it.

The following morning, March 14, we started the eight-day trek into base camp. Zigzagging up the trail above Banande led us to Taplejung. The 35 porters filed through the town in small groups, carrying close to 30 kilograms each. Mima stayed behind to wait for the final few porters who were to carry some of our climbing ropes and webbing, tinned food and kerosene. The road withered out into a walking trail at the town's end, and it was a relief to finally be away, moving closer to the mountain. When the trail had to pass a wet area like a wide creek or soak, it was maintained with large stones.

Purumbu was our stop for that night, a few farms on a wide, open hillside. Houses with red and blue painted eaves stood out between the rich green trees and terraces as I made my way down the greasy slope, struggling to stay upright. The porters that had arrived were drying out under the verandah of a schoolhouse, leaning back on the aged earth wall. Then Dudh said we were moving over to a nearby house. 'Arrr, yes, much better,' he said in his laconic way. Our new kerosene stoves, fresh from the plastic wrapping, failed to work. Dudh and his team of helpers swore away, covered in smoke and kerosene fumes.

It was 5.30 a.m. next day when we packed our sleeping bags away, ready for the porters to get going. We had finally managed to find the coffee from the mess of kitchen gear. It was freezing inside, so we wandered about the yard, waiting for the sun. Two days later we passed through Tapethok, a police checkpoint. The police huts sat on the edge of a large grassy field, dilapidated barbed wires strung around the perimeter. The Himalayan foothills rose in every direction, terraced for farming as far as we could see. Our trekking

A sign in Tapethok, Tamor Valley, marking the entrance to the Kangchenjunga Conservation Area on our way in to Jannu base camp. *Author.*

permits, passports and permit for Jannu were checked and the details transferred into the police ledger. Back by the river a sign told us we'd entered the Kangchenjunga Conservation Area, and as we started walking again we read a World Wildlife Fund-sponsored brochure about the paradise we had just entered. There was a picture of the extremely rare snow leopard, instructions 'don't destroy or burn fauna, don't throw rubbish, don't get lost or hyperthermic', where to find conservation officers and details of the snow leopard conservation programme.

The trail wound on. Birch trees and stones by the clear river. It was always exciting to turn a new corner, expecting to see snow and ice, a mountain. We stayed at around the same altitude (about 1200 metres) for several days, and began winding uphill on our fourth day of walking. At the village of Sekathum we turned away from the river we had been following, the Tamor, and began following the Ghunsa Khola. It was incredibly beautiful. Every time we stopped for *chiyaa* there would be a Western poster, often Christian, stuck up on one of the walls, with phrases like: *It's not that I don't like people, but that I love nature more.*

The Ghunsa valley was very steep and narrow, full of escarpments and hanging vines. Isolated patches of mist sitting in dark ravines, waiting for wind to move them along. Patricia, Athol and I walked up the opposite side of the river to Dudh and the porters to the small, mostly Tibetan settlement of Amjolisa, where we stopped for the night. We had risen about 1000 metres that day. During the evening dustings of snow became visible on the high cliffs above the Amjolisa homes. A small herd of yaks clumped across the terraces in the grey twilight.

Soon the magic mountain spell was broken when Mima arrived just before dark, announcing ashamedly that the gear he was bringing up had been stolen. It took us a few moments to realise all that had gone. The story of the missing gear was full of discrepancies and inconsistencies, and we weren't far from accusing Mima of orchestrating the act. Apparently the porters had disappeared in Taplejung. It was raining, it was dark. But Taplejung isn't that big a place ... The next morning we wrote a fax for Mima to take back and send from Taplejung. My sister Katherine was due to leave Melbourne for Kathmandu in a few days to walk in to our base camp with her partner, Dougal, and there was a chance she could bring two replacement climbing ropes with her. A sour feeling moved amongst us, frustration with Mima and being unable to understand how these porters had just 'gone missing'. We didn't talk about it much until later in the day, but none of us could ignore what we felt about the missing gear – that something wasn't quite right.

The trail contoured along the steep valley, and we soon left the grass and began walking through the forests. The air was cooler, evaporating sweat causing me to shiver slightly. The trail made a long series of sharp switch-back turns, and suddenly emerged on a large, smooth grassy platform – Gyapla. Athol rang the school bell here – it was an old oxygen cylinder, no doubt from an early Kangchenjunga expedition. Earlier, in Amjolisa, we had seen an expedition barrel in a Tibetan home, from a 1949 Kangchenjunga expedition, the lettering on the barrel only just visible. It was quite amazing to think these expeditions had walked up the same skinny

Taking a break in Chiruwa, near Sekathum. The porters' loads for the expedition are at the base of the picture. *Author.*

trails as we had, watching the same rolling, afternoon cloud movement, and listening to the river crashing past, the scars of rock in the nearby gorge hanging like ghosts.

The valley tightened even more above Gyapla, getting close to 3000 metres in altitude. The cold wind wrapped itself around my head and I shivered. My head ached as it had since we had left Gyapla that morning. My eyes watered and I shivered despite wearing more layers than the others. I walked slowly, sitting against tree trunks in the sun when I felt tired.

Phole was a deserted settlement on a plain. Its people had descended for the winter. Like an old Western town, not a soul

Onward and upward: a sign in Gyapla, a few hours walk below Ghunsa. *Author.*

Sorting the porters' loads outside Nima Sherpa's home in Ghunsa, while his young son looks on. *Author.*

could be seen, just creaking doorways, dust blowing about in the distance, prayer flags cracking in the wind. Soon the inhabitants would return as the temperatures began to warm again. All the homes were wooden, and clear little streams were diverted from the main river to run past some of them. Occasional smears of ice and snow marked the hard ground, usually in the shadows of rocks and houses. A woman walked out from her house offering *chiyaa* and Tibetan sheep wool rugs to sell. We sat down on the edge of her yard, holding the mugs of *chiyaa* in both hands, pulling them in closer to our chests for warmth. The rugs were exquisite, inspired patterns. The Sleeping Dragon on a rug looked as though it could have leapt out and eaten us. Athol bought one from the woman, Pema, and after another hour we shouldered our packs, and kept moving up the slope and through the riverside forest which led to Ghunsa.

The forest before Ghunsa appeared dead. All the wood was grey and wet, lumps of snow covering the ground on which we walked. A few hundred metres before Ghunsa, Athol, Patricia and I stopped at a bend in the river from where, with relief and happiness, we looked at the town. The houses, like Phole, appeared incredibly small against the mountains behind. It was a spread-out village on an unlikely plain, right before the valley tightened up again, a few hours below our 'turn-off' for Jannu.

I had read of Ghunsa in mountaineering books, the almost ancient township that is the gateway to the north side of mountains like Jannu and Kangchenjunga. One night at home, before we left, I dreamt of Ghunsa; Eskimos trudged through a village I had seen in photos. It was very cold. I was there, dressed like an Eskimo too, talking to dogs. There was ice on river edges, monolithic mountains in the background.

An American woman came along the path toward us with her guides, beginning her trek out after walking around the area for the previous ten days. We had watched her cross the narrow Ghunsa bridge to get across to our side of the river. 'Oh my, what wonderful views!' she remarked, the wind nearly pushing her over before she'd finished the sentence. She looked around, raising her arms as if to say 'here we are'. She then briefly asked us what we were 'here for' and after we explained she said, 'Well, you're going to love it!'

We had been told to expect porter trouble in Ghunsa; apparently the locals didn't appreciate porters from the valley below working above Ghunsa as that was the domain of Ghunsa locals. Dudh had told us where to go in Ghunsa, and so we headed to see Nima Sherpa, a friend of Dudh's. We stayed at his lodge, getting around the fire to beat the cold. Dudh sorted out any potential porter problems with Nima that afternoon, and we had a starting time for the morning. Some of our porters had decided to finish at Ghunsa; they would be replaced by a couple of Nima's yaks. The rest of the porters played soccer in Nima's yard, their bare feet hard on the ball.

I watched the Tibetan prayer flags on the roofs of all the houses. The 700-year-old *gompa,* a Tibetan monastery, sat on the other side of the river in the mist, almost embedded into the hill like a cave. Water turned a prayer wheel on the down-river edge of Ghunsa. As I walked past I could hear the prayer wheel groaning as the flow of water worked its way through the wooden channels to the wheel and out the other side.

A few candles lit our room in Nima's lodge. Pages from magazines, mostly Western ones, were stuck to the wall like wallpaper; I could make out Bill Clinton and others at a peace conference. How far away that information felt! We had gradually become disconnected from the mass of information in everyday life at home. Looking more closely at the pictures as I moved the candle across the timber wall it all became clearer: the intensity of violence and insecurity gripping the world.

Patricia and Athol were asleep and I lay there thinking deeply about the mountain we had nearly arrived at. The air was sharp and cold on my throat. I thought more and more, and began to betray my own confidence about the climb. The north face appeared far bigger and more violent than I had ever expected, bristling with hostility. Then I woke up, early daylight on my face, across the room. I had been dreaming.

Ghunsa was frozen, and no one moved until the sun came out from behind the mountains. It felt so desolate, grey and bleak. Smoke rose from all the rafters, and out under the eaves of houses. Then, as if on cue, people emerged from their homes, talking and working. Many layers of clothing kept the warmth in. The porters had their loads on and were away by 7 a.m. The ground was so hard it was like permafrost. My toes became cold standing around waiting for the sunlight to become warmer. Nima's children climbed all over us, and made up competitions to see who could be the first to climb to the top of a boulder out in the potato field. They ran like little Egyptian mummies, restricted by all the clothing they wore. Their noses dribbled with bronchial infections, something nearly every child we saw in the mountains had. The kids, Nima and his wife Pema lined up to wave goodbye, and I wondered how many expedition caravans they had seen pass through over the years.

Our trekking and expedition permits were again checked as we left Ghunsa. The trail followed the river for some time. Water clung to tree branches over the track, and drifts of snow sat in the shaded gullies. Late in the day we emerged from a forest we had been walking up and through onto the edge of the Jannu glacier. Snow mixed with mud and small rocks. A few minutes further on Jannu's north face headwall suddenly came into view. It was immense. The last hour of sunlight was falling across it. We tried to remember it was still winter when we thought how cold it

would be up high. As I stared at the upper part of the face, I tried
to see a physical *weakness* in it, something that offered a hint that
this extraordinary face might be climbable. I put on another top
– I was getting colder, the sun had gone. We were at around 3800
metres and skirted around the snout of the glacier to its other
side and down onto a frozen meadow called Tusa. From Tusa we
could walk up along the northern side of the Jannu glacier along
a series of rocky terraces to the site for our base camp.

As dusk approached that night so did a snowstorm. We put up
the kitchen tent next to some boulders in the dark, the last
porters coming in with the beginning of the storm. Silhouetted
figures moved against a blurry white background. Despite the
darkness and storm, most of the porters walked over to
Kambachen, a small village about 20 minutes away. When the
wind gusts hit, snow was forced in under the tent walls and
rushed about our legs.

I woke up halfway through the night, a thick coating of ice
layered the inside of my tent. It was about minus 10° Celsius.
I looked out of the door of the tent to see a big dark clear sky,
awash with stars as if someone had thrown a bucket of crystals.
My fingertips turned numb holding the flap of the tent. I let it
go and did the zip back up, and kept my eyes open, thinking,
waiting for dawn.

The porters were jumping about, cracking the ice under their
shoes. Dawn. We could see Jannu, a faint black and white image,
its colour drained by the rich dawn sun streaming down the glacier, obscuring our view of the mountain. We waited for it to
touch us, just off to the side of the glacier. I pulled my tent down
with cold hands. Once the sun was upon us, we began walking
up toward the site for base camp. Short cold breaths. Bright
white snow weighed down the leafless winter shrubs. As soon as
I tried walking fast I began gasping – we had only been above

Left: Athol during our Jannu north face direct attempt as more storm-cloud moves in. *Author*.

Below: The névé between the north face of Jannu and camp two – Athol walking back after a day's work on the lower part of the face. *Author*.

Above: Evening at our highest camp (6750 metres) on the *Wall of Shadows*, Jannu north face. From here we departed for the summit with the bare minimum of food and gear. *Author*.

Below: Climbing through the rock bands on the *Wall of Shadows*, Jannu north face, 13 May 2000. The north face direct headwall is on the right. *Athol Whimp*.

3000 metres for two days. Gradually the Jannu glacier to our right took on more scope, more scale. Grey and yellow lines, streaks of black, ran through it. It rose upward and angled further left, simultaneously narrowing.

At a shallow depression on the terrace, Athol and I hunkered down from the icy wind coming up the valley. A porter joined us. I lay back in the luxurious sunshine, drifting toward sleep, then suddenly awakening, amazed that the valley was to be our home until the end of May. Old, corroded prayer tridents and disintegrated prayer flags whistled in the wind. Out in the middle of a wide section of the terrace there was one large boulder, and under a cold, shaded overhang was the prayer site. Juniper ash lay amongst the stems of the tridents and bamboo stalks that flew the flags. It was freezing in the boulder's shade, so I walked around into the sun, crossing my arms to shield from the wind flicking around the corner of the boulder. Athol and I looked over the boulder, and all the other boulders in the area and got keen to wander down here on a rest day from the mountain and do some rock climbing. But the boulder we stood next to felt like it shouldn't be touched. We went on.

The glacier terrace was gradually narrowing. The scree-covered hills up to our left were now reinforced with broken cliffs. An eagle flew far overhead but well below the high white cloud, turning over in the wind. I followed the eagle with my eyes, and as it flew into line with the sun I squinted and lost sight of it. Jannu's north face stood in the shade. It was huge, its scale difficult to comprehend. Its features, the ice and rock, slowly revealed more detail as we made our way along the glacier's edge. From where we stood, Jannu's summit was over 3000 metres above us.

At the end of the boulder field, the terrace receded right up to the cliff line and we made our way up a scree slope, stepping on grey granite rocks, their crystals catching the sunlight. Unsure as to whether more terraces lay beyond this spot, Athol kept walking around while I waited halfway up with Patricia. Then Athol waved us on. I whistled down to the porters and they whistled back, shouldering their loads again.

We were now at around 4400 metres, and it was easy to develop a heavily pulsing head with rapid movement. I dislodged a few rocks with my ski-poles and they went rocketing down to the glacier, fresh dust rising to meet us. I fell back to walk with the porter who had stayed with us all the way up that day. 'Base camp,' he kept repeating, 'base camp.' We quickly arrived at more terraces, and kept walking to find a site for base camp. Athol and Patricia were sitting on the low stone walls of a previous expedition's shelter, their backs to the wind. We were all very happy to have arrived. There was no snow on the ground, just the very cold wind.

The porters arrived through the next hour, and were keen to get paid and return to warmer places. We put up our kitchen tent and when Dudh arrived with the last porters he got inside and worked out the porters' pay. The wind shook the tent, sucking air out and pushing it back in. Patricia, Athol and I soon realised Dudh was making a personal profit on the porters' wages, a cut out of what we had agreed to pay them. It was disappointing, but short of having a full-blown argument with Dudh then and there, there wasn't much we could do. The porters wanted a group photo taken, so they jumped and moved about in the cold while Dudh paid everyone in turn. Then, cold but grinning, they waited for the cameras to snap away before rushing down the hill into the frigid headwind and home.

Finally we had the isolation we wanted. It became colder by the minute as dusk crept in. Long, deep shadows from the cliff line near our tents reached further out towards the glacier, slowly swallowing us in cold. We stood on the glacier edge, on top of the moraine cliff, taking in the last minutes of sunlight.

★ ★ ★

The first trip across the glacier was a snowy one. The clouds sat
low. Our legs punched through the snow and into the loose, rocky
surface of the glacier. My fingers would get cold and warm up
again. We panted up and down the rise and fall of our mountain
desert. We carried light loads over to establish the first 'stash' of
gear, near where we thought we'd start climbing up the long rock
buttress to the névé, which in turn led to the foot of the north face.

It only took an hour (the same trip was only taking 20 minutes by the end of the expedition) to get across and store our
pack loads under a boulder. We then moved around nearer to the
massive icefall to the left of the rock buttress, searching for any
sign of where previous parties had gained access to the buttress.
Cold blasts of wind and snow threatened to push us over as we
probed about, the visibility getting worse. Our legs often fell
through the snow and into holes between rocks, sometimes
ending with a face full of snow. We quickly side-stepped our way
up the edge of the icefall's avalanche cone and stopped,
with heaving lungs. It was very quiet when the wind abated,
just small flakes of falling snow attempting to cover the tops of
the boulders.

Dusk was on its way, so we headed back to base camp, pleased
that we'd made a start and, in a strange way, that it had been in
bad weather. Yaks wandered about our camp as we climbed over
the moraine wall from the glacier and walked to our tents. We
often saw them grazing right up on the edge of the terrace further up the valley at close to 5000 metres. At night their bells
softly echoed against the cliffs when they stood otherwise
silently near our tents.

During those early nights in base camp, I remembered a film
I'd seen in Melbourne before we left for Jannu, of the 1975 New

Zealand expedition to the north face of Jannu. As my eyes took in the features of the thousand-metre rock buttress leading to the névé at the foot of the north face, flashes from the film came back to me, of the Kiwis in 1975 gear looking for a way up the buttress.

On our next trip across the glacier we found a shorter route and built rock cairns as we went, making it easy to find the route in bad weather. We quickly had enough rope over at 'the stash' to fix the buttress – essential for getting our equipment up efficiently to the sites for camp one, at 5050 metres, and camp two, at 5450 metres. The buttress consisted of steep, dark granite, and the route up it was of course the 'line of least resistance'. Looking up from the small col at the beginning of the buttress a few hundred metres off the glacier we could barely pick out the route, so unlikely it was.

A few old pieces of rope and some pitons revealed themselves as we made our way up the start of the buttress during the first day's work. Large clumps of snow sat over the ledges, soft in the sun, frozen hard in the shade of the overhanging walls. For anchors we would clear out snow from around cracks as if we were looking for diamonds. Carefully, deeply. The sunlight was smooth and cold, gradually losing its winter edge. The glacier creaked and then would suddenly roar, like a childhood-imagined monster. The icefall from the north face was not far away, just on the other side of the buttress: a vicious, ugly thing, pieces of it dropping away and onto the glacier like the crumbling of an ancient building.

On our second day on the buttress we emerged onto an angled rock slope covered in snow that led to a flat area where we set up camp one. Old pitons from previous expeditions hung from a few cracks, rusted, oxidising. It was obviously the way everyone over the years had climbed up, and I found these remnants far from intrusive; they were signs of passage, of moving upward. We even found a small winching point from the 1975 New Zealand expedition. I spun the little rusted pulleys, marvelling at this piece of history.

The air was cold as we clambered up the rock slope, pushing our arms into the snow, trying to get a grip on the rock underneath (we didn't have our crampons and ice tools up there). The snow would often slip away wherever we stood, leaving us standing nervously on the wet rock. Birds flew overhead, watching.

The north face of Jannu was first climbed by the Japanese, in 1976. They completed a line pioneered by the 1975 New Zealand expedition, who christened it the *Wall of Shadows*. The New Zealanders climbed most of the face leading to the summit ridge, but fell far short of completing the route. In 1976 the Japanese fixed rope up most of the face, and sections of the summit ridge.

The French – with a fine tradition in the mountains around the world – have always had a strong interest in Jannu. In 1962, after a failed attempt in 1959, they made the first ascent by the famous south-east ridge. It was 28 April '62 when they finally stood on the summit, the star René Desmaison among them. The next day, the legendary Lionel Terray also made it to the top, with Sherpa Wangdi. This ascent was an extremely strong testament to the prowess of French alpinism at the time.

In 1987, the late and great Pierre Beghin and Erik Decamp made an alpine-style ascent of the *Wall of Shadows*. Beghin had previously tried to climb the line of the north face direct (the same as our attempt), a route that would have taken them up the centre of the summit headwall. This line of rock and ice takes the steepest part of the face, much of it vertical and overhanging, especially in its final 700 metres. After realising they weren't going to succeed in 1987, Beghin and Decamp climbed the *Wall of Shadows,* up the left-hand side of the north face, through

icefields and rock barriers, reaching the summit on 15 May. The
same season, a Dutch team climbed the north face via the same
route, but tragically two men died during the descent.

The temperatures were still very cold, especially when dusk
came. At the end of March we climbed onto the small flat area
on the buttress where we sited camp one and walked up a slowly
steepening snow slope. A 100 metre-high broken rock cliff stood
between us and the approach to the camp two site, at the top of
the icefall and on the edge of the névé. A few old fixed ropes
hung, shredded and faded, half-torn, from the cliff. The icefall
passed on the left, brushing the edge of the cliff, groaning under
tension; its sudden noises sporadic but violent. We avoided passing through right next to the icefall at this point – it was just too
dangerous – and stuck to the broken rock further to the right.

As we climbed the cliff we were in the shade, and smears of
ice hung from the steeper sections. With an hour or so of light
left, we quickly abseiled and strode out down the snow slope, the
surface already freezing over. Walking back across the glacier just
before dusk the evening sun shot straight up along the moraine
and into our eyes. Returning to base camp during those early,
hard days on the mountain was always a relief: hot sweet tea,
food and sleep. Dudh had gone back to Taplejung after we had
discovered more gear had been stolen during the walk-in – food,
ropes, slings. We desperately hoped he could find it. A porter,
Ramh, stayed with us to help run the kitchen tent, an endless
battle with the fuming kerosene stoves, watering eyes.

It became light very early, yet the sun wouldn't come over the
Kambachen ridge – the ridge that links Jannu to the
Kangchenjunga massif – until later, a cold wait. I wondered
where Katherine was. It was 31 March. Athol and I left base
camp early for another day getting gear up the buttress. It was

gruelling work, especially as we were still acclimatising. As we were attempting a new route we had to take up a portaledge, haul bags and a large rack of hardware to deal with the unknown climbing. The higher we carried our gear up the buttress, the better we felt: progress.

As we began abseiling that day from halfway up the buttress, I could see a little yellow tent at base camp – Katherine. Approaching the moraine wall below the base camp terrace, I could see Katherine and Patricia standing on the edge, in the evening sunlight. Dudh had returned with Katherine and Dougal – and the stolen equipment and food, all of it as if it had never been touched. This immediately raised our suspicions – it didn't seem plausible that it had been stolen by a faceless individual. Athol, Patricia and I were becoming increasingly frustrated with Dudh and Mima – there was always something amiss, but nothing we wanted to raise for the sake of the climb, what we had really come for.

That night Katherine had severe headaches and nausea – symptoms of acute mountain sickness. Patricia dosed her up on Diamox and endless liquid, and we watched her closely, ready to go downhill to thicker air if it got any worse. Fortunately, through the night her condition improved and she soon felt fine, sleeping in the sun the next day. Katherine had brought mail from home, photos of the dog on the front lawn, flat dry paddocks in the distance. Athol had news from his brother Tristram, holding the fort in Melbourne. We also gratefully received a fresh wad of money that was going to pay for the porters going out, and transport back to Kathmandu.

We continued our work on the buttress, carrying all the gear up to the camp one site by 3 April. Here we stashed everything under a large grey granite boulder, one side undercut and just protected from snowfall. We had most of the buttress fixed with a line of rope so we could climb up and down, with one jumar attached as a security measure. Even from here, base camp looked far away, like little houses from an aeroplane.

Athol and I spent the last couple of days before Patricia, Katherine and Dougal left for base camp. The morning they departed we were going back onto the mountain to stay up there for a week or so acclimatising higher, and to establish camp two. Katherine had everything ready as I wandered across to her tent, and there was a part of me that wished I was walking out with her. As we all hugged goodbye, I suddenly felt very isolated. Patricia, who had been there from the beginning of this trip, would be specially missed but she had work commitments back in Melbourne.

As Athol and I lost sight of them between the boulders along the terrace, we went back to the kitchen tent and raided for last-minute things like drink powder to take up to camp one. Dudh and Mima were their usual polite yet reticent selves, their radio continuing with its 20-hour-a-day broadcast from the kitchen tent. Silence was far too much for them. I always got the feeling they were glad to see us leave base camp and go back on the mountain.

We were almost beginning to make a small path across the glacier, bigger rocks and moraine slopes becoming familiar. The glacial ponds were still frozen, despite the continuing sunny weather. 'I wonder where they'd be now,' we'd say to one another, myself thinking how luxurious it would be to escape all the hard work ahead on the mountain. Given the choice, I would never have left – but still the mind played these games, wanting guarantees of safety and certainty, green grass and constant blue skies. Yet even on our soon-to-be ninth trip to the buttress and above, I wasn't tired of the climbing, the same movements, the same rhythms. Each time up revealed something to me, something about the peace and resolution needed on Himalayan mountains.

By mid-afternoon we were set up at camp one. Athol found a small pool of melt-water over on the edge of the cliff and filled our cooker pots and water bottles up. Clouds drifted along at our altitude, as if looking for somewhere to rest. Over the next few days, we slept at camp one and carried gear higher, firstly to a small flat area an hour below camp two, then some of it all the way to camp two, shifting our tent up there for a few nights before descending to base camp for a rest. Several times above camp one our footsteps to the cliff were obliterated by ice avalanches from the icefall, and we would descend later in the day over blocks of fresh blue ice. On our first trip to camp two, we walked to the névé, the flat plateau beneath the north face. After only five minutes up a short slope the whole area opened out, revealing the upper part of the icefall, where it begins from the névé, gravity sucking it down. A bit further on we could see the schrunds hanging from the bottom of the north face, and the face itself, going 2200 metres up into the dark sky.

On our trip back up to camp two from base camp several days later it started snowing by 10 a.m., despite a clear early morning. As we arrived at the camp one boulder, we huddled under the overhang and brewed up, watching the heavy snowfall, feeling cold a few minutes later. We didn't have any shell jackets with us so resigned ourselves to getting wet on the way up to camp two. The snow fell more heavily as we punched our legs through the icy crust between lumps of blue ice, fresh from avalanches. We swapped going out in front, trying to drive our steps with our ski poles. There was no wind, just stillness and the gentle snow.

At camp two we put the tent up and got inside, the snow in our hair melting all over our heads. The bad weather stayed with us for two more days; we had to stagger out of the tent to dig more ice for cooking, and go to the toilet on the edge of the next cliff. We read several books several times. Cleaned our cameras time and again, stared at the ceiling, wondered what was happening up on the north face, wondered what it was like. Felt little pieces of fear in my stomach. By the time these little pieces had arrived in my mind, I'd be rationalising them, but a lot always fell down, back into my stomach, unable to be articulated. Every hour or so we'd peel back the tent door to look at the weather, and see the drape-like clouds hanging in the air, shedding snow.

As soon as the weather started clearing, we descended halfway to camp one and picked up the remaining gear. After a few heavy carries each, it was all up. We sorted what we were going to take on our north face direct attempt, enough for 14 days: the food, climbing hardware, the portaledge, ropes and gas. It all weighed too much, so we whittled it down several times, but the weight barely changed. 'Hmmmm,' we said, scratching our heads.

The first day of climbing on the face, 19 April, started in the sun, radiating warmth. We fixed rope over the schrund and up onto the wide, fan-like entrance to a shallow couloir. A large rock buttress pushed out on the left, and the wall stretched away on the right toward the west ridge of Jannu. Patches of ice stuck to the rock gleamed like dull armour in the sun. We each led a 120-metre pitch. As I jumared Athol's first pitch off the ground he yelled, 'ROCK!' – and barely a second later the frightening rush of air went past me, the rock stretched into a momentary long blur by its speed.

The climbing was mainly on ice, rivers of frozen blue. It ran transparently over the granite in many areas, a need to place crampons and ice tools gently, thoughtfully. By the time I'd finished leading the pitch above Athol's he had become very cold on the belay, and abseiled as soon as I was safe. He had been in the shade too long, for the whole area changed from intensely hot to sub-zero in literally a few minutes when we were out of the sun.

We had been gasping for cooler air, for shelter from the reflective heat – and waiting for an end to the rock-fall, the regular ricochet of rocks falling, hitting close all too often.

As I began abseiling from the high point, around 5850 metres, the rock-fall stopped, empty and cold. The bottom part of the face was cast in the long evening shadows of Sobithongie. When I arrived at the slope under the schrund, Athol had put some more clothes on and was keen to keep moving. It was suddenly very cold, just echoes of sunlight from higher on the face. We quickly strode out across the névé in the deep shadows and back toward camp two along the undulating snowy edge of the névé. There the sun was soft and low, but at least it was warmer.

At 6.40 a.m. the sunlight hit our camp two tent from over the Kambachen ridge, sudden respite from the fierce minus 15°C night. We set out to the base of the route, around the edge of the névé, across to the face, and dumped our first load as the slope began rising up the snow cone to meet the schrund. On the way back it started snowing heavily, so at camp two we got into the tent and waited for it to clear, hoping we could get another load across before dark. Clouds circled over one another, lifting higher up onto Jannu, then closed in together; tighter, heavier with snow.

By 4.30 p.m. it hadn't cleared, so we took another load over anyway, our hoods up, boots brushing through the new, loose snow. Our shallow steps from a few hours before were already beginning to fill. With heads down we plugged up the snow cone to the schrund, slowly lifting and stepping through the white. The temperature dropped and the cold started to sting my fingers. Huge, exploding clouds of spindrift avalanched down the ramp line and shallow couloir, soon arriving at our little platform at the base of the schrund, the spindrift dissipating and rushing through the area like strong wind.

On our next trip over to the route from camp two we lugged the haul bag and portaledge up to the high point, enduring another afternoon of rock-fall. It was as if tension was alive between us and the mountain. The mood was quick to get a bit further, up under a small rock buttress, for protection. We were always yelling warnings about rock-fall to one another, the continual falling rock extremely worrying, the impacts always alarmingly close. 'This is bullshit,' we said to one another. 'One of us is going to get hit and killed soon.'

At the high point Athol led away, up under the rock buttress, only about 30 metres higher. Soon we were both up there, including the haul bag and portaledge. Meanwhile, the weather had closed in, which at least brought slightly colder temperatures and, we hoped, an end to the rock-fall. We abseiled quickly, listening for the sound of cutting air, the falling rocks. As we zoomed down the fixed line, we began to notice scars where rocks had hit the surface, especially down lower, near the schrund. We resolved to arrive early when we came back to begin our ascent, avoiding the warmer part of the day when the sun was on the couloir and ramp line, causing the melt that set the rock-fall off.

The next day we rested at camp two, quietly sorting our personal gear, getting things like harnesses and camera slings just right. Virtually everything was up at 5900 metres, waiting for our return, and the big effort to go higher.

At 4 a.m. the night was already long and black, but the grey of dawn was not far away. We packed our tent away, stashed it under some rocks and trudged up the short hill and then around and across to the face. Full of food and drink, I was fighting off the urge to vomit all the way across, watching my boots slide out in front of my body. I hadn't slept much, was excited and tired all at once. We walked along the uneven and unconsolidated snow using our ski poles for balance. As we started plodding up the snow cone to the schrund, our steps fell into the familiar rhythm, lifting and pushing into the steps from the previous trip up.

We took our packs off at the base of the schrund, turning about to look at the weather. It didn't look good, grey clouds drifting ominously. 'We'll never know what the weather is doing in this place,' said Athol. The only regular pattern in the weather so far had been strong winds above 7000 metres, particularly along the summit ridge. A week's clear weather early on had given way to daily snowfall ever since.

'Let's just go,' we said to one another, and as much to ourselves. The weather always looks worse at night in the mountains, especially when you wake up at 2 a.m., stuff too much food down the throat and then wander along to climb a big mountain. So we headed up in the smooth grey light of dawn, jumaring up the fixed line, our packs light. Within a few hours the upper part of the mountain was covered in cloud. We climbed on from our high point, pitching up hard ice, weaving around areas of exposed rock. The ice kept peeling away when we landed our ice tools in, and it often took five or six blows to get a good placement, all the time standing on the crampons' front-points, calf muscles getting driven harder and harder.

Hauling up the bag and 'ledge was desperately hard work. After making an anchor, usually with two ice screws, body weight would be thrown back onto the anchor, lifting the haul bag through a pulley. After ten movements I'd be panting, my throat dry and cut. The cloud was falling lower, colder air circling around us. We could see the beginning of the 'ramp' section of the route, where the shallow couloir ended, close to 6000 metres. I finished leading a pitch and as Athol jumared it started snowing, the air thick with black clouds.

We put the portaledge up on some steep ice, just on the side of a rock buttress, anchored to three ice screws. By the time we got inside the spindrift avalanches had started falling, rolling down the 'ramp' and all over us. We arranged the haul bag as best we could at one end of the 'ledge to get access to it from inside, zipped the doors up, and half-sat, half-lay inside, panting.

Rhythmically, the spindrift avalanches tore over the 'ledge and soon we noticed the snow build-up between the 'ledge and mountain. It was horrendous trying to get organised, both of us cramped inside with our sleeping bags, hanging stove, food, bowls, water bottles, a stuff-sac full of ice for cooking. And soon the build-up of snow on the outside began pushing in on the walls of the 'ledge. Every few minutes I knocked the fly in an effort to shed the snow that came down with the spindrift avalanches, but it seemed as though I only knocked a small amount off each time. I became increasingly satisfied by knocking the stormfly, then hearing and seeing the snow drop away, but was frustrated I was losing this battle.

We got into our sleeping bags one at a time, moving all the gear onto one another as we each got our boots off and struggled into our bags. It was time consuming and eerie, getting inside the sleeping bag as the 'ledge was hammered by the spindrift avalanches, growing in frequency and weight. Soon it grew dark and after a few brews and a bowl of noodles each, we lay back, head to toe, hoping the storm would finish and leave us in peace.

I couldn't sleep very well and kept knocking the snow build-up away. When the heavy spindrift avalanches came down, snow was forced inside the 'ledge through the tops of the door zips, coating all the straps up high. As soon as we cooked all this melted, dripping over us. Thin sheets of ice coated the inside of the 'ledge and whenever one of us moved, it would break and fall. It was incredibly tight and claustrophobic.

Lightning and thunder broke heavily, right next to us. My ears cracked with the pressure. In the dark, the lightning strikes lit us up like camera flashes. We both tried to sleep through the night, but the thunder and lightning continued with growing force. The snow build-up between the 'ledge and the mountain had become worse. We could barely move anymore. As one very heavy round of spindrift avalanched over us, shaking the 'ledge, I must have had a slightly worried look on my face, and Athol said, 'What are you worried about, Andy? It's your anchor.' I smiled.

Even when it became light it was dull and gloomy, the spindrift still violently pouring over the 'ledge. We needed to clear the build-up. Around 1 p.m. Athol slowly got his boots on and stood outside between spindrift avalanches. He got between the 'ledge and the mountain, trying to kick the build-up away, but it proved extremely difficult. I tried bouncing the 'ledge out away from the mountain as he kicked the snow, but it was set like concrete. And more spindrift funnelled into the 'ledge through his open door.

The 'ledge was fast becoming unusable and moving it to another location wasn't feasible in the storm, so we decided to descend. We got organised as best we could and went out into the storm, packing the 'ledge away and leaving it and the haul bag hanging from the anchor. Despite the storm I was immensely relieved to be outside after our 24 cramped hours in the 'ledge. It was close to 3 p.m. when we started abseiling down to the névé.

We barely recognised the snow cone beneath the schrund, as a lot of fresh snow had fallen. Two ski poles we'd left clipped to the start of our fixed rope were buried deep; we didn't have the energy to try and dig them out. We ploughed through the fresh snow, down the snow cone and out onto the névé, feeling as though we'd been released from an unjustified jail sentence. As we began pushing through the knee-deep snow, I started to struggle, having to stop and rest every 20 metres. I leant over onto my knees, half-crouching in the fading light. Ath was about 50 metres behind me, taking photos as the stormclouds began to break apart, a new beginning. My eyes picked out a bamboo wand we had placed a couple of weeks back, and I resolved to keep going to it before resting and picking out the next wand. Muscles burned with hunger and dehydration. As we turned the corner to go around to camp two it became darker, just ambient light reflecting off the snow. The stormclouds slowly moved away, like animals after an attack.

We descended to base camp the next day, lifting the fixed rope on the buttress out of the new snow as we abseiled. There was even more snow at base camp than on the mountain. Walking across the glacier was quiet and peaceful, just the sounds of the rocks and ice shifting under our boots. It had started to snow again. In base camp we ate and slept, splitting time between our tents and the kitchen tent. We drank endless tea and coffee, watching the snow falling outside against the dull backdrop of the glacier. The weather up high was worsening again, with strong winds and more snowfall through the next four days. At nights after we had eaten and settled down, I could hear the BBC World Service from Athol's tent, reports from around the world delivered with urgency and efficiency while we could only wait for the weather to improve. A growing pile of read books sat in my tent. Dudh and Mima went down to Ghunsa in search of more milk powder and potatoes, so Ath and I cooked, battling with the fuming kerosene stoves in freezing temperatures.

On 1 May, we left base camp for camp two, the weather finally having improved. At least it seemed that way. As we moved up the rock buttress, we made plans to throw the haul bags off the top of the cliff when we finished, as we knew how awkward they

Looking down the *Wall of Shadows* as Athol jumars. Camp two is on the right edge of the névé, just on the rock. Base camp is on the right edge of the glacier, just out of picture. Mt Everest is at top centre on the horizon. *Author.*

Approaching the summit of Jannu: 'We discover our own answers if we have the will to do so; and if we are not afraid of the confrontation with ourselves that such a journey might entail.' Brian Keenan. Above: Athol shortly before the electrical storm; below: Athol's shot of me approaching the summit, 10 a.m., 16 May. We then faced a long journey down.

would be to bring down from camp two. We imagined and laughed at the thought of the bags flying out over the cliff near camp one, and free-falling to the glacier.

As we arrived at camp two at 1 p.m. it was lightly snowing, and this continued, more heavily, all through the next day. We spent the following two days in camp two waiting for the weather to settle, listening to the wind. On 4 May we walked out onto the névé to make some steps for when we went back on the route, we hoped the following morning. The wind stretched the cloud out over Jannu's summit, and sent spindrift spiralling far into the air along the summit ridge.

At 3.30 a.m. we left camp two for the route. The night was black, no moon. Wind had filled our steps over with snow, so we looked for their vague imprints to land our boots on, trying to avoid having to make fresh steps, especially leading up the snow cone, where the snow was far deeper. By 9 a.m. we were at our high point, knocking snow off the haul bag and anchor. We decided it was important to find a good 'ledge site before anything else, preferably higher, under another rock buttress. Once this was done, we could climb another 300 metres up the 'ramp' and abseil back to the 'ledge to sleep. The next day we would haul the 'ledge and everything else up to the new high point, and repeat the process as we went higher.

It was a clear morning, vast and blue. Athol led off from the high point, looking for a good site for the 'ledge. As I belayed, I began to shiver a little, sweat wanting to evaporate. Turning to the north, I could already see clouds building in the Ghunsa valley and rolling up the ridge line toward us. At the end of his 60 metre pitch, Athol found a small section of near-vertical rock that ran at a right angle to the face. I jumared the steep ice as Athol hauled. Around 2 p.m. we set the 'ledge up, anchoring it to a piton and ice screw at the start of the 'ramp'. We were at 6050 metres.

As I handed our sleeping mats and bags to Athol inside the 'ledge the snow started to fall, clouds racing up the side of the north face, only offering glimpses of the distance we had yet to climb. Athol's arm stuck out from the base section of his door (to avoid spindrift falling in the top, if he opened it from there), and I passed him the hanging stove, some food and brew gear. We sat in the 'ledge for a few hours, hoping the weather would improve so we could climb higher. But as evening approached the snow still fell, and the spindrift avalanches began again. Although the 'ledge shed the snow build-up far better than in its previous location, inside we were becoming increasingly frustrated with the conditions, the constant bad weather.

Through the night the snowfall became more sporadic, the cloud lighter. At 4 a.m. we started brewing up, waiting for dawn. Three hours later, we were hit by the rock and ice avalanche that forced us to abandon our route, and retreat from the face.

In base camp as we rested after our retreat from our attempt on the north face direct, we stared up at the *Wall of Shadows,* picking out the detail, looking for the best way through the two sets of schrunds and icefields to the summit ridge. We called these the 'first schrunds' and the 'second schrunds'.

We walked up the glacier terrace until its end, and up the sides of a few hills, to get a different perspective on the face, particularly how we'd gain the summit ridge from it. A rocky cliff stood between the icefield and the summit ridge, and we tried to see where the weakness in it was. Knowing that three teams had been through there before gave us some confidence.

We were meant to leave base camp early on 9 May for camp two, but I woke at 4 a.m. with violent vomiting and diarrhoea. I walked around base camp for hours, waiting for the next, inevitable bowel movement, and abdomen-seizing cramps. The

day was spent drinking as much fluid as possible and gently trying to eat some clean food in the afternoon. The kitchen tent had
gradually become more fetid; Athol and I didn't have the energy
to clean up – we just wanted to eat, sleep and get back on the
mountain. It was only with reluctance Mima would use soap to
wash the dishes, and he laughed under his breath when I became
angry about it, as I held back another wave of nausea.

The following day we were at camp two by 1 p.m., along with
the arrival of more snowfall. The first signs of the monsoon season were with us, including slightly warmer temperatures. Melt-
water ran down the cliffs beneath camp two, and small rocks
slipped from the cliff-top. Our plan for the *Wall of Shadows* was
to fix rope up the first 200 metres off the névé, getting us to the
start of the icefields. From here we would launch up the face for
the final time early the following morning.

11 May. Fixing the first section of the *Wall of Shadows* took us
a few hours; leading a 100 metre pitch each, dealing with hollow
ice over the granite, the vertical steps topped only with snow,
scraping around with ice tools overhead and getting facefuls of
powder. We had left camp that morning at 8 in clear weather, but
by early afternoon it was snowing. As I jumared Athol's pitch up
onto the beginning of the icefield, the snow was falling gently.
From where we stood we could see the way; the icefield's
expanse rising to meet the sickeningly unstable looking ice-cliffs
of what we called the 'first schrunds'. Ice-cliffs high on the north
face direct area, way up on the right, also ominously hung over
us. We had already seen two colossal avalanches from these ice-
cliffs while we were working on our direct attempt.

We left a bit of gear at the anchor and abseiled into the snowstorm, aggressive heat working through the cloud. The mountain
was full of colour and noise – rock-fall. That night at camp two
we sorted pieces of our kit, fine tuning. Athol had his shortwave

radio on, tuning into the BBC. Soothing English names like Charlotte Cooper talked to us about a world we'd left behind, frozen air pressing in on us from the outside.

The alarms went. Dread and excitement. The route, the mountain; I couldn't yet cut it loose from my mind, let it be free from the attachment of wanting to climb it. It would only be after our ascent that my sense of a relationship with the mountain reached a state of equilibrium. We needed to move, to be amongst it. At 3.30 a.m. we quietly left camp. It was 12 May. The night was black. We cruised across the undulating névé, picking out our steps from the previous afternoon. It always felt so lonely crossing the névé below the face in the dark. Isolated, on the edge of something.

We sat around at the start of the face and had a drink from our bottles. I could have gulped all my hot drink down, already thirsty, like a dog. Small parcels of pink light like laser beams cut across the mountains in the distance. But it was gloomy and cold where we sat, hunched in, arms crossed over chests. Little rivers of spindrift ran down the buttress overhead like sugar falling off a bench. We put our helmets on, pulled our hoods up.

I took my head torch off, disconnected the battery, another small mark in time. Ath jumared first. At the top anchor, we left a set of jumars and set out. Front-pointing up and across to the left, just a few metres between us, the rope away in the pack. The ice-cliffs directly above us and way up on the right sat silent, like someone about to betray us.

Even with our down suits on, it was very cold, fingers freezing and re-warming, the repeated cycle of pain. We climbed over patches of thin, close-to-rock ice and hard-packed snow. It changed from metre to metre. The crampons went in, clean and sharp. One, maybe two, swings of the ice tools. Then it would go blue and hard, scratchy.

'When we finish this expedition, make sure it really is the finish, Andy. Make sure I don't do any more of this,' Athol said as we traversed underneath the fragmented facade of the massive ice-cliffs after two hours.

'Yeah right,' I replied sarcastically, yet somehow hoping it could be true for both of us.

As we climbed over to arrive at the clear terrain on the left side of the ice-cliffs, the ice became very hard and steep. Like a deep blue ocean frozen over. It was taking up to eight blows to get a placement. Our position was exposed, the névé already a few hundred metres below us. We worked away, like cobblers, like miners. Ath pushed out onto the good ground first, and he was suddenly lit by the sun. It was a clear, still day. I moved over onto the better ice, the almost squeaky snow, and we paused for a few minutes, feeling the warmth, the new sun. It was 9.30 a.m.

For some time we climbed up the edge of the 'first schrunds', our ice tools scraping through, not really biting. The heat from the sun was becoming more intense. Clumps of snow dropped from our crampons as we kicked higher. Another 200 metres up we sat on the side of a small schrund and had some drink, a little food. Far above more ice-cliffs threatened us, so we moved right, onto the centre of the 'first schrunds': short steep sections and easier angled slopes pregnant with snow. Going knee-deep was hard; our packs pulled us down.

An hour on from our break, we could see the expanse of the upper sections of the face below the superb granite cliff lines protecting the summit ridge. Ribbons of rock, streaks of hostility, ran through the blue ice above us. We swapped going out in front, and climbed as high as we could avoiding the blue ice and fall-line of the ice-cliffs on the left.

I cut through the lip of a schrund with my tools, trying to find a way over and onto the good ice above. Ath almost heel-hooked the lip to get over. I pulled up, my face pressed against the ice, my front-points slicing through the air. We could see the place to bivvy, under the lip of a schrund, about the safest place on offer. We pressed on silently. Across another steep ice-field, heads resting on arms every few minutes, leg muscles feeling the dehydrated strain. 'Fuck, this ice!' we would often exclaim. It kept blistering in plates as we landed the tools in, peeling away like old flaky paint. The spindrift avalanche runnels were polished hard and even, dark blue, almost green.

At 1.30 p.m. we arrived at the bivvy site, 6250 metres. Ath started kicking out a platform for our little tent and I got a brew going. We drank two litres each, swishing the lukewarm drink around in our little bowls, watching it. Ath went to sleep, but I sat in the entrance of the tent looking at the sky. There was no sign of it snowing. It was stifling hot inside the tent and we peeled our down suits off. I watched the sun gradually descend, a burning jewel.

As always, the night was very cold. We talked and slept. Then the alarms again. The cooker's soft blue flame whispered as we pulled our gloves from our sleeping bags, re-inserting the inners for another day. It always felt like leaving a bomb shelter when we emptied the tent, wrappers and bits of crappy snow sitting in the corners. We moved out from the left end of the schrund at 4.30 a.m. and front-pointed up toward the rock barriers.

Ath was staying on a thin strand of sticky ice. I was about ten metres below, stopping to watch the incredible dawn light behind. It helped me to wake up. We soon ran into the first rock band. I got a rope out while Ath wound in a screw, the ice creaking under the strain. I led out to the left, hoping we would find a clear run up ice. It was brutally hard again. Ten metres out I tried to get a screw in for protection but it wouldn't bite, my arms unable to deliver enough weight. I kept going. Around the edge of the buttress my crampons slipped and settled on the granite a few inches under the now crusty ice, my arms taking the weight. But it was a clear run for at least another three pitches. I laboriously front-pointed up until the end of the rope.

We kept pitching, marking our progress against the massive schrunds on our left, the 'second schrunds'. During the final sections of the rock barriers the heat from the sun was becoming unbearable, sweat constantly stinging the eyes, draining the heart. As I hung from a belay, Athol was dealing with the closed seams of the yellow granite above. He had a sloping stance, his crampons scratching about. Ice and gravel showered me. After placing a small pin he carefully went on. 'God,' I could hear him say to himself, edging his crampons up on the rock, one tool dangling, the other bedded in a 'semi-detached' clump of ice.

At the anchor we had a quick drink, a little 'damage control' against the dehydration. More rock. The clear sky had gone, soon it would be snowing. I led off, gently balancing my front-points on edges and patches of thin ice. I tried to get my tools into a small crack, looking for *something* to pull up on. Feeling the teeth of the pick catch on an edge inside the crack, I torqued the shafts sideways and lifted. Then one tool out, looking. My left arm was locked right up until I found a small patch of ice amid the sprinkling of snow over the rock. Higher up, visibility was lost in the falling snow. I stayed on a sharp arête, probing the other side every few metres, searching for better conditions. There was now soft snow over soft ice, and it was hard to tell the difference, an awful combination. I anchored on my tools and a pathetic screw. Pulled my hood up, cinched my gloves, fingers turning numb. Athol jugged (jumared), emerging from the white blur a few metres from the anchor. It was still and quiet.

The cloud pulled away from the face for a few minutes and we saw a bivvy spot, and the top of the 'second schrunds'. Ath pushed on face-in, traversing up and left toward the ice cave we had seen. Halfway over the spindrift avalanches began. Athol disappeared in the onslaught, the rope stretched and swung by the force. It ebbed away and there was Ath, pushing onward, coated in white. I could see his arms swinging up to ten times to get placements, blocks of rotten ice ripping from the face as he did so. He just got into the cave when the rope ran out. I pulled my anchor out with ridiculous ease and moved off. I tried to move fast through the avalanche runnel but of course I was hit, like roadkill.

Vision was gone, just feeling remained. And anger. Snow poured into my neck, inside my hood. I tried moving but was pushed off-balance by the continuing force of snow. It abated and I spat snow from my lips, breathing hard.

On the edge of the cave we cleared a platform for the tent. We put soup and noodles down our throats, and I burnt my tongue as I tried to drink too quickly. The weather cleared at dusk, and we could see the amazing summit headwall of the north face direct. It looked far harder than we had thought from below. An incredible problem! I passed the sleeping bags into Athol, and we tried to get some sleep.

At 7 a.m. we were ready to go. I led off from the cave up the steepening face on the side of the 'second schrunds'. Boulders of blue ice were covered in a sheen of powder. My hands were numb and I couldn't really feel the placements, I lost track of time. Athol called out, the rope was finished. Fuck. We somehow got another couple of metres out of the system and I was perched on the top of the cliff, clipped into my tools that were belted in hard over the lip. I got in a good screw and gave Athol the call. He jugged up, moving on his front-points. I nearly lost sight of him as the wall became steeper. I tried not to move my aching feet as that would send clumps of snow and ice down onto him. My heels and toes flushed with blood and pain.

We took the rope off. Athol was a few metres above me as I put the rope on my pack and pulled over the edge, onto the softer ground. The day was clear; streaks of glaring light stretched out from behind the eastern end of the face, the sun was nearly on us. Further up, we came to the final schrund, its overhanging lip offering a perfect shelter. It was still early and stormclouds were building again. We broke through the lethargy and got ourselves under the overhang. I wondered if we were going to have any famous last words about it as we put the tent up and crawled inside. The storm was eventually split by the sunlight late in the afternoon, and we dozed and drank into the evening. It became incredibly clear, everything so far below, the sunlight soft and cold all at once.

We were at 6750 metres. We left the tent, sleeping bags, mats and most of the rack here. We took a day's worth of snack food each, a little gas, the cooker, some soup powder, one rope, three ice screws each, some pitons and 'biners for abseiling.

1.30 a.m., 15 May. The dark cold felt so familiar, little stars barely lighting the rich black sky. Our packs were light, born again. Our head torches swung about, the beams lighting the snow in pale, ghostly white. The ice was in good condition, we moved well. The rock cliffs above were surreal, floating like battleships. Talk flowed between us, aimless chatter, taking the piss. Then it all got hard again. Ath disappeared into a narrow chute between the walls of a short cliff. I saw a few green sparks light from his picks bottoming out, his shoulder pressed on the wall. Once through, he called down where it was good and I moved through and onto the icefields above. It was a relief to have more weight back on the feet.

Then it was up, on and on, steeper than it looked from base camp. Those hours climbing up to the summit ridge were incredible; nowhere to sit and rest, just moving higher, everything dropping away. The glacier below, alongside base camp, was deep and dark. The cliffs on our right were streaked with ancient, dark ribbons. After four hours on the go, in the bone-coloured light before dawn, we stopped at a foot-wide shelf and had a quick drink, took some photos. It was cold, little shivers under the down suits. We had gradually started veering right with the cliff-line, heading toward the rock band below the ridge. Then it all started burning with orange light.

At the rock band we got the rope out and Ath led up a faint near-vertical groove, swapping between numb hands and tools. My hands and feet also turned numb, waiting for and fighting off the bouts of shivering. At his belay I moved through for the next pitch, front-pointing up the ice and snow, gasping for breath. I sat down on the flat and Ath climbed up. The sky and sun were out, clear and blue.

The summit was far away. We sat down, staring about, feeling stunned; the summit ridge was longer and more intricate than we expected. We would be up here for at least one night, maybe two. A weird part of us, deep inside, wanted it this way, to shed ourselves of all the links to safety and certainty. I felt exhausted already, the altitude having a strong effect. High cloud was streaking in. 'Let's just go a bit more and see,' said Ath. I had become worried about our situation: the weather, the possible nights out. But as we stood and moved off along the ridge toward the summit a great sense of peace came over me, that somehow we would deal with whatever came our way, an acceptance of the future.

We steered clear of the cornices, running the rope out through the steep sections, traversing face-in across the slippery snow. Heavier, darker cloud moved onto us and the snow flew about, stinging our faces. We sat and rested, hanging our heads, our hoods up. After 30 minutes we set off again, thinking we could get to the top by dark. The snowfall was passing through, off and on. The 2000-metre cliffs of the north face started a few metres below us.

At 5.30 p.m. we were again in a storm, but we kept going. We had climbed up the side of some rock, on the edge of the north face, and higher onto the thin, snowy ridge. I was just passed Athol's belay when I heard him yell out through the wind, 'Andy! Get back!'

I heard something different in his voice, and front-pointed back around to him, my lungs burning. Athol was totally alive with electricity, like a light bulb shorting out. There was a constant buzzing noise, a loud and sharp electric hum. There was no lightning, just the eerie electric-charged air. Athol could feel it running all over his body. We didn't know what was going to happen next. Then he could hear it on me. We frantically looked around for somewhere to go. So much was going on. The wind chaotically whipped the rope and snow around our legs, snapping at us. 'That slot down there on the edge of the cliff,' yelled Ath, pointing.

Inside the slot a few minutes later, between the ice and the cliff-edge, we sat on our packs, exhausted and relieved, almost giggling. We even had a roof, but snow blew up through a hole on the north face, like a blast freezer. Soon it was dark. Our feet went cold all too quickly. We put chemical warmers in and put our feet into our down mitts. Ath tried various combinations for warmth for his feet as the hours wore on. We had one bar of chocolate each for the night and an energy bar each for the next day. We didn't really want to eat our chocolate, preferring the security of just having it there, in case. Despite being in pain from lack of food, we both just played with the chocolate, like uninterested children. Our talking, our reactions, were slow. With great satisfaction we melted ice with our little cooker and had hot soup, a whole litre each. I threw the soup packet into a large crack in the ice. Then I leant over, my head in my arms. The cold kept searching deeper into us, looking for our hearts. The watch told us it was minus 20° Celsius.

I leant against Ath's legs and tried to sleep, but the cold was too much. Out of the whirring of the wind and snow outside, Ath said, 'Andy, I wouldn't be here with anyone else, mate.'

'Same,' I replied, and felt an enormous sense of gratitude towards him, for the years of climbing together, the nights out like this.

We murmured softly, and with a profound sense of detachment, about home, about getting back to base camp. Both of us couldn't seem to stop dribbling. 'I can see some stars out there,' said Ath, almost whispering. I leaned over and peered out into the black; soon a few stars glowed faintly as the thin cloud running over the ridge ran out. We had hope for the morning, for getting to the top and getting down the mountain.

Slightly after dawn and a miserable amount of lukewarm drink, we left for the summit. Our bodies were deeply cold, shell-shocked. The sky had cleared – a hopeful sign. We were pitching the ridge, but never putting any gear in. The snow and ice conditions were horrible; it took a lot of effort to keep placements in. We took the rope off and kept moving, turning the ridge to the south side as we approached the summit, frontpointing all the way.

'That's it. End of the road,' Ath called out from along the ridge. When I arrived we peered over the summit, down the north face, and back around to Kangchenjunga. It had taken us four hours from the slot. I felt emotionally devastated.

As we descended to the slot we had spent the night in, Athol fell. I was belaying him as he down-climbed when I heard him yell. Simultaneously, the rope began rapidly looping in front of me. I jumped down into the slot and saw him fall past, upside-down, a dark blur. We were literally on the edge of the north face. The rope went tight. Soon my fingers were cramping from holding the rope so tight, holding him on. Luckily, Ath had landed in a narrow, icy groove, wedged against some rock. I yelled out, but got no reply. I yelled again. Then his weight eased from the rope. I was filled with relief. Ath slowly climbed back up to the slot, breathing hard. His eyes were bloodshot, his face pale. Feathers stuck to his face from a tear across the shoulder of his down suit. We got inside and sat down where we had spent the previous night, and I kept asking Ath if he was OK, if he felt anything broken. 'It's OK,' was all he said, feeling his body over for something that the shock might have hidden.

We sat there for a while, listening to the hum of the wind outside the slot. We had to go, to keep going. We reversed the summit ridge. I was staggered I couldn't even remember some sections. The sun was out, and the wind pushed patches of snow through like clusters of stars, glinting in the light. As Athol front-pointed along below a cornice I heard him swear loudly, almost comically. Twenty minutes on, he asked me if I saw it, the car-sized block of cornice that had dropped off, a couple of thousand metres into the East Kumbhakarna glacier. I hadn't seen or heard a thing. Ath was a metre below the break when it happened.

By 6 p.m. we had arrived back at the area where we could descend from the ridge. Kanch was covered in black, curling cloud, the wind on us was freezing, spindrift tore about our faces; the air a whirling mass of snow crystals. We abseiled the rock band as the sun dropped over the horizon, jets of light streaming through the clouds. We made another abseil off some old Japanese fixed rope at the top of the icefield, even though we couldn't see where it was anchored. As I put the rope away, I watched Ath rhythmically descending, facing-in, the whole scene lit by the last sun, a roaring vivid orange, spindrift pouring down from the ridge. I will never forget it. On we went, into the dark.

I marked my descent on the silent cliffs we had passed in the early morning nearly two days ago. We made an abseil over a short cliff as we approached where we thought the tent was. Ath had climbed under the lip of a schrund further down, looking for our little home. I couldn't remember what the area looked like. At 9.45 p.m. we arrived. We drank and drank, then fell asleep.

The next day we lay in the tent for hours on end, trying to drink, wanting to get down. We waited, hydrated more. That afternoon we ran out of gas. I kept having bad dreams – perhaps they were nightmares – about getting down. At 5 a.m. the next morning we left. We abseiled the top icefields on single screws, pins, slings, whatever we could use.

As the sun hit the face we arrived on top of the 'first schrunds'. I was amazed how far we had dropped already. The last liquid from our water bottles, a mix of malt powder and 'dirty food water' smelling like off milk, nearly made us vomit. More descending, down-climbing and abseiling, eating snow, wanting to sleep. Then, after a few massive free abseils off the schrund ice-cliffs, we were back on the first icefields. Then we strung a few more abseils together under the ice-cliffs as another storm hit.

We brewed up on the névé, sitting on our packs as the snow fell. Athol vomited it all up as we began slogging it out to camp two, what should have been a half-hour walk. But the monsoon had nearly arrived. We crawled and sunk waist- and chest-deep for nearly five hours, all the way to camp two, the snow-filled clouds pulsing in front of us like an aurora. A lightning storm played out on the horizon, the flashes bright, like flicking channels on the television in a dark room. It all felt rather unceremonious, as if those stormclouds were part of a distant, disconnected battle. We kept pausing to watch until all the colour had gone.

The morning we left Ghunsa on our way home it was drizzling, the earth soft and loamy. We crept around the Tibetan *gompa,* trying to feel its 700 years. Cold air rushed through the open building. Faded prayer flags, stories of people on horses, flew gently. And the stone and wood, it also told stories, slowly eroded by the mountain rain and snow.

A day uphill – up the Ghunsa Khola and Jannu glacier – was Jannu, Kumbhakarna, on whose summit snows and ice we had so briefly been. Our time up there was marked by but a few footprints, scrapings from our crampons in the snow. I knew that as the years came to pass there would be more. For as each journey ends, we realise *that journey* was part of a deeper search for experience and meaning.

Never before had I felt such a strong sense of communion between the cautious, rational mind, and the deeper, profound, 'life force' as I did during

Andrew Lindblade at the gompa in Ghunsa, on the way home from Jannu, already looking toward the next mountain. *Athol Whimp.*

our time along Jannu's summit ridge. Jannu had become our beloved companion, our object of affection.

Yet, paradoxically, Jannu was looking hard for us to relinquish all our defences during our time along the ridge to the summit and back. It was as though the mountain wanted this sense of 'communion' to be full, for us to rest and sleep, finally.

Still I can feel it: the wind snapping at us, the spindrift stinging our faces, the enormous, approaching black clouds, the crackling electricity in the air, the ridge dropping away into thin air, the desperate night, feeling eerily concerned yet deeply calm. Lips blue from lack of oxygen, not feeling quite alive yet very aware of something, our 'burning jewel' the sun; dreamy, sleepy, stopping to rest, waking with a start, looking upward, outward and around.

Something inside was always connected to a belief and acceptance of all; something, somewhere, absolute and pure.

Above left: Back on the glacier after descending Jannu, very happy and relieved the job was done. *Athol Whimp.*

Above right: Athol at the beginning of the long –20°C night in the ice slot at 7600 metres on Jannu, just after being caught in the electrical storm. *Author.*

Below: Gearing up for the walk-out from Jannu base camp: Nima Sherpa (back centre) organises the porters. *Author.*

Descending Mt Cook following a night out near the summit after climbing the north ridge, winter 1997. There is a lifetime of amazing alpinism to be had in this area; sadly, many Australasian climbers miss the opportunity. *Athol Whimp.*

GOING AND RETURNING:
Aoraki Mt Cook, New Zealand

3753 metres
1992–2000

FROM A PLANE at 5000 metres the detail one can see of mountains below is staggering. Yet still it is hard to immediately recognise those places where we have stood. Only after my eyes rush over the scene do they settle on a place; and the memories, the experiences, from that place come zooming to the front of my mind.

It is just after dawn, only a half-hour after take-off. I am on the way home. I recognise a small crest along the summit ridge of Mt Cook where we paused to rest a week before. And also the summit, the apex of all the routes and corresponding experiences, can be seen glinting like the peak of a diamond. The plane rises, accelerates through 700 kilometres per hour, leaving Mt Cook as a freeze-frame memory. We are in a capsule moving through the light, the earth receding. I have a feeling for how cold it might be outside. I wonder when I will be back, and remember seeing the jet-stream of a plane from the summit of Mt Cook a few weeks previously, a thin white line evaporating like the wake of a boat.

Waiting for the boarding call I could feel my feet overheating, victims of much abuse during the previous weeks in the mountains. Drizzle hit the windows and ran down to the sills, and as I watched the water I felt strangely detached from home, of what I was going back to, of things that no doubt meant so much. Desire for the familiar and safe mixed with a sense of dread about facing the responsibilities like money and work. How distant the brittle cold of the mountains suddenly seemed!

I anxiously sorted through the slides once home, hoping for something unseen at the time, an expression, a perspective, to come to light. The projector warmed the room, the wall awash with a flow of images. There is one shot of Athol's from 1999, when we were resting on the summit ridge of Mt Cook in a schrund to get out of the sun and heat. It reminds so much me of that particular day. So much happened.

Surrounded by ice, I was dizzy from the reflected heat. We had climbed along the ridge from the summit, having to pause every few metres to bury our heads in our arms and close our eyes against the oven-like heat. We were trying to keep going for a long time, so we would get to the Middle Peak as soon as possible, where we could sit down. I sucked on small pieces of ice I broke off in a losing attempt to stay hydrated. I noticed Athol doing the same. Inside the schrund, as I lay down on my pack, I stared out and all I could see was a massive section of blue, the sky. We caught drips of water falling from the roof of the schrund in our waiting water bottles. Two hours later we were nearly killed.

Overheating

The morning we set out it hadn't been that cold for the mountains. Moving up the upper Hooker glacier area from Empress Hut to the base of the Sheila buttress, the frozen crust we started out on gave way every few steps, leaving us knee-deep in the snow. We were roped together, picking a path through the crevasses. Sweat washed over my body as my legs broke through the crust time and again. Still very sleepy from a 3 a.m. wake-up. The small amount I had eaten rolled through my stomach and I waited for the coffee to have more effect. We paused briefly to work out a way around a crevasse, our head torches casting light in narrow beams. I caught Athol's eyes and he looked like he had just walked into the kitchen to make a coffee after waking up.

It was quiet, just a few small ice avalanches across the way toward the south face of Mt Hicks. We stood at the hard blue lip of the crevasse for a minute or two listening to the mountains, the distant roar of the glaciers. The 'tightrope'-style walk along a very

thin fin of ice linking the two walls of the crevasse was good reason to 'switch on', each watching the other as we crossed, hoping
the 'fin' wouldn't collapse. Then another upward stretch, waiting
for my steps to fall into a rhythm. We were heading east, but our
view was only of the huge dark ramparts of ice and rock rising
thousands of feet above us, the sides of Mt Cook.

A section of perfect ice allowed us to rapidly zig-zag up the
slope, like rising on an escalator. Dawn was edging toward a
brighter light, but we barely noticed the change; only when we
accidentally turned to the west did we see the brilliant colours of
dawn spread over the mountain La Perouse and beyond. After
that, every few steps, without stopping, we turned and looked west
again, disbelieving. The rope between us slid along the icy crust,
causing tiny ice crystals to tumble away. Then, again, more steps
up, our upper bodies slightly curled toward the slope. I was drawn
into my unconscious, as the sounds of my crampons slicing
through the ice reverberated in my mind. Watching my boots and
crampons take another step I wondered if the sounds were out
of sync with my vision, as if it were an old movie. Pausing and
standing straight again, my sense of balance and equilibrium
were regained.

Looking up into the narrow couloir between Mt Cook and Mt
Dampier, commonly known as Fyfe's Gut, we saw scars lining its
length. These black lines were evidence of rock-fall from the
Sheila Face, and from high on Mt Dampier, funnelling into the
couloir with gravity's help. The present long spell of fine weather
at Mt Cook was very unusual, melting a lot of snow and ice, loosening the rocks and making the slopes dangerous.

When the sunlight fell over the western side of Mt Cook's
summit ridge, Athol and I were about halfway up the buttress, and
felt the instant warmth. From the base of the buttress all the
climbing had been on rock. We had changed from plastic boots
into rock shoes, stepping off the snow with our plastics in our

packs, and our ice tools cinched down the packs' sides. We could move faster with rock shoes on, even if it meant cold toes while standing still on belay. When the steep climbing on the rock finished, we took the rope off and put it away in one of our packs. We sat on a small ledge, our feet dangling over the edge, then carefully moved up to where the buttress merges with the steep icefield to the summit. At the base of the short gullies beneath the summit ice-cap, we changed back into our plastics, and snapped our crampons on; the first placements in the ice were solid and reassuring.

Athol and I probed up different gullies, looking for the quickest route through the rocky area. As I moved up a tight, rocky gully, pieces of ice flew off and tore away toward the ground far below. I could hear Athol breathing only a few metres away to my right, but I couldn't see him – hidden by the rock buttress between us. Small stones scattered from my crampon placements as I moved my legs around to get positioned right to climb higher. All the rock was loose, but fortunately some of it was bedded down by ice, stopping it from moving when I put weight on it.

I placed my ice tools alternately in small patches of ice and the rock, hoping I was going to exit the gully very soon and emerge onto solid ice above. Suddenly I realised both of my ice tools were on the same piece of ice as I was moving my feet up – and it was loose. The ice rocked around on the little shelf where it sat and become disconnected from the gully's two walls, as if watching me and laughing. I felt panic and amazement all at once – amazement because the piece of ice hadn't shattered when I had dug in two ice tools at once, although it had become disconnected from the walls.

Even though I couldn't see Athol, I called out. I needed to know he was there. 'Wait a second,' he replied, and I felt a little calmer. 'Are you right?' he called out, louder. 'I think ...' and my voice faded out, my mind totally absorbed with fixing my problem. By removing one pick from the piece of ice and balancing it

on the small rock shelf, I was able to get my feet higher, my crampons' front points sticking into a small crack, and my back leaning
against the left wall of the tight gully. A couple of minutes later,
after nervously pulling out of the gully, I stabbed my front points
into the ice, made my ice tool placements solid. I rested, my
breathing rasping the back of my throat.

Athol was a few metres to my right and was also relieved to
have arrived at the icefield. I explained what happened and we
both managed a small smile, a way of putting it in the past. We
climbed beside one another after that, talking as we moved higher.
Both of us had sweat burning our eyes and running freely from
our heads. The final metres to the summit were quite agonising –
the ice had become very hard, making placements tedious and
physically difficult. The summit of Mt Cook had become very
precarious since a massive rock and ice avalanche down its East
Face (the opposite side to the Sheila Face) in December 1991,
which had left the summit a bit lower than it had been. We
approached the area with caution, and peeked over the top like a
couple of burglars looking for the best way to get into a house.
After about 30 seconds we began descending down and across to
the Middle Peak, the first possible place we could sit down, under
the mid-afternoon sun.

It was just below here we slumped in the schrund, exhausted
and dizzy from the heat and dehydration. The shade was very cool.
It was just like sitting in a freezer after slogging through a desert.
We sat on our packs, happy to have arrived at our little oasis. We
each forced down two litres of freezing melt-water caught from the
dripping roof in our well-balanced water bottles, sparking a nausea
like air-sickness. I fell asleep and woke to hear Athol outside the
schrund casually swearing at his phone which wouldn't log onto
the network, pointing it into space, hoping for a connection.

It was a clear day, no wind. We could see forever. As the sun
dropped lower in the sky we left the schrund. I had put the rope

at the top of my pack in case we wanted it out for a quick abseil down from Porter's Col. The first few steps of our downward journey I was fresh, I felt energy inside. But after only a few minutes I felt dehydrated again. The whole area was beginning to take on a deep, surreal glow from the evening light, cast out over the Tasman Sea toward us, rippling over the snow and ice. Within a few minutes we were at Porter's Col, a small area barely big enough to sit down. The Caroline Face dropped away for thousands of feet a few steps from where we stood at the top of our descent route. My lips were cracked, sun cream stung my eyes. We both had strong headaches, hardly numbed by painkillers. I could feel the skin on my fingers splitting. After briefly looking about the scene, we began heading down, facing into the hard ice.

After a hundred or so metres of descending facing-in to the ice, we made a short abseil over a rock band, then kept front-pointing down, unroped, heading out down and right to avoid the large bank of a long schrund. Athol was a few metres above me. I heard a faint whistling, that distinct sound of sucking air, looked up and saw a single rock ripping through the air, silhouetted high against the evening sky. It passed high overhead in a blur. I looked into the slope again, and wished I could rub away the sweat stinging my eyes under my sunglasses and helmet. It felt very claustrophobic not being able to take my glasses and helmet off easily, to wipe the sweat away and feel the fresh air on my head. Athol suddenly screamed, 'ROCKS!', and I looked up again to see a mass of large rocks crashing down the cliff, out into the sky, then straight in toward us. I felt an elastic surge of panic tear through my body. I can barely remember thinking, only moving. I remember seeing my legs turn sideways and attempting to run across the icefield. Within a second I was falling down the icefield and across in the direction I had turned and moved. I tried to leap further away from the rock-fall and self-arrested, one ice tool biting into the ice, the other hanging free from its leash. As I fell I saw Athol moving to the right as well, lunging out with his ice tools, his legs following almost simultaneously. The last thing I saw in those frantic seconds was Athol curling his upper body inward and hunching down, ready to take the impacting debris.

A ringing crash sounded from my helmet – my head felt undamaged but very insecure. Massive rocks tore into the ice about half a metre away to the left. The power and momentum of the rock-fall was incredible. I kept waiting for the final blow, hunched and curled inward, thinking I had to *stay on* if I was hit, that I couldn't be pushed off. At least if we got hit but managed to stay on we might be able to get out alive, but being hit and knocked off meant a certain end.

As soon as the rock-fall seemed to have stopped, we both kept moving to the right, towards an overhead rock buttress that might guard us from further rock-fall. A few metres later we stopped, panting, our legs shaking. 'Are you okay?' Athol asked. 'Fine,' I replied. 'You okay?' He was.

Our communication seemed to be limited to the essential, both feeling there might be more to come from above. After a frustrating search for a place to rig an anchor we made another quick abseil. Then I pulled the rope and dragged it with me – not wanting to spend time coiling it. Finally, down at the schrund, we inspected the mess of rocks that had fallen past us half an hour before. Television-sized, dark red and grey, they seemed spent of their energy as they sat half-buried in the snow. I picked up a small, fist-sized rock that was shockingly heavy. 'Feel the weight of that fucking thing,' I said and passed it to Athol. We both turned toward the Tasman Sea, turned bronze in the late evening light, then back to the upper Empress Shelf.

We had a few hours to go before we would arrive at Empress Hut. The amount of rock and ice fall debris scattered across parts of the shelf was sickening. We considered the best line to take and headed off, looking up regularly, our steps often turning into a run, the incredibly clear day growing dimmer and the temperature dropping. It was like we were rushing to a plane we were likely to miss, yet it all felt so calm.

Approaching the hut a few hours later in the darkness, I watched Athol's steps; frozen clumps of snow tumbled down the low-angled slope before stopping against other embedded clumps of blue ice. He slowly came to a stop at the back of the hut and let out a sigh of relief. Both of us were suddenly unburdened.

Belongings

Northerly wind rolled down the Hooker glacier, bringing with it the sounds of glacial melt-water gurgling amongst a myriad of underground chasms and tunnels. The thunder of ice avalanches broke the sound of the gusting wind. The trickle of point-and-shoot camera-snapping tourists ebbed as the terrain became more hostile. As we rose up the glacier and trod rapidly over the white ice studded with small stones, it became harder to see.

Yet despite the onset of night, we moved faster, needing to be able to pick some sort of route through the crevasses that guard Pudding Rock before it was too dark. All our actions were very relaxed and certain, and despite the darkness everything shifted into focus. We were guided by ambient light from high on Mt Cook and the tops of the ranges on either side of the Hooker Valley. Only when the body and mind sense their own rhythm does the familiar feeling of being home in the mountains come around again. At that point one can leave previous trips behind and embrace the new.

Seeing the familiar again – a certain rock, the hut door – becomes a reference point that allows us to embrace a new journey without hesitation. Even the sound of the sliding bolt on the door – it is just like turning the key of your own house after being away for a long time.

We arrived at Gardiner Hut after quickly climbing up Pudding Rock, trying to out-run the approaching mass of cloud and freezing air. Athol had a brew on the cooker within a few minutes. It had begun to snow. We had the door slightly ajar to let out the cooker fumes, the snow a slow-motion white blur outside. After sitting for a while, warm from the hours of walking and climbing, I began to feel cold, my hands wrapped around the brew Athol had put into my hands, looking at dates years old in the log book.

The sweat was evaporating and leaving me cold. Sitting there, my back trying to lean against the curved inside wall, I notice old hardcover thrillers with pages askew and the bindings torn. The books had been sitting there for years. Old candles were melted into corroded candlestick holders, or bits of broken plate. The wind pushed against the hut in violent surges. My hands got too cold to read ungloved. In the morning, under gentle snowfall, we moved out and up to Empress Hut. The sun was trying to break through, but we were grateful for the cloud and snow, saving us from the overpowering heat of the sun.

Some time ago

1992. On the bookshelf in Jeremy Strang's house in Dunedin, New Zealand, was a small, slightly bent metal frame housing a black and white print, a shadowed figure silhouetted against Empress hut – a young Andrew Milne looking out to the sky. Jeremy told me when it was, but I can't remember. He was sewing, repairing his windsuit at the living-room table. Jeremy showed me Long Beach, a local cliff, salt-air slick rock, *Crime and Punishment* the route of the day; the sea out and below the climb looked strong as bed-rock, the sand bleach-white under the January sun.

As I ran through the forests with his brother Tim, we talked about Jeremy getting his kit ready at the house, the evening covering the ground with dark light, our steps becoming harder to see. Driving across the South Island from Dunedin towards Mt Cook, the wind outside the car was louder than the engine. I approached Mt Cook, frightened but inextricably attracted in a way I naïvely denied, my fear outrunning the desire. We walked up the Tasman Glacier, and then up the laborious Haast ridge to the plateau below Mt Cook and Mt Tasman. The next day we headed up Mt Tasman, my first time using ice tools and crampons on a mountain. After a small shield of rock, Jeremy took the rope off. My sense of exposure and vulnerability suddenly increased. As we neared the summit of a satellite peak called Silberhorn, on the ridge to Mt Tasman, clouds rolled in and we couldn't see. We kept climbing to the top of Silberhorn; when we got there we could barely stand up in the blizzard. For a few seconds we got a glimpse of Mt Tasman and its Balfour Face.

Jeremy stared out into the oncoming cloud and snow, then belted his ice tools into the wind-packed ice. We had a drink and ate chocolate, our backs to the spindrift and wind. We waited for about half an hour, hunched over, hoping the cloud would dissipate. Then, eventually, he pointed back down the ridge. I yelled out to Jeremy, 'How do I climb down?!', and he just said 'Go in reverse'. It was that simple, so we began climbing down. Half an hour down the ridge the wind had eased, and we paused for a rest as the snow fell all around us. Snow poured from the summits of Silberhorn and Tasman in long plumes.

Early morning a few days later, Jeremy left me at the campsite near Mt Cook village and drove around to the Tasman glacier, the walk-in to the Grand Plateau of Mt Cook and Mt Tasman, and the Balfour Face – he was going to climb on his own. I was uncertain about what to do. Unable to pack and leave, yet too scared to move, I was caught in a void between where I stood on the alpine grass, the mountain above me, and home. Late that night he was back, and selfish relief flooded through me. I hoped he would take me into the mountains again. 'I turned around near the foot of Haast ridge,' said Jeremy. He laughed about eating all his food, sitting on the glacier.

In the morning he left, the last time I saw him, a fine shallow shingle dust trail rising in the car's wake. In the cold morning light I was instilled with an appreciation and acceptance for the mountains all around me, and this was enough for me to continue. Knowing that Jeremy, with all his experience, had turned around, lifted my self-imposed guilt and opened the door for me to return, still innocent, still green, but a little bit aware.

A few days later, I walked up the Hooker Valley with someone I didn't know, talking to myself. Hard hot sun reflected off the grey glacial stones and the silty water of Hooker Lake. We had arrived at Empress Hut at 4 a.m. after a night and storm-bound day at Gardiner Hut, half-way house of the Hooker. Ascending to Empress Hut at 1 a.m. I could hear the wind up high on Cook, precursor to the distant curling hog's backs, just visible scuttling in from the south-west. I was so excited, yet still holding myself in reserve, unsure I even knew what to do to climb higher, and of being with someone I didn't even know.

A pale pre-dawn light showed the way across the lower Empress shelf. I had a borrowed ice-axe in my left hand. Jeremy's crampons on my plastic boots bit to half-depth – what I would later come to know as perfect conditions. If I didn't lift my crampons out cleanly, the front points would catch at each step.

Crevasses arced and dropped along the shelf like crumpled white sheets, and I couldn't believe how frozen it all was. I knew then that I wasn't going to climb a route during that first trip up the Hooker. It felt right, within my knowledge, that I was going home instead once I'd walked out. I felt there were immediate dangers everywhere I stepped, and wanted safety. It was only as I made my way back home that a peace flowed from within, confidence gained, the lesson emerging.

A phone call was all it took to dispel my innocence, my looking forward to climbing in the mountains again. My return to Mt Cook was going to be a meeting and climb with Jeremy again. I was away from home down on the Victorian coast, and as my father relayed the message about Jeremy's death from Andy Milne a sudden emptiness circled through me – a hollow shock. Then came the sensation that perhaps I never really knew him that well. He had been a member of a Kiwi rock contingent to Arapiles in '89, when I was 17 years of age, and his mountaineering stories enthralled me. Photos of climbers descending in a blizzard, crampons scratching around on the rock while trying to get an abseil anchor in, the whole bit.

At that stage I had not been able to resist the call of naïve, imaginary journeys. After I'd said one night at Arapiles that it must be fantastic in the huts at Mt Cook, New Zealand alpinist Dave Fearnley said, 'Believe me, people do an awful lot of talking about Arapiles in those huts ...'. In my innocence I was unaware of the mountaineer's predicament – the potentially long periods of waiting out bad weather, the dangers, the very intense nature of mountaineering. Talk of faraway warm places is a way of escaping the present before opening the hut door and heading up onto the mountain again.

Often I have thought of that first visit here in January '92, up in the wind and snow on Silberhorn, and walking through the tussock around Mt Cook with Jeremy. All the trips meld into a conglomerate when I am at home, but on the mountains my mind is filled with freeze-frame memories. Even now, as I recall running up to the Hooker foot bridges with Jeremy in a fierce wind and cloud, sleet spitting into our faces, I can remember the absence of our shadows on the ground. Looking up at the beginnings of the Hooker glacier was like observing a distant planet, small patches of the glacial white ice showing through the cloud in light patches. The second time I was there should have been the meeting-to-be with Jeremy that wasn't. His death was made very real by suddenly having to confront Mt Cook on my own, and needing to find a climbing partner I could trust. I constantly expected to see his car approaching along the shingle road, dust plume curling behind.

Ten days on, at the foot of Silberhorn ridge above the Grand Plateau, I climbed alone past the place I'd first launched up a route in the mountains the previous year with Jeremy. He'd not been long perished, yet the only way to acknowledge him, even to say thank you, was to be here putting into practice the lessons learnt from him.

As I climbed above the height of Silberhorn it was as though I had let go of something, however unfocused and distant. I looked back and forth between Silberhorn and Lake Pukaki to the south, where Jeremy had died. The southern aurora pulsed simultaneously close and distant out past Lake Pukaki as I moved through the summit rocks, the east face of Mt Cook stretching away to the south. A brief wait on top for dawn, then down to Plateau Hut.

Nothing for it

Making this same descent from the summit of Mt Cook after climbing the East Ridge early one summer with Athol signalled the passage of a lot of time and distance. Movement in the mountains had gradually become more instinctive for me, unspoken. All the little steps, facing in and then turning out again, all within a few metres, scraping around for a decent crack to secure a piton to abseil from, and sending clumps of blue ice groundward. The body's temperature going from hot to cold in five minutes, and vice versa; either pining for the sun or attempting to hide from it.

Below the summit rocks we abandoned the idea of trying to string 25 metre abseils together (we carried only one 50 metre rope) with sporadic anchors, and plunged into down-climbing. I watched Athol put the rope away in his pack yet again; so far it had been a descent interrupted by short abseils and jumping over some steep, messy schrunds. My hands went through the very painful re-warming process, the blood gradually pulsing and shifting from the heart, through the arms to the fingers with increasing efficiency. I'd abseiled with bare hands, and my 'summer' gloves were frozen with sweat when I put them back on.

It had been another long, hot day in difficult conditions. Descending the Linda Glacier to Plateau Hut was tedious work, abseiling into crevasses to climb out the other side, out of water, out of food, the whole route taking twice as long as it would have normally. When we topped out onto the summit ridge after climbing up the East Ridge, we briefly paused to get the weight off our front points and toes. As we climbed the final 50 metres of the East Ridge, we clambered over and through some pale grey rocks, clearing the snow and ice away to get a hold. On the summit ridge, the view opened out to the west, and it seemed a long time since we had weaved our way up the bottom slopes off the Grand Plateau at 3 a.m. that morning.

Ten days before we'd climbed the route *Desolation Row* on the steep south face of Mt Hicks. The route itself passed without too much drama, excepting the loose rock. On the upper sections it was vertical climbing with all four points of contact on loose blocks. A bit like standing on a toppling pile of bricks with your hands tied. Protecting the pitches became pretty much cosmetic. Numb fingers and threats from the nearby, snowing clouds completed the picture – but we were thrilled to be going up. It was only while belaying I thought how dangerous the route was, how vulnerable to rock-fall we were.

All through the upper pitches, the restless clouds had brushed snow crystals against us, keeping lines of sunlight at bay until the clouds backed off again, opening up the sky. Athol's helmet took on a yellow glow as he crested the end of the upper rock buttress and climbed up to my belay. The light was strange, as if it was refracting through the threatening storm-clouds. The foreshortened summit ice-cap rose straight above us. Here we put the rope away: 150 or so metres of clean front-pointing on good ice beside each other up to the summit. Five minutes after landing on the summit we felt the full effect of the westerly cloud-bank that had followed us up the mountain; snow pellets showered down, all the while the heat of the sun was still working through the storm-filled clouds.

Eventually, down at 'the book', a long open corner, we ran into some trouble. Abseiling into it, we found no anchors. There had just been a terrific amount of rock-fall into the base of the corner. If we'd been a few minutes further ahead we would have been killed, trapped at the base of the corner, still with another abseil to go, confined by a small, sloping platform of slithering, broken rock. With only one 50 metre rope, we strung a few abseils together from single wire anchors, the last putting us on the ice, a final escape from the 'fall-line' of rocks from above.

Ath stuffed the rope into his pack, and we moved fast out of the area. As we approached the saddle from where we could descend to the upper Hooker glacier and Empress Hut, we desperately tried to see where any crevasses might be hidden under the snow. We slowly and carefully moved about, staying close to the ridge-line. After half an hour of tedious work, we arrived at Harper saddle in a fierce wind.

I looked at Athol front-pointing around the lip of the wind scoop and he was coated in wind-blasted ice. He still managed to smile for a photo. We paused and assessed things in the dying light. 'There's nothing for it,' said Ath, my ears only just catching the words from the wind. We plunged into the blizzard off the side of the saddle and kept descending: probing, probing, probing. Our bleary eyes battled the horizontally driven snow. After only a few minutes we found a thin track of ice that provided a link from the rock barrier to the icefield further below.

I heard Athol caution me as I dry-tooled off the rock and onto the ice. Thereafter it was all work on ice and, further down, snow. A long traverse followed, and then the eventual arrival on flat ground, our head torches sweeping through sweet, gentle snowfall.

We followed our noses through 50-metre visibility, slowly drifting to the right of the field until we crested a small rise and landed at the 'Mother Ship', Empress Hut.

Some years ago we were traversing the summit ridge of Cook after climbing the central buttress of Cook's Sheila Face. We had been rewarded with clear, cold conditions after patiently waiting five days in Empress Hut for a storm to clear. As we sat eating chocolate on the Middle Peak, a Hughes 500 helicopter passed by a couple of hundred metres out to the west, another sight-seeing flight, passengers staring out with complete joyful innocence.

Sensations of wanting to be like them, safe and certain, while committed on an alpine route, have mostly faded for me now – once they seemed to come out of nowhere. During that moment – seeing those little faces staring out of the chopper windows – I was able to luxuriate in the present. The pain of ascending the summit ice-cap only an hour ago in the heat had already become a memory. Descending was the new beginning, moving deeply into detachment. An intense awareness of the present became my driving force – the awareness of some sort of freedom.

Dawn still eastward

It was a dark evening; in winter the light always fades quickly. We didn't want to sit still and wait for the dark in the place where we had eaten our last food. We needed to keep walking, to make use of that food – a couple of chocolate bars in a stashed bag, their unwrapping a little unceremonious link in the chain. Turning back to Mt Cook as the last fragments of sun lay on the summit ridge was undeniably strange. For only two nights before we had spent the entire night up there on the summit, with no more than the clothes we were wearing. And now, here we are, in the arms of safety.

How I have felt the drive to keep walking harder and harder under a heavy load as we leave our mountain home once more!

Down through the crevasses below Gardiner Hut, generating a powerful stride down the white ice, and then onto the moraine and up the short gullies. By this stage another little hill doesn't hurt at all because we want it more than before; it is with a sense of completion we drive our legs down with each step. And then, looking down the line of the East Hooker terraces, in a state of dehydrated calm, all is peaceful.

We had climbed the north ridge of Mt Cook, reaching the summit as the fireball sun dropped over the horizon as quickly as a coin down a slot. We had left Empress Hut late – 8 a.m., in the wake of southerly front, sans bivvy gear. During the last pitches the rock felt like cold metal, and there was the tingling in the fingers that belongs so distinctly to deadening tips. But on we went. It was all rather serious, verglassed steep rock – crampons *de rigeur.*

Athol had the last pitch before the ice. I followed, fast and efficient. I felt so happy to be pulling a Friend out up there, feeling the cams stick in the cold, clipping it carefully onto my harness with gloved hands. I cinched down the leashes on my ice tools and traversed around a crumbling rock tower held together by ice, and up the final 20 metres to the belay. Even as I belted out the last few metres Ath began stripping down the belay. We were warm in that cold air. At the end of the rock , where the ridge merges with an ice field, we took the rope off and put in fast short bursts toward the top. There wasn't a breath of wind. We had neglected to take a cooker, or anything that might offer us some comfort, mainly because we thought we wouldn't need it. What little water we had left was frozen. An energy bar each and a few dried bananas was all we had until we returned to Empress Hut.

From the summit we headed towards the summit rocks. The dark shadow of Mt Hicks' summit sat far below sat like a discarded bowler hat. It was too dark to see the big south face. A few days before we had stood on Hicks' summit, striding out along the small area at 9 p.m. We had sat and rested there, waiting for the cold. Soon we had set off down. Athol had probed down a steep gully for an abseil anchor when we reached the second descent area; his rhythm down the chute had been textbook stuff. He had yelled a quick affirmative and I was on my way.

Soon we had got down, but not before having to address a stuck rope. At Harper Saddle we had dropped into the wind – we were moving quickly, unroped, an ice tool in each hand, everything on automatic. We had made a final abseil to get us to the very toe of the south face. With the rope quickly stuffed into the pack we had stridden across toward Mother Empress.

I worked up the last remnants of saliva into my mouth and checked the watch as we went along under the starlight. 12.30 a.m. Things take longer in the dark. We paused every now and then and had a quiet laugh. We felt as still as the breath of the night as we walked. I could hear my heart in my ears, yet still hear the faintest tinkling of ice on the cliffs behind us.

'It's so far down there,' I thought, and Hicks disappeared from view as we approached a schrund. We decided to sit down for the night. This schrund was about a hundred metres down from the top, and the last time I checked, a couple of months ago, it was still there. Up there on my own recently was like returning to the scene of the crime, looking for clues I knew weren't going to be there.

Athol had been up Cook a couple months before me, and when I got home he asked, 'How was the schrund?'

'Yeah, fuck, it's still there,' I replied.

We cut in and made a bench to sit on, and tied into an ice-screw above and outside the schrund should the floor blow out through the night. Already it was minus 10° Celsius, and on the way to minus 16°. We wanted to descend the northern icefields to Green Saddle, and then down to Empress. For this we needed a good moon, and we weren't going to get one. I remember feeling a short-lived panic rise within me upon realising the weight of our situation, the length of the night ahead. However, I soon experienced a peace I shall never forget – perhaps that is what we had really gone there for. We sat on the foam from our packs, slouched over, wishing we could collapse on our knees and sleep, if only for 30 seconds at a time. Soon I was woken by Athol urging me to deal with my feet – maybe I was complaining about them in my sleep. It was too sad to turn a torch off, just too desperate.

Time became a blur, spurning our hold on reality. Even though we looked at a watch every five minutes, I cannot remember that time passing – slowly or quickly. Violent involuntary shivering occurred as a cycle. Once our bodies had warmed themselves through shivering, it would lapse until we had cooled too much, then the convulsive shivering would begin again. I tried to welcome the night and to hear my breathing, to know we had ourselves in good hands. A long way below and out on the ocean abalone boats' lights twinkled, their crews no doubt bedded down, their radios crackling to life every so often.

The night, black as ink, offered no respite from our predicament. Out there was the universe: timeless, boundless, immeasurable. But in the schrund the watch offered us a countdown until light. Eventually we noticed a faint bone-coloured light on the eastern horizon. It became dark red, like blood from a fresh cut, fading to a pale grey overhead.

At 7.30 we crawled from the schrund to try and absorb any warmth from the sun. With no energy in our bodies, we began to stamp our legs, do anything to try and get the blood to move into the feet again. After another half-hour, I felt something. I felt my heart pushing blood, doing its job. We tried as hard as we could to help our hearts by stamping our feet, but they were on their own. Even before we moved off, we were exhausted. However, we had light, we could see, we had the small excitement of losing height. We had a new cause. We had at least another six hours until we were back at Empress.

After much descending and a couple of abseils we began to traverse to Green Saddle, only 200 metres away. The sun was warm, our throats cracked and dry. As I front-pointed around to Green Saddle I saw Athol lining the camera up towards me and snapping a couple of pictures. It was a good thing to be back at the start of the north ridge, where we had been a day ago. Down on the upper Hooker glacier we put the rope on and motored through to Empress, the afternoon empty save for the small, cold waves of snow blowing around our legs. We didn't stop for anything, reading the slots with precision and speed. Mother Empress, base station. We made a quick radio link with park HQ after we chipped the ice off the antenna and told them all was well – 'Thanks for that Nine Empress, base clear and listening.'

From the ice-encrusted grass under our weary bodies we took photographs, even when we knew it might be too dark, the meters registering at one-fifteenth of a second, too slow for numb-tipped fingers and unsteady limbs. Down to our left Hooker Lake lay motionless and began to freeze over, twilight reflections from the mountains on the western side of the glacier settling in. Our packs were now laden with the whole deal: ice tools, crampons, jackets, the rack – our artillery. But for a two-week winter effort up the Hooker they were light as can be – clean lines, nothing unnecessary, certainly not *de luxe*. Walking in, we had done a double-gear carry to Empress Hut, Athol's brother Tristram shouldering food up the terraces for us in the driving snowfall.

Not until we were literally stumbling from misplaced feet in the dark did we stop to put our head torches on, so keen were we not to break the rhythm of our weary steps. Our 'exile' on the mountain now broke loose in my mind, and I began to realise it was there, if only for a few moments, that we were free. But even this hardly occupied a few seconds as the momentum of reaching the end was at its height. We were channelled down and through the tussock toward the gravel path by the Hooker foot bridges and into the car park. Tristram was there, and I felt as if he could be my brother.

Staying, to be sure

During July '93 Athol and I flew from Australia to New Zealand for a predicted period of fine winter weather, a big high-pressure system slowly making its way east from south of the Australian continent. Usually, high-pressure systems drift north-east once under the Great Australian Bight, but this time it all worked out. Loading up the plane at Mt Cook village to head up to the Grand Plateau was a romantic vision turned real, the 15-minute flight ending in a propeller-stirred flurry of spindrift as we unloaded the gear. The smell of aviation fuel, mixed with the steep, pre-landing turns, filled me with nausea. After asking us twice whether we were sure we wanted to stay, the pilot slapped the door shut and flew away, Athol's mother beside her.

We had the mountains to ourselves, and made the ceremonial stash of food for our return (without any bamboo wands 'X marks the spot' had to do) and began climbing toward the Balfour Face, up the lower slopes of Mt Tasman, in the dying light. It wasn't long before the bag was a mere black dot. 'Imagine getting back to those goodies,' we said. We progressed up toward Silberhorn ridge in a blue, dusky gloom. Athol was out in front. As soon as the slope steepened enough we put our crampons on and took the rope off, crevasses no longer a danger. I felt a bit clumsy as I stood next to Athol, who was efficiently snapping his crampons on. By the time I arrived on the ridge it was dark and Athol nearly had our bivvy shelter up – a lightweight, single-skin tent. We finished kicking and stamping a platform out for the tent and bedded it down, our ice tools serving as anchors.

Some time towards dawn I heard myself gasping in pain and holding my left ear until Athol produced an 'advanced level' painkiller. I gulped it down without water, wrapped my ears in a loose piece of fleece clothing and with some measure of futility waited for sleep. The futility was borne out of the nervousness of knowing the new day, the burning cold, was only a few hours away. Wanting to preserve the warmth of the sleeping bag *eternally,* not to have to face the cold of rising in the soon-to-arrive minus 20°C morning. The luxury of sleep was lost as soon as it was gained, once asleep we were on a fast-forward track to another day on the mountain.

The day on the Balfour Face was cold, clear, shaded and bleak. The iron-hard ice took multiple blows to penetrate with our ice tools. Warmth remained a memory until we arrived in a schrund just below the summit ice-cap and stood in a post-activity glow, eating dried whole bananas and putting another insulating layer on. The angle of the face below lessened after the final vertical pitch and we encountered loose snow over the same insecure ice we'd climbed below. The loose snow was frozen over with a hard crust which body weight only just seemed to penetrate. The rope became a cosmetic interference as we both climbed carefully toward the schrund. We took the rope off for the final, knife-edge arête to the top.

On the summit of Mt Tasman at 7 p.m. I watched tiny snow crystals scatter over my plastic boots and crampons as a little bit of wind pushed them over the summit crest. I remember the camera flashes going off, and putting more layers on our hands to combat the increasing cold. After ten minutes we were starting to shiver, so began our descent. Descending the classic steep ice arête to the Silberhorn col was a test, my head torch battery dying, the picks on my ice tools loosening. The rope was off. It was a relief to arrive at the large schrund at the col to find the abseil rope already anchored by Athol. A quick inspection of the ice screw and I was on my way.

Athol coiled the rope as I re-arranged some gear and we moved off again, gradually closing in on a roaring cooker and eventual sleep. Ath had out-run me back to the bivouac site, and I lost sight of him somewhere as we closed in on the bivvy. Despite a temperature of minus 20 Celsius, I sucked on icicles, staring at the icefield under the starlight; it looked like the snap-frozen, rippled surface of an ocean. It wasn't until the next, sunny morning that I realised I'd taken the long way. After jumping over a schrund downhill from the bivvy site in the darkness I suddenly realised where I was. The relief the violent, lurching jump gave me, once landed, was immense. I soon rounded the bend of the schrund to our bivvy site and heard the cooker. Then I saw Athol, resurrecting the tiny tent.

I talked to myself in big, bold words that trip, my first hard experience. I have never forgotton Athol's implicit trust in me – it was our earliest mountaineering trip together. Viewing the face the day before the ascent, I told him I didn't really know what to expect, not having climbing a steep ice face like the Balfour before. 'You'll be right,' he said.

Memorial

In early 1996 I first felt a ghostly morbid sensation about the mountains. After nearly coming unstuck from a cold, wind-blown, waterfall-ridden Pudding Rock as we went up the Hooker glacier, I'd struggled for the remainder of the trip. After climbing the Sheila Face, I just needed to walk out.

In late '98, the news was out that the Alpine Memorial at White Horse Hill, originally built in memory of the guides killed by an avalanche in 1914, would now accommodate plaques for others who'd died on Mt Cook and surrounding mountains. On a hot February afternoon Athol and I walked up with our cameras. Surrounded by rocks and scrub on the crest of a moraine ridge, the memorial, a sharp pyramid, stands only a few feet high. I could imagine families who'd never truly understood their son's or daughter's death in the mountains, stumbling up here and finding, more than anything, relief in it as a place for them to project their grief. Somehow, it allows one to peer into the mountain, into Mt Cook's upper reaches.

Tristram Whimp had told me he always found something 'a bit eerie' about being here. Many times he'd dropped his brother Athol or both of us off, or picked us up, amid summers of many fatalities. He once waited at the village, pacing, for Athol to walk out of the Hooker valley from a north-west storm. Athol was two days overdue from a solo climb of the *Direct* route on Mt Cook's south face. He of course emerged physically unscathed after an experience that pushed him toward 'the limit', and Tristram felt the relief of one connected by blood.

A few weeks before, in the darkness of Plateau Hut, Athol and I talked ourselves toward sleep. Somehow the conversation approached death, and of feeling an empathy toward others in the mountains. Once, from Empress Hut, we saw four people traversing the summit ridge. It was 9.30 p.m., a summer evening, and the final stretches of light blasted out of thin cloud, highlighting the ridge like a giant fang. I remember empathising with them – they'd obviously had a very long day, and all they'd want was to get off the summit ridge, a serious place of sometimes seemingly unending front-pointing.

'Within the next 15 hours or so *we'll* be up there,' said Athol as we shivered in the evening cold. As we lay in our bunks inside Plateau Hut we numbered up all the people who'd been killed on and about Mt Cook since we'd been around, and it was frightening. The day before we'd climbed Mt Cook's east ridge, and felt this strange association with those who'd fallen off here in recent times. The empathy comes with knowing how easily it can happen. As we moved across the Plateau after descending the Linda glacier following the ascent, I had trouble reconciling it all in my mind, the people *never seen again,* the failed anchors, people roped together when they shouldn't have been. So many symbolic warning flares have been fired for the rest of us by those perished.

Surrounded by evidence of disaster, we continue to move into the fray, time after time.

The recent finding of human remains on the Hooker glacier by two climbers in late '99 led me to the story of their disappearance in 1964. The two men had tried to make the first ascent of the then greatest unclimbed face on Mt Cook, the Caroline. Somewhere along the way, against a week-long storm, they met their end. Their remains were found on the opposite side of the mountain to where they started, bringing the conclusion they had made the first ascent of the Caroline Face, but failed to make it down the mountain and out the Hooker glacier alive. Inspecting the gear found with the remains felt strange; it had been lying next to Michael Goldsmith and John Cousins for nearly 36 years, yet it felt as though it could have been lost and found a week ago. Handling the gear felt invasive, yet it spoke to all of us who are inextricably drawn to the mountains. I could understand how it might have happened, the onset of storm, of being cold and damp, looking for a way down, of desperately willing the height to fall behind, to arrive in a safer realm. Reading through the obituaries from the time filled a few of the factual gaps, but the single photos I saw of each of them said so much more. Hands on the rock, sun on their faces, and smiles that spoke about climbing higher. For the families, there was a final, if ironic, answer: that after being accepted as missing for so long they had been found. Many other families have unfortunately not had the privilege.

Retreating from a route only means we can go back again when the time is right. In midsummer we had climbed five pitches up the Bowie Ridge on Mt Cook before abseiling off. We had been battling much fresh snow, and upward progress was turned into a deep-seated, prolonged struggle. Anchors were slow and tedious to find, the rock very loose and most of the holds were covered in snow and ice. The remaining, visible edges were often peeling off under the weight and force of the crampons' front points. The decision to abseil down came about without tension or concern for giving up. Such smooth transition between potential success and failure doesn't seem to occur at home. Failure on the domestic, career scale can be all the more crushing when one knows one is far happier contending with the often serious scenarios played out when in the mountains. Eventually we are led to the weeks and days running into a departure for the mountains. Romantic excitement dies out to a little apprehension, an appreciation for the risks. Then the overwhelming peace, the realisation that we are returning once more to somewhere larger than life.

Cast

Athol's mother drove slowly up the shingle road to pick us up, so we left the memorial and cut across the grass toward the hut where our gear was. Athol was re-united with Steve Elder, an alpine activist at Mt Cook from the '80s. They talked for a while about what they and others from the time were doing with their lives. Small tributaries of the Hooker and Tasman glaciers running into Lake Pukaki glinted in the sunlight as we drove away from Mt Cook. The car briefly shuddered as we drove over a stock grid. I turned back to see Mt Cook with a hazy, cloudy backdrop. A neat road sign dominated the foreground – *Dead Horse Stream.* On our way in a month before Athol stopped to photograph the sign and Mt Cook, the narrow timber rails along the stream edge splitting, the slight warp from years of weather.

Images of Jeremy's father's handwriting faded in and out of my mind, his writing on a card sent to me in Melbourne. Sometime in late 1997 I sorted through a whole lot of papers when moving house, and found Jeremy's letters, blue ink scrawls across A5 paper. Of trying to get the money together for an expedition to a mountain called Bagarathi in the Indian Himalaya. Rock climbing in the U.S.; buying a wood-panelled vehicle on the West Coast and heading away tuned in to the local radio. Climbing at Hell

Cave, a postcard photo of him falling off in a blur trying to make the final move to the anchor. A letter from myself to his father followed, just to say I'd re-read all these letters, what a sterling person he was. His response warmed my heart, I could just about feel his father walking up to Jeremy's memorial beside Lake Pukaki.

After swimming in the warm blue surface water of Pukaki, we drove toward where I thought the memorial might be, believing it to be a tree. Unbeknownst to us we were driving in the right direction, but didn't know exactly where to stop and walk down through the tussock. We made a U-turn on the loose shingle and headed back into our own cloud of dust. A phone call from Christchurch at the tail end of a recent trip put me in contact with Jeremy's mother in Dunedin, faint pauses evident between her kind words. I was relieved she remembered my name. She informed me there was a memorial stone by a willow tree. The willow tree used to be the largest one, but others had grown up around it. 'Just look for it in the grass,' she told me, 'it's there.'

Later that year, in winter, Jeremy's father sent me a map of the area so I could find his memorial stone. As I read his map sitting at my desk I imagined how cold and hard the ground would be over at Mt Cook, and I thought of the times I had been there in winter, of the hard trips I had done with Athol. It all sat three-dimensional in my mind. The cold water of the glacial Lake Pukaki formed the foreground of the picture; the rest was filled with vast expanses of snow and light, the massive sky that always sits behind Mt Cook.

November of that year: I was on the way in to Cook with Gigi, what turned out to be a storm-bound nine days in the Tasman Saddle area. Every few days the clouds opened out for 20 minutes or so to reveal the bright, endless mountains. Then we were closed in again, and the wind would pick up, trying to lift the hut away. Tristram had driven with us, and we parked the car along the edge of the dusty road and slowly walked across the undulating green grass toward Lake Pukaki. The willow trees next to Jeremy's memorial stone had grown fresh and strong, their low-hanging branches sweeping the grass. It was a still evening, and the sunset cast its faint light across the higher sections of Mt Cook.

As we wandered about, the sunlight retreated over the ranges to the west. The plaque on the stone was shadowed by the grass, light resting on some of the letters. Parts of my memory came forth; of those first steps into the mountains, the nights of no sleep because I didn't quite know how to deal with the new unknown. And the earlier, terrifying, experiences lived out on the granite rocks near my home at age 15, when I often only realised I was in trouble halfway up the wall when it was too late.

All the days and years since suddenly formed into the most powerful sensations; as if I were in the middle of reading a long book, unable to put it down. Looking back up to Mt Cook again, the sun had gone, and only the twilight remained. How amazing it was to be on the verge of going in again! Everything felt so alive, so infinite and boundless.

The acceptance is found
in facing up again
to leaving the ground,
to find a bearing
yet still missing,
somewhere out there
where midnight passes,
and dawn is still eastward.

GLOSSARY

Abseil (rappel): to slide down a rope using a friction-controlling device, such as a belay device, attached to one's waist harness.

Aiders (etriers): the stepped slings that allow a climber, by clipping the aider with a karabiner to a piece of protection, to step in the aiders to gain height. They are particularly useful when there are not enough features on the rock or ice to climb otherwise.

Alpine-style: a mountaineering 'ethic'. An alpine-style ascent is usually made by a small team, say 2–4 climbers, going from the bottom to the top of their chosen mountain and down again without fixed rope (or minimal use of fixed rope, very low on the mountain), or any other support. It is the most committing and admirable form of mountaineering, especially in the Himalaya where conditions and complications of climbing at altitude make this sort of style very risky.

Anchor: one or more (ideally three) pieces of protection placed and arranged in rock or ice from which to belay or abseil from.

Arête: a sharp, pronounced 'ridge', usually very steep.

Belay: to pay out rope to the leader as he or she climbs away from the anchor (also sometimes known as 'the belay').

Bivouac (bivvy): a temporary sleeping place, usually without tent, and sometimes without sleeping bags.

Bolt: normal construction-type bolt of narrow diameter fastened into a pre-drilled hole. A form of protection. Very common in rock climbing where places for 'natural' or 'passive' protection, such as wires or camming devices, can't be found.

Col (saddle): the lowest point in a ridge where the ridge is higher on each end.

Cornice: a lip of snow or ice that overhangs the slope underneath. Very typical of alpine mountain ridges, often formed by the prevailing wind. It is important to climb below the level of the cornice when near one as they can break off, potentially taking the climber as well.

Couloir: a gully, often steep. Can be narrow or wide.

Crampons: metal 'plates' with sharp points that attach to the soles of mountaineering boots for climbing ice and snow. They attach by 'snapping on' to the boots with front and rear bails. The 'front points' of a crampon are the primary point of contact between the crampons and the ice when the ice is steep, usually more than 30–40°, but this can also depend on the condition of the ice being climbed.

Crevasse: a break or split in the surface of a glacier, anywhere from a metre to hundreds of metres deep. Crevasses can be hidden by bridges formed by snowfall, and can be hard to see in poor weather. Thus climbers rope together when moving through crevassed areas.

Down (jacket/suit etc): down is still the best insulator against extreme cold. Himalayan mountaineers will wear down suits almost exclusively above 7000 metres.

Fixed rope (line): the rope that is attached to the mountain or rock cliff by a series of anchors to facilitate climbers efficiently ascending that particular section of the mountain by using a jumar connecting him or herself to the fixed rope to safeguard against falling. Often used to make load-carrying to higher camps faster and safer.

Haul bag: an extremely durable, duffel-type bag for carrying supplies and equipment up a very steep, multi-day route. Climbers haul it up the face, often with their portaledge, as they climb.

Ice tools: the mountaineer uses two ice tools, a 'hammer' and an 'axe'. These are the same except a 'hammer' has a small hammer head at its top rear while an 'axe' has an adze at its top rear, a small fan-like blade for chopping ice and snow. Both the 'hammer' and the 'axe' have picks exactly the same. It is the picks which are struck into ice or snow (or even balanced or wedged in the rock, known as dry-tooling) to gain purchase. Most modern ice tools for climbing steeper ice and snow are about 50 cm long. For less-steep mountains, like Mt Everest, where the body is standing near-straight for much of the time, climbers will use longer-shafted tools so they can use an ice tool like a walking stick.

Ice screw: tubular metal screws with sharp teeth at one end and an exterior thread that can be screwed into ice. Usually about 15–17 cm long. Used as protection while climbing, or to make an anchor for belaying or abseiling.

Icefall: the often steep part of a glacier, where the névé beneath a mountain face breaks down to eventually form into a glacier. Icefalls are usually always very unstable and dangerous, and mountaineers avoid them if possible.

Jumar: a generic name for lightweight 'ascenders', clamps that clip onto a rope. They can slide up a rope, but a cam locks on the rope when downward force is applied to the jumar. This enables the climber to ascend a rope by alternately weighting each of two jumars.

Karabiner: generally oval-shaped metal alloy 'snap-link' or 'clip' device that is used for many climbing purposes, such as connecting rope to an anchor, or a belay device to one's harness.

Moraine: the vast amounts of rocks and boulders found on a glacier.

Névé: the snowy area, often plateau-like, at the head of a glacier.

Pitch: a section of climbing between anchors or belays. Usually 50 or 60 metres in length (the length of most climbing ropes), although can be any length up to the length of the rope.

Piton: metal 'pin' that is hammered into rock cracks for protection. Various versions exist such as 'knifeblades', 'angles' etc., but all follow the same principle.

Plastic mountaineering boots: similar to downhill ski boots, but far more suited to walking. Insulated inner-boots provide warmth. Crampons clip easily to these rigid-soled boots.

Protection: A climber places pieces or points of protection such as a 'wire' or 'piton' in the rock or ice and clips the rope to them while leading a pitch. If the leader falls, the belayer (see 'belay') locks the rope which is passing through his or her belay device (see 'abseil'), which arrests the leader's fall. If the leader falls, the distance he or she falls depends on how far above their last point of protection they are. For example, if the leader falls when two metres above the last protection, they will fall that two metres plus another two metres below the last protection, plus the amount the rope stretches. Climbing ropes are designed to stretch slightly when under severe stress such as a climber's fall, thus absorbing the shock. The amount the rope stretches depends of several factors, such as how much rope is between the belayer and the climber, and how far above the piece of protection bearing the impact the climber was when they fell. There are many factors which can complicate this scenario, but this is the overall principle.

Portaledge: a portable, collapsible ledge anchored to the cliff or mountain face used by climbers to sleep in, and live in during bad weather. They are used on routes where there is nowhere to pitch a tent, or natural ledge to sleep on. A portaledge usually has a stormfly covering the entire portaledge, proofing it from snowstorms, for example. When it is being hauled, the portaledge is usually packed up into a tubular bag and hung from the haul bag.

Schrund: The large break in a snow slope, often at the foot of a mountain face. Similar to a crevasse, although instead of walking around or jumping over (as is the case with a crevasse), the climber has to climb up and over, or around, the schrund to gain the slope or steeper face above.

Spindrift: Loose snow that is blown by wind.

Wire: a form of 'passive' or 'natural' protection. A high load-rated loop of steel wire with a shaped metal head on one end. Placed in rock cracks. Many sizes exist.